RIDING SCHOOL

RIDING SCHOOL

PAM & LIONEL DUNNING

Macdonald
Queen Anne Press

A Queen Anne Press Book

First published in hardback in Great Britain in 1989 by Queen Anne Press
First published in paperback in Great Britain in 1991 by Queen Anne Press: a division of
Macdonald & Co (Publishers) Ltd
Orbit House,
1 New Fetter Lane, London EC4A 1AR

A member of the Maxwell Macmillan Pergamon
Publishing Corporation

Dunning, Lionel,
Riding school,
1. Show jumping
1. Title 11. Dunning, Pam
798.2'5

ISBN 0-356-15824-1

This book was designed and produced by
Quarto Publishing plc
The Old Brewery, 6 Blundell Street
London N7 9BH

Project Editor Sally Taylor
Senior Editors Dennis Kennedy, Angela Gair
Editor Mary Chesshyre

Designer Carole Perks

Photographer Kit Houghton
Illustrator Stephen Frisby

Editorial Director Carolyn King
Art Director Moira Clinch

Typeset by Ampersand Typesetting (Bournemouth) Ltd
Manufactured in Hong Kong by Regent Publishing
Services Limited
Printed by Leefung Asco Printers Ltd, Hong Kong

CONTENTS

INTRODUCTION

For my family and me, horses are not just a part of our lives; they are a way of life. We are all involved, from Pam and myself to our ten-year-old son Robert, who, in his first year of show-jumping, is winning many more rosettes than I did at his age. And Pam's father, eighty years young, still hunts twice a week throughout the winter. A quick look around our yard confirms the picture: the horses there are completely dependent on us for their health and welfare, so really there is no way that they could not come first.

This book is written from the heart. The joy that horses have given us, and the knowledge that we have gained through them, are things we have always wanted to share, and that is how this book has come about. Together, Pam and I have set down what we believe to be the principles of learning to ride, not only drawing on the experience we have gained in teaching and training young riders and horses, but also taking into account the questions we are constantly being asked, even by experienced riders.

Learning to ride should be above all an enjoyable experience, and the first essential is for you to feel confident on horseback so that you can work with, not against, the horse. From this must follow the physical coordination that is so important, and the technicalities will begin to fall naturally into place. As you venture out of the school to enjoy your first rides in the countryside all this will be consolidated: the learning – and the enjoyment – should continue.

Having acquired the fundamental riding skills, you will sooner or later want to learn to jump. For me, jumping is when I feel most intimately involved with a horse, and although at the time of our marriage Pam was an experienced racing jockey, not a show-jumper, she soon excelled in this field as well. We hope it is an enthusiasm that all readers of this book will come to share.

Advanced riding techniques and dressage movements are important in developing and expressing the increasingly refined relationship that you have with your horse. In writing this chapter we have been very lucky to have had Judy Bradwell's help. Judy is a highly successful event rider who has recently been concentrating particularly on dressage. She is an extremely talented horsewoman and specializes in bringing on young horses; we are very grateful for the assistance she has given us.

It is not only riding skills that have to be developed for competitive riding; a horse must be physically fit to meet all the demands that may be made on it. Here Pam has contributed her knowledge of lungeing and long-reining, with the emphasis on how they can be used to help get a horse fit. She is a great believer in the value of both as a means of exercise. We also look at other aspects of preparing for competition; something we know almost too much about, since competitive riding has played such a major part in our lives over the years.

Then we have given you an introduction to the show-jumping competitions themselves, explaining how to assess and ride courses, how to overcome jumping problems and how to cope with the procedure and the etiquette of competitions.

Finally, there is the day-to-day business of looking after horses – stable management or horsemastership. Rather than devoting a single, separate chapter to this aspect of riding, we felt that it should be a theme that continued through the book alongside the "riding lessons". The way a horse is cared for affects its well-being, its physical performance and thus how it responds to you. Looking after a horse properly is just as important as riding it correctly and sensitively: the two are inseparable. With all that horses can give to people – the fun and the friendship as well as the sport – keeping them comfortable and happy doesn't seem a lot to ask.

GETTING STARTED

When, like us, you spend your whole life with horses, riding them, competing in major events with them, and helping others to get the same satisfaction and enjoyment from an association with them, you find you have developed a certain outlook, a kind of philosophy if you like. We believe that the whole basis of successful riding is a sense of balance and coordination. This is the major thing to think about, both as you learn to ride, and later, whether you progress up a competitive ladder or simply enjoy recreational riding. Just keep asking yourself the questions, Am I balanced on the horse's back? Are my body movements coordinated with its body movements? This is far more important than worrying about the correct position of your legs, or how you are sitting in the saddle, or whether your back is sufficiently straight and upright. Providing you get the balance and coordination right, every other aspect of riding will follow and fall naturally into place.

Developing a relationship with a horse is important, but once you are confident of your ability to ride and have achieved a sense of balance and coordination you will find that an understanding between you and a horse becomes spontaneous. With the confidence this brings you, you will find you are able to get up on a dozen different horses and ride them as easily as if they were a dozen different bicycles. There will inevitably be a certain type of horse with whom you find you have the best rapport – I always like rather sharp, quick-thinking horses. Others prefer horses that require the rider to do all the thinking for them. This has nothing to do with the shape or breed or size of the horse in themselves; it is simply a matter of how your temperament and the horse's relate to one another. But once you are confident of your riding ability, you can ride any type of horse; each one will be an individual and the challenge for you becomes how to get the best out of it.

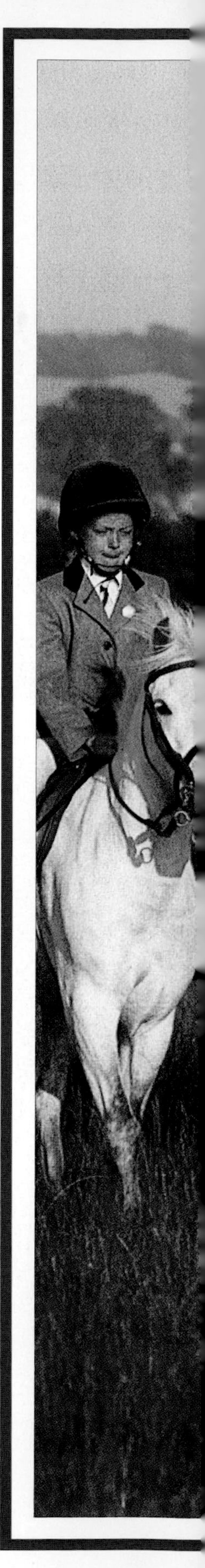

Riding is for all ages! Here Pam's father keeps control of some youngsters out for a ride. His grandson, our son, Robert, is on his immediate left. There's a gap of some 70 years between them, and yet they can share the joys of riding together.

WHEN TO START

A great thing about riding is that you can take it up at almost any time of life. Each year I run a number of show-jumping "clinics" in the UK and all over the world, and one of the great joys is to find the mix of ages among those who attend – from the very young to the recently retired. All of them, whatever their level of experience and expertise, enjoy their riding to the full.

Having said this, however, it is of course also true to say that there are advantages in starting young, as there are in any sport. Youth has so much on its side: suppleness, enthusiasm, and a wonderful lack of adult and worldly commitments and responsibilities that allows for greater confidence and a greater degree of abandonment to the sport.

You will often hear it said that good horsemen or women are born, not made. Well, there's a lot of truth in this, but by "good horsemen" we are referring to the David Broomes, Bill Steinkrauses and Lester Piggotts of this world. We believe that anyone can learn about the fundamentals of successful riding – balance and coordination. And in any case the gift may be there, dormant and waiting to be discovered. Paul Shockemohle, the famous show-jumper from Germany, did not begin riding at all until his late twenties; when Nick Skelton first started working with Ted Edgar he spent almost more time on the ground than he did in the saddle. What he had was total dedication, a huge capacity for hard work and a terrific talent waiting to be developed. Now he is one of the very best riders in the world, perhaps of all time, but it would have been hard to predict that success for him when he was sixteen.

Learning to ride – "going into horses" – is a commitment. There is no doubt that it's an expensive sport both in terms of time and money, but if you've bought this book we'll presume that you've thought about these things and are ready to press ahead, which is great. In our view you've made the right decision; it's all well worth it!

Above *Nick Skelton, a member of the British team at the Seoul Olympics in 1988, is one of the most brilliant of today's international show-jumpers. It is fair to say he has worked extremely hard for the success he now enjoys.*

Left *One of tomorrow's successes perhaps? Whatever the future holds for this eight-year-old rider, she has had the advantage of learning to ride while she is still very young.*

***Above** Paul Shockemohle, from Germany, is one of the most brilliant and successful show-jumpers of all time, yet he did not begin riding until his late twenties. Here, he and Lorenzo clear the 'Devil's Dyke' at Hickstead.*

RIDING – THE INTERNATIONAL WAY

Riding is a living art, and like all living arts it is subject to constant review and change. If someone who first learned to ride, say, thirty or forty years ago, went to a good instructor and had riding lessons now, he or she would find that much had changed, that some old techniques would have to be discarded and new ones learned instead.

What has developed in those thirty or forty years is a world-recognized, international style of riding. There are two main reasons for this. One is that riding as a recreational and professional competitive sport has really taken off in this time. The other is that more widely available travel has enabled people interested in horses to visit other countries and ride and compete in different areas of the sport, thereby effecting a ready exchange of ideas and techniques.

Now, different styles of riding are associated with different areas of the sport itself rather than with different countries of the world. Dressage riders the world over will ride in the same style, and that style will differ from a show-jumping, eventing, racing, or even recreational riding style. There may be slight national variations within each discipline but they would be unapparent except to the most expert eye, and there would be few differences between the teaching techniques of each country.

In our world of show-jumping the style that has evolved over the years and is practised now by all top riders came from the USA. At Ascot Horse Show in 1968 Harvey Smith and I wandered over to the collecting ring and to our amazement found it was littered with poles seemingly scattered all over the place. Ted Williams, a great show-jumper of the time, then in his sixties, was solemnly trotting his horse in an even rhythm over these poles. Harvey and I laughed, and shouted over to him, "What are you up to, old feller?" His reply was, "You'll see; this is the way of the future". From there, he went into the ring and won every jumping class he entered. What Ted was doing were the elementary grid exercises that are the foundation work of all show-jumpers today and which teach the technique of maintaining a constant and even rhythm when going round a show-jumping course. All top show-jumpers ride and jump in this way today: it is an international style.

Above *In flat racing, jockeys ride in an easily recognizable style. Their stirrup leathers are very short so that they can stand up and lean right forward, taking the weight off the horse's back. This leaves it with complete freedom of movement.*

Right *Show-jumping the American way (top). I admire American riders most of all; they are completely dedicated to riding in the correct style. They pay particular attention to the position and use of the lower leg, which helps to consolidate the rider's overall position, and spend long hours working on the flat, not only over jumps. Contrast this with the traditional hunting seat (bottom), though this is equally effective when galloping across country.*

Left *The Western style of riding is quite different from a standard British, American or European style. It was devised as a working style, when long hours had to be spent in the saddle and great distances had to be covered. The Western saddle is considerably larger than most other types of saddle, so that the rider's weight is spread over a larger area of the horse's back.*

Below *The dressage style of riding differs from the Western style and also from the way a show-jumper, for example, would ride. No jumping is involved in pure dressage riding; instead, the rider aims to develop the horse's range of movements and paces. All styles of riding have one thing in common, however: the rider is always positioned over the horse's centre of balance.*

THE INSTRUCTOR'S ROLE

Riding is a very difficult sport to teach yourself, and to be honest, few people are able to begin it on their own anyway. To ride, you have to have access to a horse or pony, and generally you would not think of buying one until you knew how to ride it and what was involved in looking after it. Even children born into families where older brothers and sisters or parents ride, and horses and ponies are around, still need lessons in how to do things the proper way.

Before learning to ride, it's a good idea to spend some time if you can with horses and ponies – at a friend's stables perhaps, or at a nearby riding school if the owners are willing, just looking at and learning about horses, how they tick and what care and attention they need. You'll learn a lot simply by watching the grooms at work catching up the horses from grass or attending to them in the stables, grooming them and getting them ready to be ridden. It's a sport in which you need to know what goes on behind the scenes as well as having the "on-top" view.

The role of this book is to act as a supplement to an instructor giving you practical lessons. Besides being an active sport, riding as an art is both technical and theoretical, and the theory is highly important. Reading about it, when you've got time to think and digest the information, can be an enormous help. The chances are, though, that you will have your first riding lesson from a qualified instructor. In fact you never, never reach a stage in riding when you no longer need lessons. The top riders who achieve regular success in any of the competitive equestrian sports are those who have regular sessions with a qualified trainer.

Your instructor is most likely to be at a local riding school and you should be confident that you like the atmosphere of the school, that its general appearance and upkeep, and that of the horses, are pleasing. If there is a feeling of disorder and disarray it is likely there will be a lax attitude towards everything – including teaching! You should also like and feel able to get on well with the person who is going to teach you to ride.

Do listen to your instructor and try to do what he or she tells you. I always say to the people at my clinics when we are getting started, "You've paid your money to come here for me to try to improve your riding, so for the next few days do it my way. At the end of the time, modify it to suit you and your own specific riding requirements, but for now do it the way I tell you. It's worked for me over the years; some bits of it will work for you". I think it's good advice; the instructor must know more than you do at this stage. And if you don't understand anything he tells you to do, ask him to demonstrate it to you. If he's not good enough to show you, he's not good enough to be teaching you.

All riders, however experienced, benefit from having advice from a trainer on the ground now and again. Pam and I have ridden horses for as long as each other, yet we will still help and criticize one another. Here I recommend Pam should lengthen her stirrup leathers by one hole to give her a slightly longer leg for the work she is doing with this horse.

Above *Trainers have to be adaptable to cope with all ages! These young riders are having a little talk about tack and equipment, as the bit on a pony's bridle was too low in its mouth. Even young or novice riders should have an understanding of the equipment their horse or pony is wearing, what its purpose is and how to adjust it properly.*

Above *Now I'm schooling young riders over a simple jumping grid. This is an exercise for control; the rider nearest to me sets the pace and the rider on the other side has to control his pony to keep level with his partner.*

Left *If ever you are having difficulties or problems in your riding and jumping, always take advice from someone experienced rather than trying to solve the problem yourself. It is much easier for someone on the ground to see what is going wrong than it is for the rider on top.*

RIDING CLOTHES

As with nearly every sport, you will need some special clothing when you start to ride. Initially, there's no need to go overboard and buy everything you see the top riders wear; you only need a few basic essentials.

First among these, as you will undoubtedly know, is a hat. All good riding establishments will insist on your wearing a proper hat and it is the law that hats must be worn in competitive riding. Their importance cannot be stressed enough and we have our own personal experiences to make the point. In 1975 I had a horrendous accident in the show-jumping ring, in which my hat came off and I collided, head first and at speed, with the solid wing of a jump. I received a blow on the head which rendered me unconscious and kept me in a coma for three days. It took me literally years to fight my way back to the top after this, and it is why for many years I was one of the few international show-jumpers you would see wearing a proper chin strap on my hat. Much more recently our son, Robert, was out riding with us on the road when his pony shied and put him down on the tarmac. He had a broken collar bone and was badly shaken; on the side of his hat (which stayed on his head) there was a sizeable rip.

Various types of approved hats are available and you will probably find you have a preference, but I personally feel that skull caps can be reserved for serious competitive riding; they seem too heavy and cumbersome for recreational riding. An ordinary velvet peak cap of a reputable make is fine and it should be a snug and firm fit without being so tight that it gives you a headache. For young people and beginners in particular, it should have a proper chin strap attached at two points on either side: a hat made by a reputable manufacturer will automatically have this.

Next you need a pair of boots. You can invest in long boots if you like, but jodhpur boots are perfectly satisfactory. Some people maintain that stout walking shoes are good enough, but they do not protect the ankles as jodhpur boots do: a bang from a loose stirrup iron on the ankle bone is achingly painful. Jodhpur boots are also designed not to slip through the stirrup irons, which shoes can easily do. Trainers – worn at all other times, perhaps – should never be worn for riding!

Jodhpurs are a good investment because they are comfortable; failing these, a thick pair of jeans that are close-fitting around the leg will do. A tough jacket will give protection if you fall off or get hit by overhead branches.

Experienced riders wearing correct riding clothes that are practical and comfortable as well as smart. On the left, the rider is wearing breeches, long boots, a thick tweed hacking jacket, hat and gloves. On the right, the black coat and white stock make the turn-out a little smarter, suitable for most competitive riding.

The correct dress for a novice rider. She is wearing a properly fitting hat with a chin strap, a thick padded jacket which will give her some protection should she fall, riding breeches and long boots. It would also be perfectly acceptable to wear jodhpurs or closely fitting thick jeans and jodhpur boots instead of breeches and long boots.

Alternative riding gear for a young, but more experienced rider. She is wearing suede chaps over jodhpurs and "muckers" – all-purpose working and riding boots, which are very popular. Available in three different lengths, they are waterproof and tough, and do give some support to the ankle. As it's a hot day, this rider has chosen not to wear a jacket; but remember that when you begin learning to ride, you should always wear a jacket for protection, however hot the day.

FALLING OFF

It may seem strange and discouraging to talk about falling off before you have even got on a horse. But the fact is that as you learn to ride, and all the way through your riding career, you are going to fall off: there's no avoiding it, and anyway everyone will tell you that you are no kind of rider until you have fallen off – many times. However, it is possible to learn how to fall off so as not to hurt yourself, at least from a simple fall.

The trick is to go to a local gym and practise learning how to fall on a trampoline; tuck your head in as you fall so that you roll, and don't put your hands out to break your fall – that's when arms and wrists get broken. This advice was given to my parents when I was learning to ride by the late Phil Blakemore, a great horseman and one-time international show-jumper.

If you ride, you never stop falling off! The important thing is to learn how to do it properly. This huntsman has parted company with his horse, after unexpectedly finding a deep ditch on the landing side of a large hedge. However, his experience is showing; he has rolled over so that he is now sitting on the ground, still holding on to the reins, and he will be back on his feet before the horse.

APPROACHING A HORSE

Before you can get up on a horse's back and begin to learn to ride it is important to know how to approach it. Approached incorrectly, from behind, a horse will not be aware of you coming towards it, and will be surprised to find you suddenly standing beside it. This could result in it jumping to one side, even kicking out, both bad experiences for a novice.

Go up to it quietly from in front, have a bit of a chat with it, patting its neck or stroking its forehead if you see it doesn't mind its head being touched. It just helps you to get to know and trust one another.

A final piece of advice for when you start to ride: if at all possible, try to engineer an introduction to a top-class horseman or woman and go and pick their brains all you can. Their knowledge is invaluable and will have been gained through a love of horses and a lifetime of working with them. You will find such people are only too happy to share their knowledge with someone else who has that love, and every bit of knowledge you can acquire will help you. And you can also learn a good deal by studying some of the educational videos now available on all aspects of riding and horsemanship.

1 & 2 *The correct way to approach a horse. Always approach a horse from the front, so that it can see you clearly. Here, I am holding the horse's head, ready to introduce horse and rider to one another.*

3 *As you can see, I am signalling to the rider not to approach the horse in this way. Already it has its ears back because it is unsure of what is happening. Startled by someone coming up behind it like this, a horse is likely to jump forward, or even to kick out.*

2 THE FIRST LESSONS

We believe that if you are interested in horses you should learn *all* about them – about their moods and needs and how to look after them as well as just how to ride them. In fact, if you don't spend time simply being with horses, watching them and taking care of them, you will never really be sufficiently in sympathy with them to become a truly good rider.

Many books about horses, like many conventional riding stables, separate the business of riding and horse management. Because we believe the two go together, and that one day you may own your own horse and be responsible for its welfare yourself, we shall include aspects of horse care as they occur naturally in your developing relationship with horses.

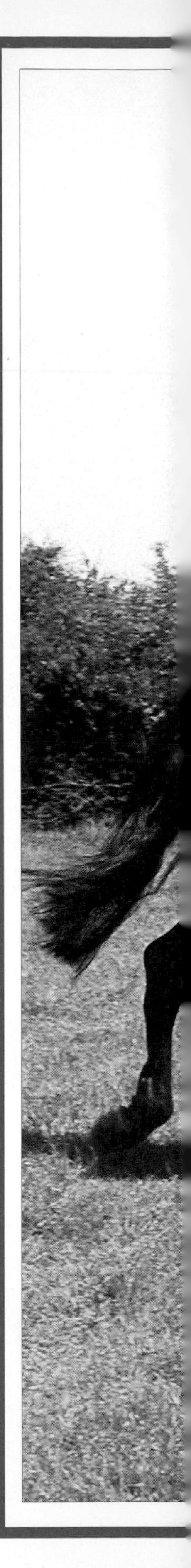

The important thing when learning to ride is to understand and begin to develop a sense of balance. There is no better way to do this than by having lessons on the lunge, with the instructor at the other end of the lunge line, controlling the horse and explaining to you what you should be doing.

SADDLING

Now that you are correctly kitted out for riding and know the right and wrong way to approach a horse, you should next learn a bit about the saddlery, or tack, a horse wears when it is to be ridden.

The saddle, which fits into the hollow of the horse's back, provides the rider with a support, making it easier to maintain a balanced position when riding. There are many different types of saddle and at any stage of riding it is important to have the right one for the job.

A novice rider should have a general purpose saddle. This is designed for recreational riding, not for serious jumping or competition riding of any kind. It should have a *spring tree;* this is the inside part of the saddle that lies across the wither and makes the saddle feel "alive", allowing it to move in harmony with the horse. A solid tree saddle tends to be rigid and sits like a lump on the horse.

As you will see from the pictures, the saddle is put on a horse from the nearside – that is, the horse's left side. There happens to be a belief among many horsey people, including ourselves, that it is bad luck to tack-up from the offside.

The saddle should always be worn with a numnah – a shaped pad – underneath. This makes the saddle more comfortable on the horse's back, helps to prevent any rubbing and also absorbs sweat.

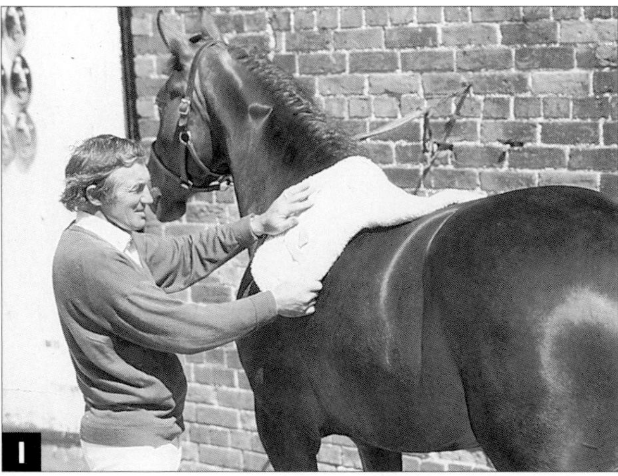

1 *Place the numnah evenly over the horse's back under the saddle area. The best types of numnah are made of sheepskin; nowadays, however, most people favour the man-made fibre types. Never use a foam numnah unless it is covered with some absorbent material.*

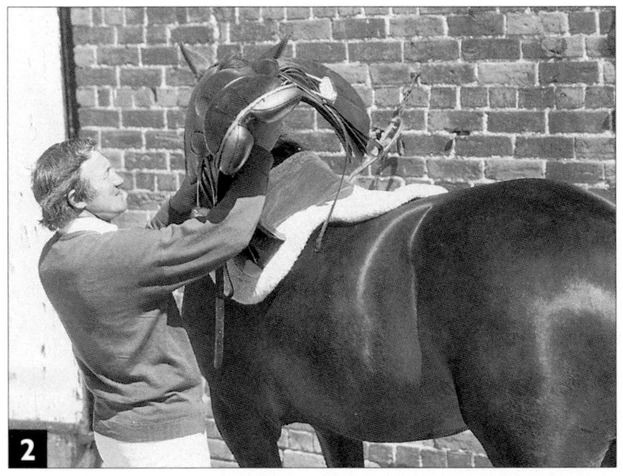

2 *Lift the saddle up over the horse's back and lower it gently so it fits snugly over the numnah.*

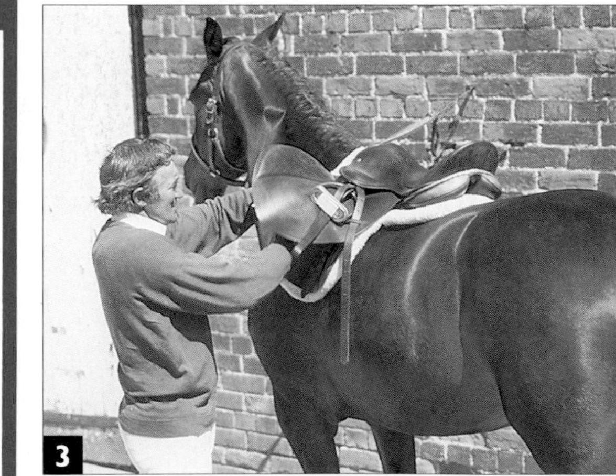

3 *To keep the numnah in place, loop the tapes at the front around the girth straps under the saddle flap. If you don't do this the numnah will soon slip and will do more harm than good.*

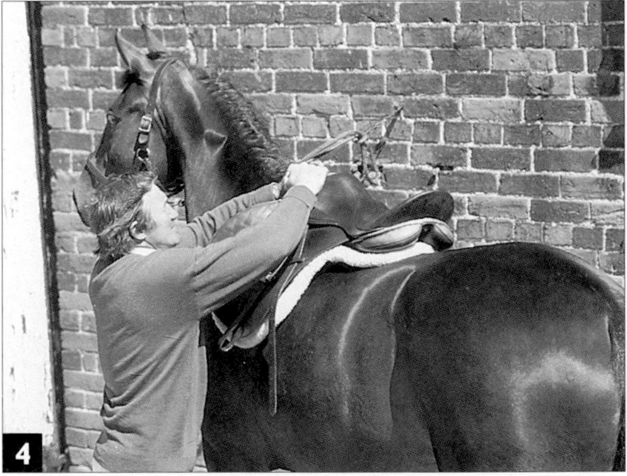

4 *After fitting the tapes, pull the numnah up into the arch of the saddle so that it is not stretched across the horse's back. If the numnah is too tight across the wither it can do as much harm as a saddle that pinches across the back. You should be able to get three fingers between the arch of the saddle and the horse's back at the wither.*

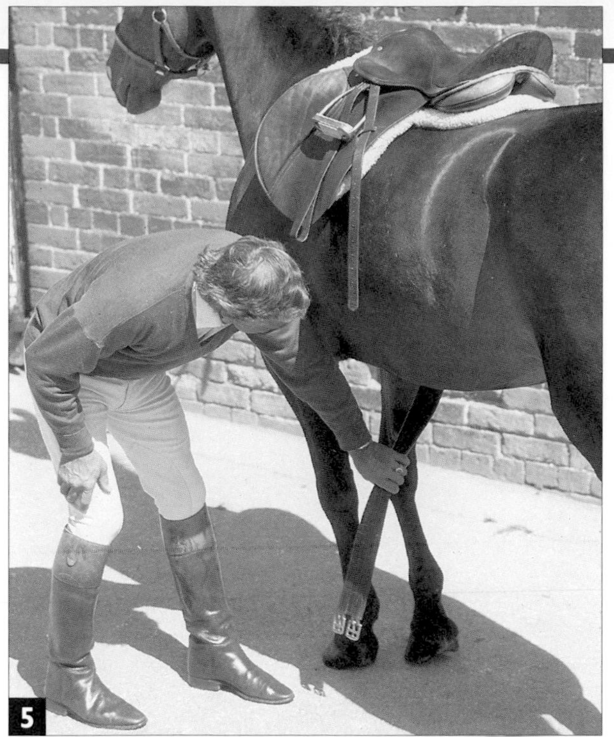

5 *Buckle the girth to the straps under the saddle on the off-side, then bring them under the horse's belly.*

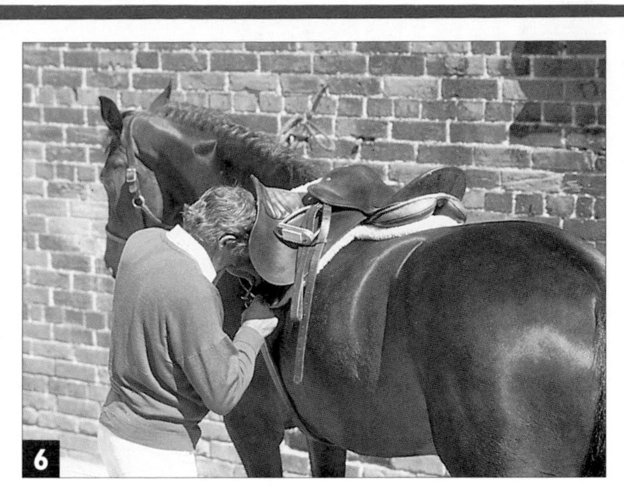

6 *Buckle them quite loosely at this stage, and run your hand down under the girth, to make sure the coat is smooth and the skin is not being pinched.*

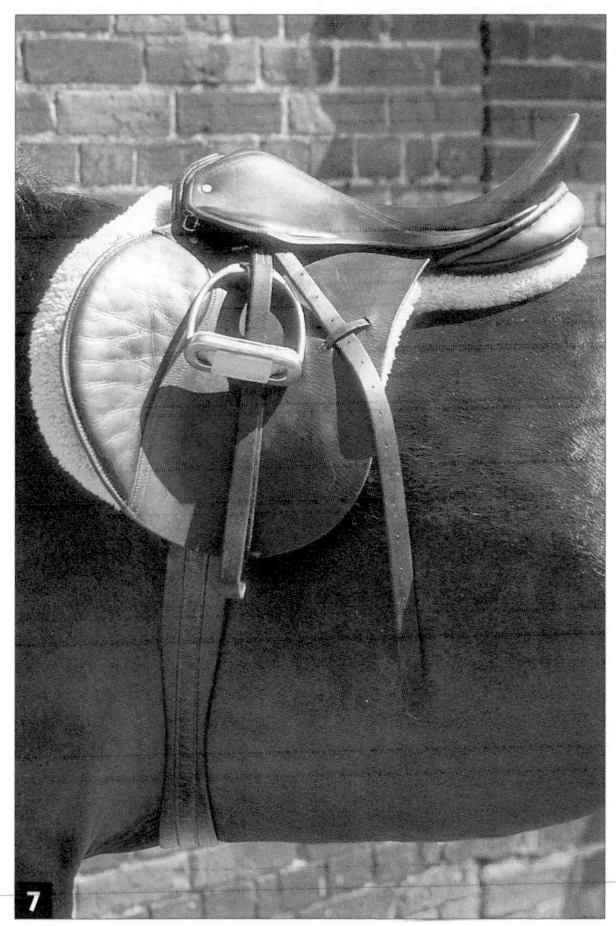

7 *A correctly fitting saddle and numnah, with the stirrups run up the leathers.*

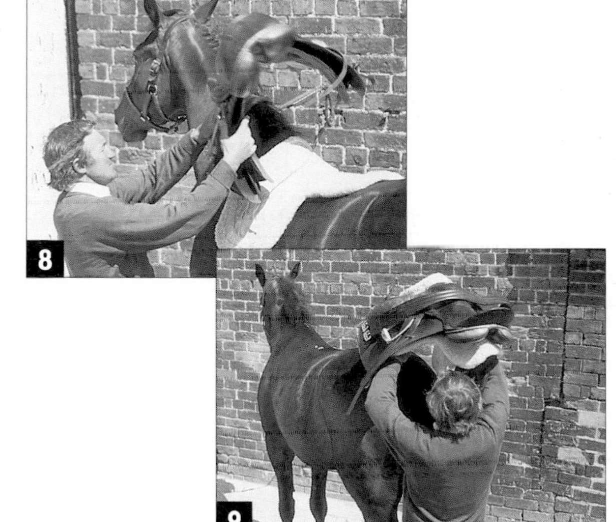

8 *"Throwing" the saddle up high in the air and letting it come down on the horse's back with a thud. At best, it will frighten the horse; at worst, it might bruise its back. Either way, it's not going to be happy about being tacked-up in future.*

9 *A sure way of encouraging a horse to kick out at you. Never try to put on a saddle this way; even if you could guarantee getting it in the right place, the horse's hair would be ruffled up the wrong way.*

BRIDLING

The bridle, fitted on to the horse's head, links the rider through the reins to the horse's mouth, which is its nerve centre. Thus it is one of the principal means of control the rider has over the horse. The part of the bridle that the horse holds in its mouth is the bit, and there are many different types which vary in the effect they have on the horse. As a novice rider, you will be likely to be riding a horse with one of the types of *snaffle* or *pelham* bits which have a mild action on the horse's mouth.

As you learn to put on the bridle you will have a better understanding of its function and the effect you can have on the horse through it. Whatever the type, its correct fitting is very important to ensure that the horse is comfortable and does not sustain any injury.

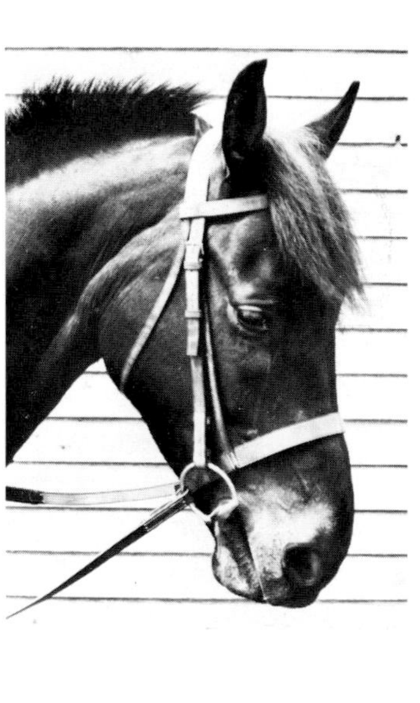

Top centre: *an ordinary cavesson noseband. Unless used with a standing martingale, this noseband performs no real function, but helps to improve the appearance of the horse's face.*
Top right: *a cavesson noseband fitted with a flash attachment. This is for horses that tend to open their mouths and get their tongues over the bit; the flash attachment keeps the mouth shut.*
Left: *a drop noseband also keeps the horse's mouth shut. It is important not to buckle it too tightly, or it will press on the nasal passages and impede the horse's breathing. It is only used with a snaffle, whereas the flash attachment to the cavesson can be used with a pelham.*
Bottom right: *a slim-looking, slightly padded noseband which is used on horses and ponies purely for show purposes.*

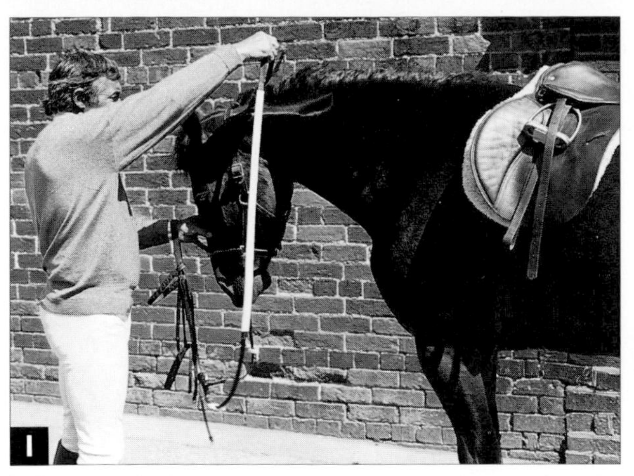

1 *To put on the bridle, again stand on the horse's nearside and put the reins over the neck before taking off the headcollar. This gives you some means of hanging on to the horse should it decide to move away.*

2 *Holding the top of the headpiece in your right hand, spread the fingers of your left hand along the bit, and hold this up to the horse's mouth.*

3 *Use your fingers to open its mouth and slip the bit in.*

3a *Slip the headpiece over the ears, gently pulling them through above the browband.*

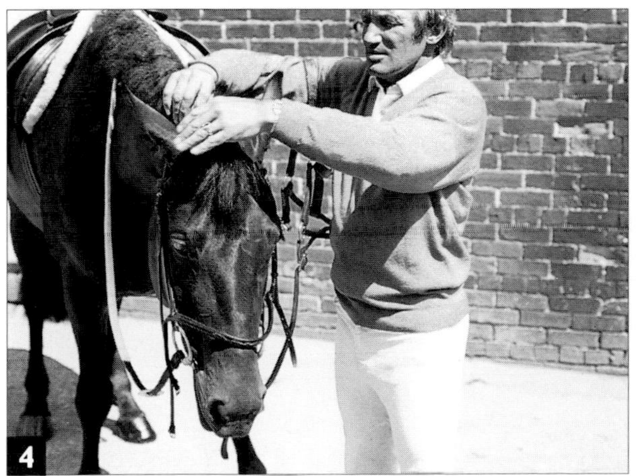

4 *Pull the forelock out so it lies flat over the browband.*

5 *Buckle the noseband so that you can get two fingers between it and the horse's nose. It should lie comfortably above the bit so that is does not hamper the bit's movement.*

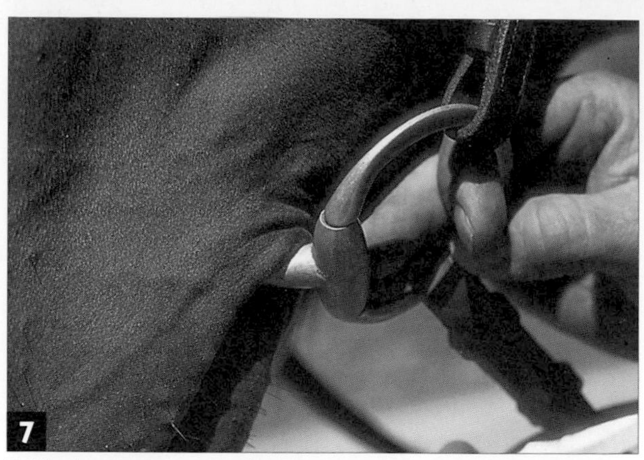

6 *Buckle the throatlash so that you can get the width of your fingers between it and the gullet. If it is any tighter than this it can seriously impede the horse's breathing.*

7 *The bit should lie comfortably at the corner of the mouth with just a very slight crease at the corners.*

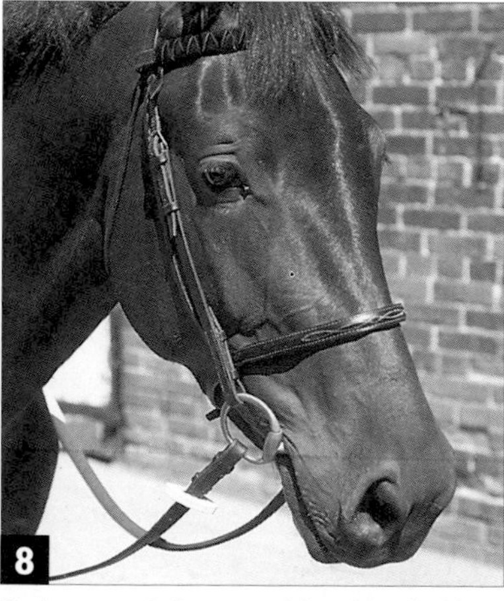

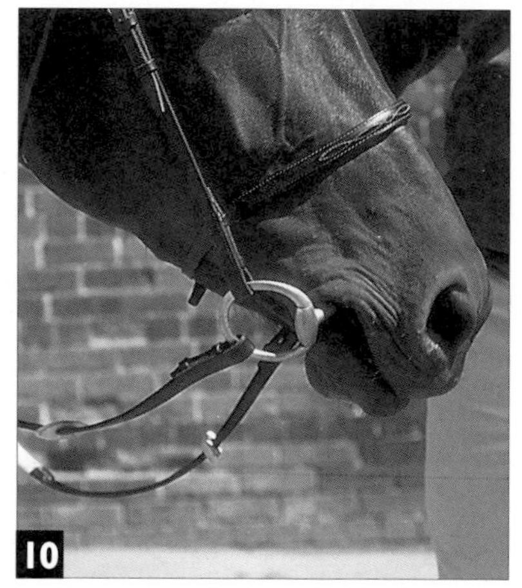

8 *A correctly fitting and fitted bridle. You can see the horse is quite happy and content.*

9 *This picture shows the bit far too high in the horse's mouth: the cheek pieces have been buckled too tightly. The horse is going to resist the bit as much as it can. The snaffle works with a nutcracker action – this high in the mouth means the bit will pinch the mouth severely.*

10 *Here the bit is far too low in the horse's mouth. It will soon get its tongue over it, which reduces the rider's control. Once a horse starts doing this it is very hard to break it of the habit.*

11 & 12 *This bit is too big for the horse's mouth. The ring of the bit is dropping down – compare it with the bit in the perfectly fitting bridle. Many people think horses' mouths are all the same size, but they vary considerably even among horses of the same height. It is essential to use the right size of bit for the horse. Here you can see how greatly bits vary in size.*

MOUNTING AND DISMOUNTING

Before you make your first move up on to the horse's back, check the girth and get into the habit of checking the stitching around the buckle on the stirrup leathers. If this is allowed to become old and worn it may suddenly give way, and you will lose the support of the stirrup irons. This would be an unnerving experience for a novice and an extremely dangerous one for a more competent rider who might be jumping or galloping at the time.

The first time you get on to, or mount, a horse, someone will be holding its head, so you won't have to worry about it moving away. It is probable, too, that you will be given a leg-up. This is the easiest way to get up on to a horse, particularly a large one. Learn to coordinate your movements with the person giving you the leg-up so that you spring up off the ground when you are given the command.

Even before you settle in the saddle and learn the correct way to sit, you should get off, or dismount, so that you can then learn to mount on your own. There is a right and a wrong way to dismount so learn the correct way now and never do it any other way. If you cross your leg in the front of the saddle you lose all control of the horse as you drop the reins, and you are also balanced very precariously should it take it into its head to move. If you keep your left foot in the stirrup iron, you could easily find yourself on the ground, with your foot caught in the stirrup and the horse moving off, dragging you behind.

Practise mounting and dismounting on your own a few times at this stage, so that you feel happy with the movements. It's good for your confidence to know that you can get off the horse whenever you want to – using your own free will and ability!

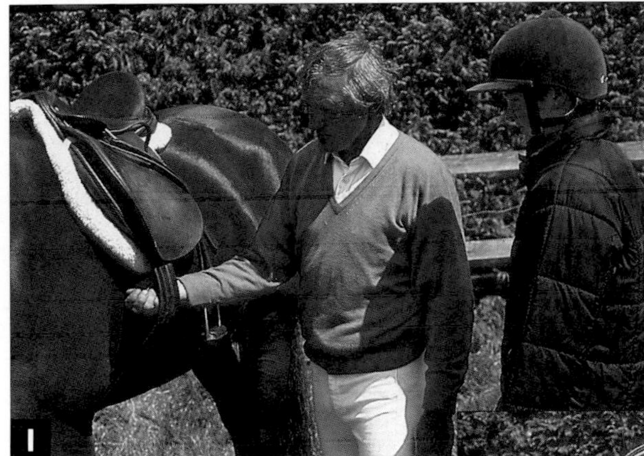

1 *Before mounting always check the girth. If it is loose like this one the saddle will slip over or move out of position on the horse's back as you get on.*

2 *Tighten the girth if necessary, buckling it as tightly as you can. If the horse blows out its tummy, give it a tap in the ribs to make it breathe in.*

2a *It is a good idea to adjust the stirrup leathers to roughly the length you will find correct when sitting in the saddle. To gauge this, place the fingertips of one hand at the buckle and hold the stirrup leather along the underside of your arm; the stirrup leather should fit snugly into your armpit.*

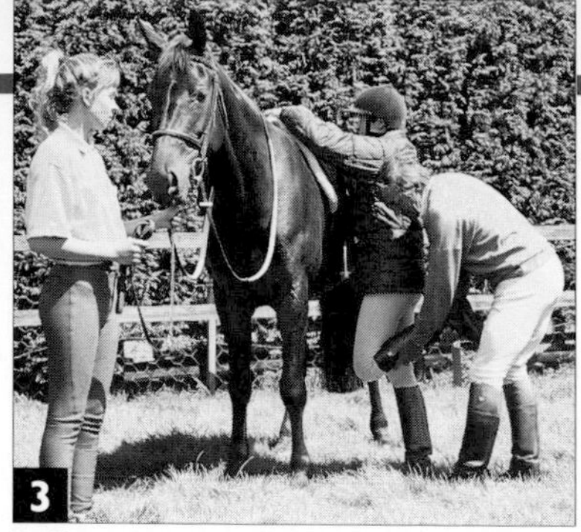

3 *To mount by a leg-up, place your left hand on the pommel and the right hand across the seat of the saddle. Then bend your left leg from the knee so that the helper can support your leg at the ankle and the knee.*

4 *At the helper's command, spring into the air from your left foot, and then throw your right leg across the saddle, taking care not to brush the horse's back.*

5 *Settle into the saddle as gently as possible, ready to put your feet into the stirrup irons.*

Mounting

1 *To mount without a leg-up, stand close to the horse's shoulder and face towards the tail. Hold the reins at the wither in your left hand and with your right hand turn the stirrup iron towards you and put your left foot into it.*

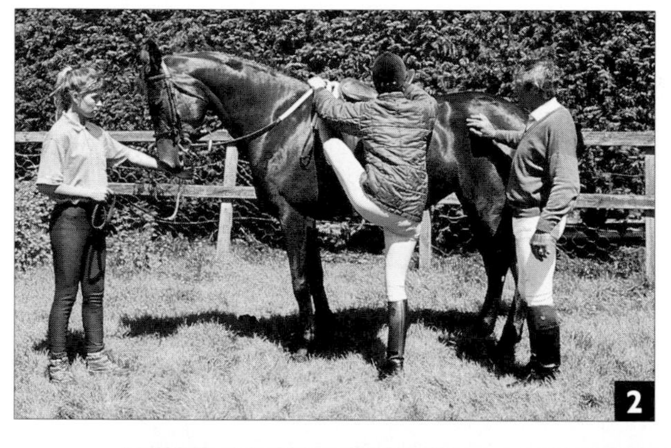

2 *Hop round to face the horse's side and move your right hand across the back of the saddle.*

3 *Spring off the ground, move your right hand forward and swing your right leg across the top of the saddle, again taking care not to brush the horse's back with your leg.*

4 *Lower yourself gently into the saddle and place your right foot in the stirrup. Here I am just steadying the horse's hindquarters, and feeling for any tenseness in the horse which would indicate restlessness.*

Incorrect mounting

This is the wrong way to get on. The rider is not holding the reins so would have no control if someone was not holding the horse. Facing towards the front of the horse like this makes it possible for it to strike forward with a hindleg catching the rider as she puts her foot in the stirrup iron. In this position it is also harder to spring off the ground so that the extra pressure she has to exert on the saddle is pulling it over to the horse's nearside.

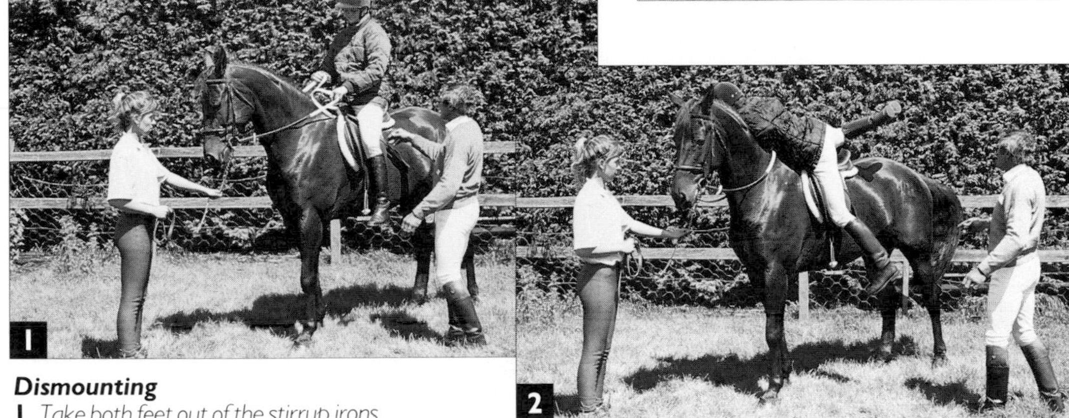

Dismounting

1 *Take both feet out of the stirrup irons and hold the reins in your left hand.*

2 *Leaning forward, swing your right leg up in the air behind you, bringing it over to the horse's near side.*

3 *Move your right hand so it rests across the back of the saddle and bend your knees to take the impact as you land. Stand up straight as quickly as you can.*

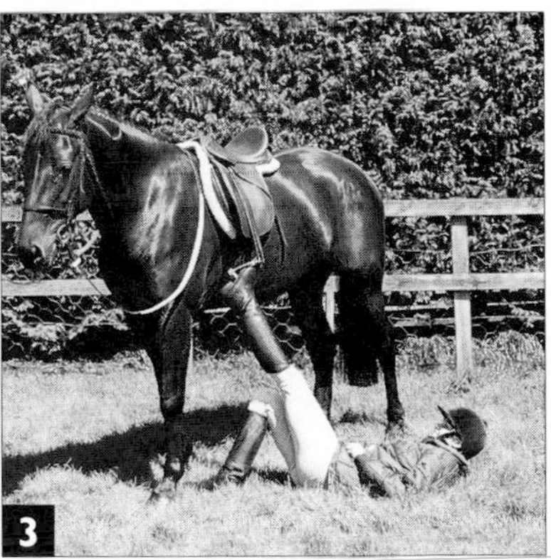

Incorrect dismounting

1 *Never dismount like this. By putting your right leg over the front of the saddle, you are balanced very precariously and you have no control over the horse should it move away.*

2 *Nor should you leave your left foot in the stirrup iron as you swing your right leg up behind the saddle to dismount as the horse might suddenly move forward and unbalance you.*

3 *This could very easily be the result, and it is highly unlikely that the horse would just stand still. It would be likely to move, dragging the rider behind it.*

SITTING IN THE SADDLE

As we explained earlier, our whole philosophy of riding has to do with the rider being in perfect balance with the horse at all times, both when standing still and through all the various movements. The ability to achieve this balance is, of course, governed by the rider's position as he or she sits in the saddle.

The first thing to understand – and something that is perhaps not always explained – is that the horse's point of balance, or centre of gravity, is its heart. The rider, therefore, must be evenly balanced over and around the area of the heart. A correctly placed saddle will put you in this position in principle, but you in turn must sit in the saddle correctly in order to maintain the balance.

The pictures on these pages show the correct way to sit in the saddle in order to achieve a balanced position. When you look down, without moving your head right forward you should just be able to see the points of your toes. Providing your legs are in the correct position, being able to see your toes now will be determined by the length of the stirrup leathers. Having used the rough guide to give the right stirrup length for you, adjust the leathers a hole up or down if you find you can't see your toes as you look down.

It is important to know the correct way to sit in the saddle, but don't worry about it too much at this moment. If it becomes your major preoccupation you are likely to become tense with concentration, and there is no way you can ride in balance with your horse if you are tense. So try to relax, and let your concentration be on being balanced. Sit upright without being stiff and rigid, and look between the horse's ears. Let your body weight fall down on to your seat and your leg weight drop down into your heels.

Hold the reins in either hand so that they run in a straight line from the bit to your hands and pass up through your hands. Your thumbs rest lightly on the top of them. They should be at a length which allows the horse to hold its head naturally, not so tight that its head is tucked into its chest and its mouth is open, nor so loose that you have no contact with its mouth.

1 *A good position for the novice rider. Both she and the horse look quite relaxed and happy. She is in the centre of the saddle with her legs close to the saddle, and her stirrups are the correct length, so that if she looked down she would just see the point of her toe. Her hands are quite relaxed. The only possible criticism is that she could be sitting more upright; however, for a novice this is not at all bad.*

2 *This is a typical novice position – and quite wrong. The rider is round-shouldered and slouching, and way in front of the horse's centre of balance. Her feet are pressed into the stirrup irons and are pointing down, which will make her lower legs quite useless. Although the horse's ears are pricked, you can tell by the way the bit is pulling at the corners of its mouth that the rider is holding the reins too tightly. If she were to ask it to move forward, it would be confused and unhappy.*

3 *Here the stirrup irons are too long, so that the rider is having to fight with her feet to keep them in the irons. Instead of her knee nestling easily against the saddle in the correct position it is too low. It has also shifted her position to the back of the saddle and will have rendered her calf muscles useless. She is holding on to the mane with her right hand and to the pommel with her left hand to balance herself. The moment the horse moves away her feet will come out of the stirrup irons and she will lose her balance completely.*

4 *This is just as incorrect. The stirrup irons are far too short, so that the rider's knees are too high – coming almost higher than the saddle – and her heels are still up in the air. She has shifted her seat right back to counteract the short stirrups so that she is balanced on the cantle of the saddle where she could do real damage to the horse's kidneys. Although the horse looks happy enough, it would soon resist if asked to move because of the pain in its back.*

THE WALK

The walk is the horse's slowest, easiest pace, and the one you will first experience. It is a pace in four-time; that is, each foot leaves and comes to the ground in turn, making it an easy, smooth movement with no jolting.

At this stage of learning to ride, your mount will be being led within a confined space around the school or field so you have no worries about control, or even steering, initially. Simply relax into the saddle, maintaining the correct position. Feel the horse's movement as it takes each step and let your body movement coordinate with the horse's. Thus your body will move very slightly in the saddle to the swing of the walk. You shouldn't be perched in the saddle: the saying goes that you should not be sitting up on the top of the tree but down in its branches. Your aim is to feel that you are part of the horse, rather than a separate entity.

Aim to hold your hands naturally in front of you, just letting them move very slightly with the horse's head. Resist the temptation to hang on to the reins for dear life; they are not there to hold you in place in the saddle or to help you keep your balance. If you pull on the reins continually, the walk will be jerky and unrhythmical or the horse will stop. Either way, it is not going to think much of you as a rider.

Feel confident and happy with the walk, trying it in both directions and being led in a circle before moving on to faster speeds.

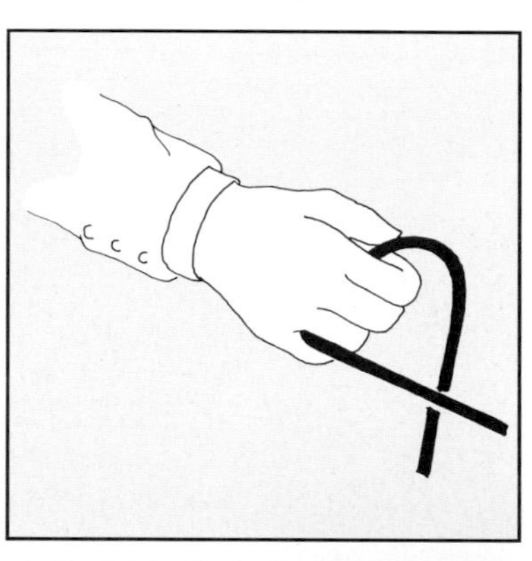

Far left *Here the rider is sitting correctly at the walk, with back straight, hands relaxed at the wither, heels down and feet pointing forward.*

Left *The normal way to hold the reins involves passing them inside the hands, from the third finger to the crook of the first finger and thumb. The thumbs are on the top of the reins, holding them down onto the fingers.*

1 *Being led at the walk, the novice rider is in a good, relaxed position. Her knees are pressed lightly against the saddle, her heels are down, her toes are pointing forward and she is sitting quite upright in the saddle. She is perhaps exerting a little too much tension on the horse's mouth, as you can see by the way the bit is pulling up in the corner of the mouth.*

2 *In this picture, the rider has become rather tense. Her legs are still in a good position, but she has tensed her upper body, stiffening her arms so that they are too far forward. There is no easy harmony between horse and rider.*

3 *You can see the difference between the novice and the experienced rider here. Pam's horse is going forward in a happy, relaxed movement. We have attached an Abbot Davis to the bridle; this is a piece of equipment joined on to the reins and girth which helps to position the horse's head correctly without bending the neck too much. It is ideal for novice riders to use and it is also good for a young horse like this. Notice how Pam's hands are held easily, just above the saddle, so that her arms hang naturally in a straight line down to her elbow.*

4 *Here is another picture of Pam and her horse walking with relaxed movement, displaying good head carriage and perfect harmony with one another.*

THE TROT

The next movement to experience is the trot. This is a much bouncier pace, in which the horse moves diagonal pairs of front and hind legs together. The bouncier rhythm makes it far more difficult for the novice rider to feel in harmony with the movement.

The person leading your horse will take it forward into a trot, which you are likely to find a fairly bone-shaking movement to begin with. Initially try to relax as much as you can with the movement, while still sitting up straight in the saddle. As you feel the rhythm of the movement, so you can begin trying to rise from the saddle with it, just moving your body forward very slightly supported on your knees for one stride, and coming back into the saddle for the next. Try it going in both directions.

It will take you a little time to master the rising trot, and for the first few times you ride there will be moments when you can do it and others when you can't. Persevere; eventually you will find it is as comfortable as walking.

1 *You can see the rider is feeling very insecure in this photograph showing a trotting horse. The movement is bouncing her about, so that she is leaning forward. She is using her hands and legs to hang desperately on to the horse – her hands are pressed against the horse's neck and her legs are hugging its sides.*

2 *Here, the rider's legs are in a good position, but her hands are much too far forward up the horse's neck and she is now using her reins as lifelines to balance herself. She is balancing precariously on the horse, rather than riding it, and she is not using her knee as a pivot in the way she should.*

3 *Here she is beginning to relax a little more. She is sitting nicely and has brought her hands back closer to her body. If anything, her reins are a little too loose, but at least she is no longer hanging on to them to help her balance.*

4 *You can see the contrast between a novice and an experienced rider at the trot here. Pam is just moving off into an easy, balanced, rising trot. Her leg is correctly positioned, hanging down straight, her hands are held correctly just above the wither. Her weight is just slightly forward to counteract the horse's movement at the transition. In the next step, she will reposition over the centre of balance.*

5 *Here is the next step, and you can see Pam is back sitting in the saddle over the centre of balance.*

LEARNING TO STOP

By this stage, you will find that most books about learning to ride have discussed the *aids* in some detail. These are the signals a rider gives to his horse to let it know what is required – to go faster or slower, perform some refinement of pace, stop and so on. In this teaching programme, however, I don't want to discuss the aids in isolation. I believe a novice rider should learn to achieve and experience that all-important balance with the horse's movement before he starts thinking what signals he should be giving at any given time. The aids can be discovered and considered as they occur naturally and necessarily within the learning process.

At this stage of learning to ride stopping will be controlled by the person leading you. Now, as you begin to feel happy with the movement, you can start telling the horse that *you* want it to stop, so as to experience this with someone else in control rather than finding out about it all on your own.

When you want to slow down or stop, just close your hands around the reins to increase the tension on them and hold your hands still, so that as the horse moves its head in time with the movement it feels a resistance from your static hands, rather than feeling them move with it. Don't actually pull on the reins. If you do this, you will find your body automatically leans back which actually pushes the animal forwards because your seat muscles will be pushing harder into the saddle. Instead, as you close your hands on the reins, try to lean forward very slightly.

As soon as you feel the horse respond to whatever it is you have asked it to do, settle back over the centre of balance and relax your hands to hold the reins normally.

Remember, however, that you should not be attempting to slow down or stop, i.e. giving positive signals, even at a walk, until you are feeling confident at a trot.

1

2

Compare this sequence of Pam bringing her horse to a halt with those of the novice rider opposite – and try to emulate Pam! In **1** *the horse is walking forward freely and easily. In* **2** *Pam begins to ask for a halt by closing her hands gently on the reins so as to resist the forward movement. In* **3** *you can see the horse has raised his head very slightly, as if to resist. However, in* **4** *Pam has him back under control so that he has come to a perfect balanced stop.*

3

4

This is how not to stop a horse. The rider is leaning back which has the effect of pushing her seat muscles into the saddle. In turn this tells the horse to go forward. At the same time she has pulled far too hard on the reins so that the horse's head is pulled into its chest.

This is a horrible halt! The rider's legs have shot forward, and she is leaning back, braced against them. All her weight is positioned over the horse's kidneys and, not surprisingly, it is extremely unhappy.

This is an incorrect attempt to slow down and stop from a trot. Again the rider is resisting the movement by leaning back in the saddle, holding her hands high in the air as she pulls backwards. Her seat pressing into the saddle, however, means the horse is still receiving instructions to move forward.

LESSONS ON THE LUNGE

Having an experienced instructor give you some lessons on the lunge rein at this moment in your riding career is the best possible thing for your progress. It is a step up from being led; the instructor holds the horse on the end of a long lunge rein attached either to the bit or to the noseband of a special lungeing cavesson, so that horse and rider circle around him. He is able to stop it careering off but he does not have all the control as the person leading you at the very beginning did. If, for example, you keep kicking the horse's sides, it will go faster, regardless of what the instructor says, and, similarly, you can pull it up yourself.

The instructor will begin by walking the horse around in a circle and your concentration, again and always, is on feeling in perfect balance and harmony with the horse. When you want to move forward into a trot, just squeeze very slightly with both legs evenly to push the horse forward. When you feel it respond, yield with your hands, relaxing your fingers on the reins so as to give it a little more freedom with its head which it needs for this pace. Practise both a sitting and a rising trot while on the lunge and remember to work evenly on both reins.

When you are feeling confident at a walk and a trot on the lunge, try pulling the horse up, using the signals discussed on the previous pages. You will see how the responsibility for slowing the pace or coming to a complete halt rests more with you now. The instructor can slow the horse only with his voice, if this is something to which the horse will respond, or by shortening the lunge rein and bringing the horse into the centre of the circle towards him. To stop the horse as it moves on the circle will be entirely your responsibility.

1

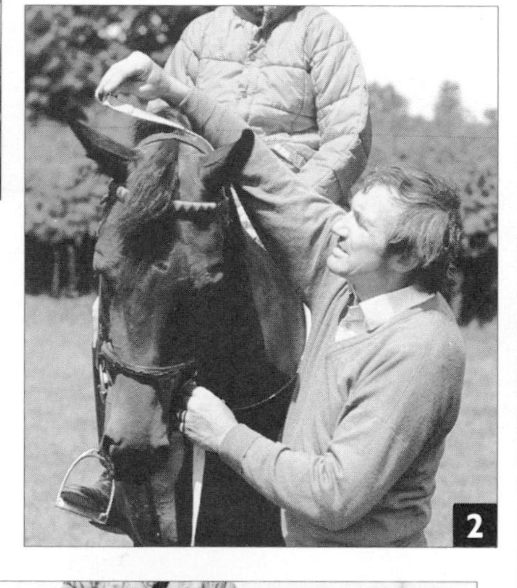

2

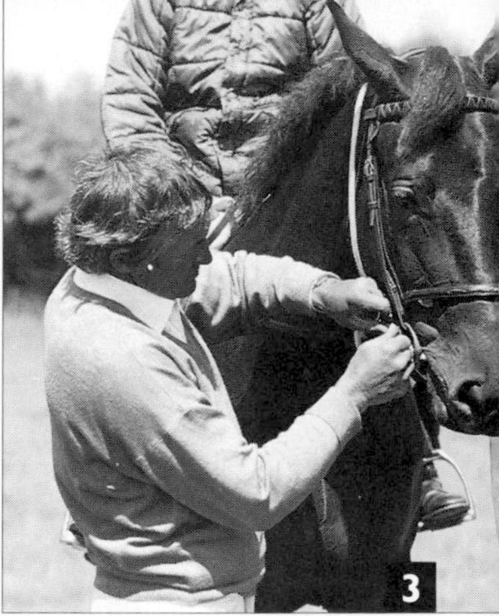

3

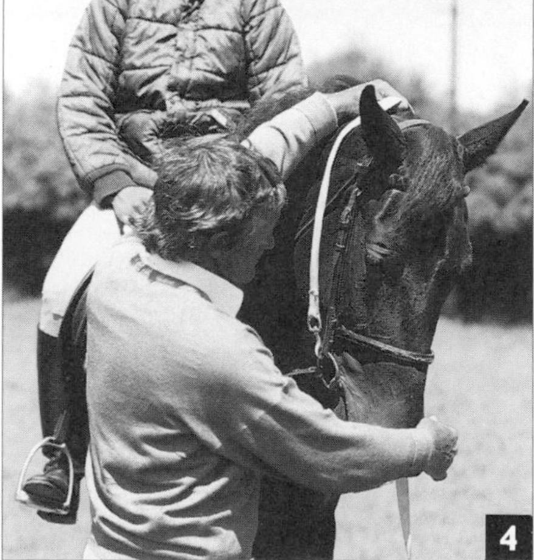

4

The lunge line can be attached to a special lungeing headcollar known as a cavesson, *or it can be attached directly to the bridle. I prefer this latter method, but it is essential that the line operates on both sides of the bit, to give equal control and pressure. To achieve this, the line is first threaded through the bit ring on one side (**1**), taken over the horse's head (**2**), then clipped on to the bit ring on the other side (**3**). The line should be positioned close to the headpiece of the bridle (**4**). To work on the left rein, the line would first be threaded through the nearside bit ring.*

1 *Lessons on the lunge are invaluable for the novice rider. He or she has to be a little more in control than when being led from the ground and, because the horse has a little more freedom, the rider is better able to experience the feel of the movement. This in itself tends to be very rhythmical as the horse is moving steadily around the instructor, thereby giving the rider every chance to consolidate his or her position in the saddle. Riding on the lunge, therefore, is an ideal way to work on balance, to gain confidence, to learn to use the legs as independent and positive instruments, and to begin to understand the basic control of a horse.*

2 *You can see in this picture how the novice rider is beginning to increase in confidence. She is trotting forward easily. Most important of all, her hands are relaxed – a sure sign that she is feeling happier.*

3 *It is important for horse and rider to work equally in both directions on the lunge. Here I have asked the rider to slow to a walk, then walk towards me in the centre of the circle so that I can change the rein.*

EXERCISES ON THE LUNGE

Pictured here are some exercises you can do on the lunge, riding without stirrup irons and without holding the reins. These are tremendously valuable for helping with your balance. You will find, too, that as your balance improves as a result of them so your seat muscles begin working correctly.

I can't emphasize enough the value of lessons and exercises on the lunge for a novice in helping to improve balance. At the trot, for example, because the movement is so difficult, a novice rider will often rely on the reins as balancing agents and lifelines. In fact, what happens is that the horse receives a jab in the mouth, which breaks the rhythm of the trot and makes it even harder for a novice to find his balance. Riding on the lunge at the trot and not holding the reins really allows a rider to feel the movement of the trot and discover the point of balance for his body.

1 *Once the rider is feeling more confident it is time to try a few exercises on the lunge. Here I have taken away her stirrup irons, and you can see that, robbed of their support, she is now hanging on for dear life. Her knees have come off the saddle, her toes have dropped and are now facing the ground and she is balancing by resting her hands on the neck. Although she is very uncomfortable at the moment, this is an excellent exercise to help a rider develop a balanced and secure seat independent of the stirrup irons.*

2 *At a trot, matters are even worse! You can see how she is being bounced about in the saddle and is using her hands even more to balance herself.*

3 *Although she is still hanging on to the mane with her right hand and leaning forward a little here, she is beginning to have more control over her lower leg, which has dropped down a little but is in a pretty good position. She still has to learn to be able to work off her knees without using the stirrup irons for support.*

6

4, 5 & **6** *Three exercises with the rider riding without using her reins as well as without stirrups. In the first, she rests her hands on her thighs; this is the easiest exercise to do. Secondly, she puts her hands on her head and finally, hardest of all, places them behind her back. In no way can she now use her hands to hang on, so she is really beginning to develop the sense of independent balance which is so important. Throughout these exercises the rider should also try to maintain control over her lower leg, keeping it still and in the correct position. Incidentally, it is important in these exercises either to use shorter reins or to knot them at the place you would normally hold them so that they do not hang down.*

THE CANTER

After the trot in a horse's repertoire of paces comes the canter. This is a pace in three-time, in which one hind leg takes the first step, followed by the other hind leg with its diagonally opposite front leg, and finally the remaining front leg (which actually looks as if it is leading the pace to an observer).

Many riders find the canter a more comfortable pace than the trot. You should not attempt it, however, before you feel wholly confident and balanced at both a sitting and a rising trot, and ideally the first time you do experience it should be while riding on the lunge with your instructor at the other end of the lunge line. You should also canter in this way before you begin attempting to control a horse entirely on your own – at any pace.

The best sort of horse to experience a first canter on is one that will canter slowly and evenly around the instructor on the lunge. I once sold some circus ponies to a riding school and the school kept them for years because they were so good at just going round and round in a circle at one pace, just as they had been trained to do for the circus ring.

When you are feeling sufficiently confident to try a canter, sit down in the saddle to the trot and squeeze with your legs against the horse's sides. As it moves into a canter, relax into the saddle as best you can to keep at the point of balance. Here, you will find that many books and instructors tell you to try to sit down deep into the saddle during the canter stride. I advise riders to let their bottoms leave the saddle with each stride – no more than 2 to 4 cm (1 to 1½ in) – but this helps you to find, and balance over, the centre of balance. If you do try to sit deep and still in the saddle, you will probably bounce around even more and will find you are rigid and set in one position, from which it is impossible to achieve balance. You should "work off your knees", an expression you will find used quite often in this book. It means staying in the centre of the point of balance and using your knees as a support and pivot for your thighs and body, and you should still be relaxed and not gripping tightly.

This position also helps when you want to slow down. If you are sitting deep in the saddle you are in effect pushing the horse forward with your seat muscles, so that when you come to resist the forward movement, keeping your hands still and closing your fingers on the reins, you will be giving conflicting commands.

During the canter pace, you may find you need to think about using your leg aids a little now. Few horses will canter evenly and rhythmically without constant encouragement from the rider in the same way that they will maintain a steady trot. So keep applying a squeeze-pressure with your legs in time with the pace. Listen to the pace, and keep squeezing with your legs – with your legs – with your legs – to the rhythm of the pace.

1 *A beautiful transition from a trot into a canter. You can see Pam is using her right leg just behind the girth to ask the horse to canter forward with its near fore leading. She is positioned right over the centre of balance, with her seat just slightly out of the saddle as I recommend.*

1a *Compare this picture of the transition from a trot to a canter with the one of Pam. Our novice rider is doing everything wrong. She is leaning forwards and into the circle, her hands are halfway up the horse's neck, her legs are far too far back with her toes pointing down, and her knees have come off the saddle. You can see by the horse's expression and ears that it is confused and unhappy about the instructions it is receiving.*

2 *Here our novice rider is on the lunge and experiencing canter for the first time. She is making the common mistake of leaning into the direction of the circle, in this case to the right. Her leg isn't in too bad a position, but basically she is simply hanging on with this leg and also with her hands on the mane. She's also too far in front of the centre of balance.*

3 *Here she is gripping with the back of her leg instead of her calf, so her foot is pointing out sideways from the saddle. Her elbows are also sticking out and she is still too far in front of the centre of balance.*

4 *In this picture she is beginning to get the hang of it. She is a little too high out of the saddle, her knee is also a little too high and her hands low, but she is in better balance with the movement.*

5 *Having got more used to the canter, the rider is now cantering on the lunge without stirrup irons – an excellent exercise for improving her balance. She is sitting a little deep in the saddle, not working off her knees, and is also a little too far forward, rather relying on her hands,which are pressed down on the neck.*

6 *This picture shows Pam in a nice relaxed canter – rider and horse working perfectly together as a team. Note the position of Pam's hands, held correctly just above the pommel of the saddle. In this position it is easy to flex the fingers for subtle nuances of control.*

MORE EXERCISES

I want to emphasize again the importance of riding and doing all exercises – walking, trotting and cantering with and without stirrups – equally on both reins. Most horses will tend to move and walk better and more easily to the left, and riders, too, quickly develop a good side on which they feel more comfortable, balanced and relaxed. You really want to guard against this as much as you can, because once established it is very hard to change.

When you begin to feel in control of yourself and aware of what you are expecting of your horse at any time you can begin to practise more exercises in the confined space of a school or small field. But before you do this it is a help to go for some gentle rides at a walk and trot in the country with your instructor leading you from his horse. This gives you the feel of some free forward movement instead of going round and round forever in a circle, but without the rather awesome responsibility of being left to control your mount entirely on your own.

You can use the time to do some useful exercises. At a walk or a trot, push your horse up to and just past the instructor's horse so you are moving slightly in front of him, then slow down again, coming back to a point where your horse's head is just level with the instructor's knee. When he tells you to stop make the initiative come from you, so that you stop in coordination with one another.

Riding out of the school in this way is very pleasant. Enjoy the beauty and peace of the countryside, look around, breathe the air, listen to the sounds. After all you are learning to ride because you want to, because you like being with horses and in the countryside, and you'll find you learn more quickly if you enjoy yourself and relax a bit, rather than concentrating hard and narrowly on your riding.

1 *Riding in pleasant countryside surroundings while being led by an instructor is a great way to improve your riding. You should have a basic knowledge of how to control your horse, but because the instructor has some control you can concentrate on improving your balance and coordination.*

2 *You can see from this picture that whilst our novice rider is now feeling quite relaxed in the saddle, she is actually sitting lop-sided. It is very easy to get into this habit, so guard against it by being aware of your position when you are riding.*

3 *This is a very good exercise; at the trot, Pam, as the instructor, has told the novice to use her legs a little more strongly against the horse's sides in order to move her horse forward in front of Pam's horse.*

4 *Here Pam has instructed the novice to bring her horse back so that its head is level with Pam's knee. The rider has concentrated so hard on pulling the horse back that she has allowed her knee to come away from the saddle. In this exercise the rider learns to increase and decrease her speed with no fear of the horse taking off with her.*

5 *Now the rider has pulled back a little too far so that Pam has had to check her horse suddenly in order to keep hold of the lead rein. This illustrates the importance of keeping up with the instructor at the same time as trying to do what you are told.*

6 *Here Pam is teaching the rider to get the feel of the horse moving away from her leg. By applying more pressure with her left leg behind the girth, she is moving the horse slightly to the right away from Pam's horse.*

7 *In this photograph she has brought her horse back closer to Pam's by applying pressure with her right leg.*

BACK IN THE SCHOOL

When you first start learning to control your mount entirely on your own, it should be in a confined space – no more than about 20 m (22 yd) square. This provides enough space for a horse to trot and canter, but not enough to work up the kind of speed at which bad accidents generally occur. Because the space is so small there really is not room for other riders and their horses and ponies and now, even if you have shared your early lessons with others, it is time to think for yourself and to begin to experience a real rapport between you and the horse. Your confidence will improve, too.

So practise all the paces you have learned, moving in both directions and making sure you are in complete control at all times. Think about balance, coordination and control and make sure the horse is doing what *you* want it to do at any given moment.

Practise making turns to the left and right at a walk and trot. To turn to the left exert slight pressure on the left rein, while yielding with the right. To turn to the right exert slight pressure on the right rein and yield with the left. Don't worry about any specific leg aids for making these turns; use your legs only to change the pace from a walk to a trot, or to maintain the pace if the horse is beginning to slacken when you don't want it to.

After these exercises, try cantering in a circle, again on either rein.

When you are happy in a small confined space, move up to a large *manège* or *school*, either indoors or outdoors, but make sure you are still working in an enclosed space. Really get the feel of riding without someone telling you what to do all the time; you must learn to make decisions for yourself. What you need now is to get more experience, to keep on feeling what it is like to be on a horse's back while it is moving through its paces, to feel what it is like to be in control, and able to stop at any time.

But do keep everything simple. Practise the basics only. I find over and over again at my clinics, and it is the same the world over, that the simpler everything is the quicker and more successfully people learn.

Our novice rider has progressed sufficiently to enjoy and benefit from practising school work on her own in the manège. Here she is quite relaxed, and both she and the horse are enjoying themselves and beginning to understand what it is all about. Don't undertake these sessions in the school aimlessly; work out a little training programme incorporating the different paces and movements you have learned so far, and vary them as much as possible. The only comment I would make on our rider here is that she is not looking where the horse is going!

The figure-of-eight exercise is one of the most useful schooling figures. It ensures that both sides of the horse are exercised equally, that the vertebrae in its spine are being rotated in both directions, and that the hocks are strengthened evenly. Also, horses with a high head carriage will tend to drop it naturally if you give them lots of work on the diagonal. So that you ride the figure-of-eight smoothly and evenly, place two barrels, oil drums or posts in the arena, as here, with a distance between them that suits you.

1 – 5 *Here Pam is in the field demonstrating a figure-of-eight exercise at a nice balanced trot. In (**1**) she is trotting on a left-handed circle. In (**2**) and (**3**) she is coming across the centre of the movement, ready to change the rein to the right. In (**2**) she is using her left leg to keep the horse straight and in (**3**) she has released that pressure and is now just gently pulling on the right rein against its neck, and using her right leg to bend it round to the right. In (**4**) and (**5**) you can see how she has got the horse going forward bent gently round her inside leg, so that its body is forming an arc of the circle. Pam is doing this exercise in a field so that we can see it easily; for a novice rider it is best to try these exercises in a small space so that there is no risk of an accident in which the horse may gallop off.*

COLLECTED AND EXTENDED WALK AND TROT

In no time at all you are going to be sufficiently competent to learn some refinements in the paces with which you are now wholly familiar.

When a horse walks naturally it will do so with the length of stride it finds most comfortable, with its neck stretched forward and its head nodding slightly as it takes each step. It is possible, however, to alter the walk, and the whole appearance of the walk, by shortening or lengthening the stride.

When the stride is shortened, the horse moves at a *collected* pace. At a collected walk and trot the horse covers less ground with each step, but the step itself is springier. To achieve this, the horse must "shorten" its neck and body, making itself more compact. Its outline – the whole shape of its carriage – becomes rounder, and the carriage of its head becomes higher and more composed.

When the stride is lengthened, the horse moves at an *extended* pace. In this it covers more ground with each step and its outline, correspondingly, becomes longer to allow it to achieve this. It gives the impression of pointing its toes; in

In these photographs Pam is riding the same young horse which appeared earlier in the book, but now she is demonstrating how to shorten and lengthen its stride. It is important to understand, however, that we are training this horse to be a show-jumper, not a dressage horse, so it does not have to reach the same precision of pace as you will see demonstrated by Judy Bradwell on her dressage horse.

1 *Here Pam is moving forwards freely at an ordinary walk. In (**2**) you can see from the fact that the horse is beginning to lift its knee a little as it takes a step that Pam is beginning to ask it to gather itself in and shorten its stride. To do this she has sat up straight in the saddle, keeping her legs relaxed. Then she makes a slightly firmer grip on the reins whilst pushing with her legs just behind the girth. This makes the horse use its hocks which it must do to get elevation into the step. Because of the resistance from the reins as the horse goes forward the energy created by the rider's legs, instead of making the horse go faster, goes into making its step bouncier.*

3 *In response to Pam's request, the horse has gathered itself together so that its neck has shortened and its whole outline appears shorter. It is taking slightly higher steps – raising its knee a little more – and is demonstrating a collected walk.*

4 & **5** *Now Pam is asking the horse to use its shoulders more to really stretch out its step into an extended walk. She has relaxed her hands a little and as its left foreleg goes forward she uses her left leg against its side to indicate that she wants it to work that shoulder. As its right foreleg goes forward, so she uses her right leg against its side. You can see how its outline has lengthened as it reaches forward to cover more ground with each step. Remember it is a lengthening of stride that is required, not a quickening of pace, and that it will be necessary to keep up the pressure with alternate legs to maintain the step.*

fact it is really using its fetlock joints, almost throwing them forward to help achieve the greater length of stride.

Practise these changes in pace for a few turns of the school, then in a figure-of-eight movement. If you just keep going round and round the school, you will work one rein for a longer period of time. Working in a figure-of-eight means you are constantly changing the rein and thus working both sides evenly.

After feeling the changes in pace at walk and trot a few times, allow the horse to come back to an ordinary walk. Then move it up to an ordinary trot; you won't even have to think about the aids you are giving now – they will have become second nature. Be aware of your contact with the reins, and begin to use your fingers more, flexing them on the reins all the time. As the horse feels this contact, it will begin to arch its neck more, holding it in an almost half-moon shape.

__1, 2,__ & __3__ Here Pam is just beginning to ask the horse to do a collected trot. She has applied a little tension on the reins, whilst applying pressure with her legs, so that the horse has to gather itself in. You can see how it has arched its neck in response – in fact almost too much – and is really using its knee and hock joints to take springy high steps. (__2__) As it takes the next step, it has adjusted its head carriage and is now performing a beautiful, balanced collected trot. (__3__) Now Pam is asking the horse to lengthen its stride in the same way that she did at the walk. It is beginning to respond by taking longer steps and slightly lengthening its outline.

4 *As it takes the next step in this picture, you can see how it is throwing its toes out in order to cover as much ground as possible with each step.*

5 *A lovely picture of an extended trot. You can see how the horse has really stretched its whole body and appears to be pointing its toes, covering as much ground as possible. Note how it is over-tracking with its hind legs – that is, they are coming into contact with the ground some distance in front of the forelegs in the same stride.*

COLLECTED AND EXTENDED CANTER

In just the same way, you should be able to perform a collected or extended canter. But before this, we should talk about cantering on different legs.

In the canter pace, a horse is said to be leading with his near-or off-fore, according to which front leg appears to be leading the pace. When cantering on a right-handed circle, the horse will be most correctly balanced if it is bent very slightly along the length of its body to the right, with its inside – or off-fore – leading; on a left-handed circle a horse should be slightly bent to the left and lead with the near-fore.

As you ask for a canter, therefore, you should now be thinking of this and ask the horse to strike off on a specific leg. However, there are two ways of doing it and it depends a bit on who is teaching you and how the horse has been schooled.

Ordinary canter

1 *An ordinary canter. Note how the horse is looking easy and relaxed along its length; its head carriage is quite natural; it is balanced and moving forward freely.*

Dressage and event riders, and probably most recreational riders, will use *diagonal aids* to tell a horse which leg it should lead off. This means that if you wanted to canter left-handed, with the near-fore leading, you would exert more pressure with the right (or outside) leg, placing it behind the girth, in order to influence the off-hind leg. In a left-handed canter, the horse actually takes the first step of the stride with its off-hind, the second step with near-hind and off-fore together and the final step with the near fore, which appears to be leading the pace. Diagonal aids, therefore, influence the horse's hindquarters.

As a show-jumper, however, I always use and teach horses and pupils to use *lateral aids.* These influence the horse's shoulders, and as it is the front legs that land first over a jump it is important to a show-jumper, where the first stride over a jump is the beginning of the approach to the next fence, to have control over the horse's front end. To ask a horse to canter with the near-fore using lateral aids, exert a little more pressure with your inside, or left leg, on the girth, rather than behind it, thereby giving the instruction that it is the left shoulder and left foreleg you want to move.

Practise changes of leg at the canter in a figure-of-eight, coming back to a trot for a few strides as you go across the diagonals and then asking the horse to lead off on the correct leg for the circle.

After this, try collecting and extending the pace, but this time use the full length of the school, asking for a collected canter along the short sides and an extended canter down the long sides.

Collected canter

1 *Now Pam is asking the horse to do a collected canter. She has eased its head in to shorten it up and it is moving off with its near-fore leading. At the moment, it is resisting the command slightly – note how it is swishing its tail and its ears are back.*

2 *Here Pam has settled the horse into a balanced collected canter, in which, if anything, it is a little overbent. Note though how it has shortened up its length and is lifting its knee high as it moves.*

Extended canter

1 *Now Pam is beginning to ask it to lengthen its stride for an extended canter. You can see she has allowed it a little more head and is keeping up the pressure against its sides with her legs.*

2 & 3 *The result is a lovely free and easy swinging canter in which the horse's body is stretched to its utmost and it is really using its shoulder to help it throw its legs forward. It is covering more ground with each step, but not actually increasing the speed at which it is moving.*

PULLING UP IN A STRAIGHT LINE

If you watch a horse in its natural environment, it very rarely pulls up in anything approaching a straight line. In fact it nearly always pulls up in a circle, and usually going round to the left. So when you ask a horse to pull up it will usually do so at an angle, or at least bent to a greater or lesser degree, probably to the left.

Pulling up in a straight line is really quite a difficult exercise. At the clinics I held every week in a recent winter, not one of the riders attending for the first time could pull up in a straight line. And they were not novices. Even watching top riders in any equestrian sport – show-jumping, eventing or racing – you will be surprised how few of them pull up in a straight line. Many don't because they have simply never thought about it, but it is actually very important to be able to do so, particularly in the sports of dressage, showing and show-jumping.

In dressage, coming to a halt in anything but a straight line in a test will mean marks against you, and in showing classes, at whatever level, the judges will be looking for the same thing. In show-jumping, where big jumps are placed at tight and tricky angles often in a very small arena, and time is often of the essence, it is essential to be able to keep your horse straight at all times. These are not the only times it is important though; out hunting or riding across country you may find yourself in a situation when you must pull up quickly, perhaps even in the middle of a full, extended gallop – if hounds suddenly check, if you come across growing crops, or if you find yourself in a confined space.

Begin by walking in a straight line along the long side of the school and aim to pull up in a straight line, halfway down. Then try going from trot to halt in a straight line. Finally, canter along the long side of the school and come to a halt so that the horse stops straight.

There are all sorts of exercises you can do to help you perfect this technique. When you are happy about coming to a halt in a straight line from ordinary paces, try it from collected and extended ones. Ask for a collected trot, push forward into an extended trot and ask for a halt from there. Then try going from a halt straight into a collected trot. Then from a halt straight into a collected canter.

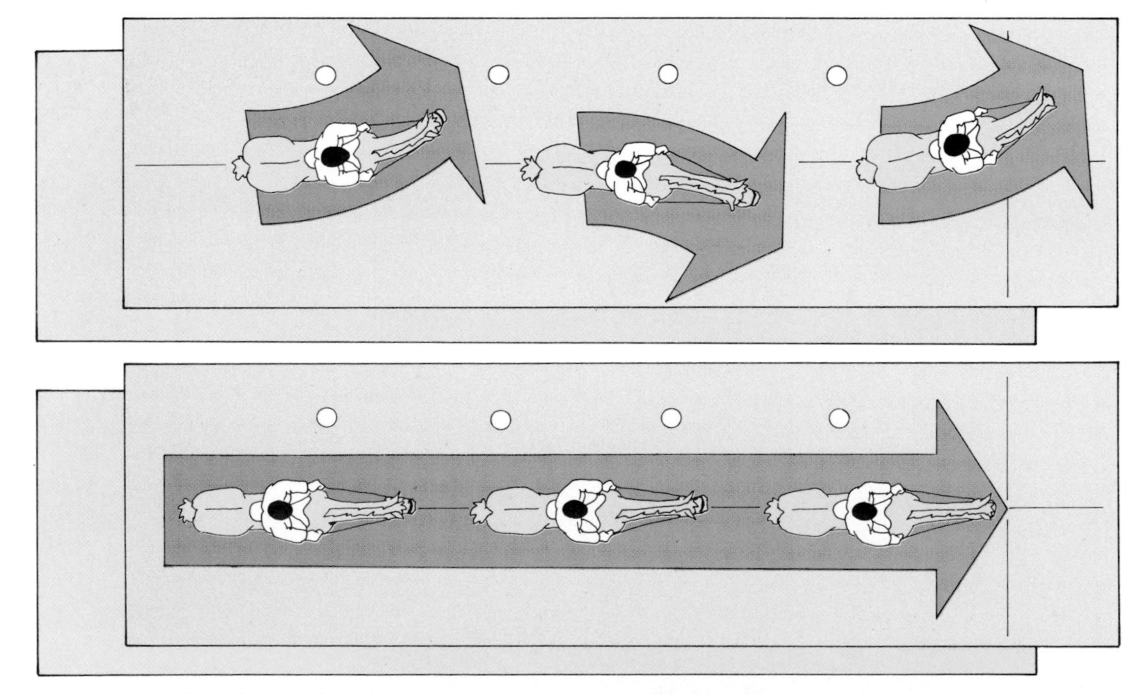

__Top__ The horse is being allowed to wander because the rider is not using the lower leg to control it, and it stops with its body askew. __Bottom__ The rider keeps the horse in a straight line between hand and leg, and it stops in a straight line.

1 – 5 *This is one of the hardest exercises of all – to walk and trot in a straight line and then pull up standing absolutely square to the movement. European riders attach a great deal of importance to a horse and rider's ability to do this and often when they come to the UK to buy horses they will turn down a horse that won't pull up in a straight line and stand square. In this country, however, I am constantly surprised at how difficult even experienced riders find it – so the earlier you start trying the exercise the better. Here Pam is trotting up the field in a perfectly straight line and she achieves an extremely commendable square halt considering she is riding a novice horse. Note that she is using her legs as well as her hands to steer the horse as she indicates she wants it to stop by resisting with the reins. If she were to use her hands only, it would stop, but would be likely to come to a halt and drift all over the place at an angle to the line it has been taking. To achieve a straight halt, work slightly off your knees – remember that means staying in the centre of the point of balance, using your legs to support your body – so that your seat muscles are not pushing the horse forward. Then close your legs gently against its sides so as to keep the shoulders and hindquarters in a line.*

2

3

5

4

FINISHING OFF

You will have had a number of lessons by now, and taking off the saddle and bridle and attending to your horse after a lesson will soon become a familiar routine. The pictures here show you the steps in this routine. Do everything quietly and calmly, talk to your horse and enjoy these peaceful moments after your work together. You have come a long way since your first lessons and no doubt you were aching after each one of them! I always ask my pupils at the end of a session if they have any aches and pains, and it is those with the most – especially aching legs – who I know have been really working. But such aches and pains obviously get less as you become more experienced and exercise and develop the right muscles.

If you are now able to do the exercises we have discussed, particularly the pulling up in a straight line from a trot and canter, you are way ahead of many experienced riders. You must now have gained confidence in yourself, in your ability as a rider and in your control over your horse. Hopefully you are aware of some sort of rapport and partnership with it, too. Using your aids with confidence will come naturally as your experience increases. You know already that it is not just a matter of kicking the animal to go faster and pulling on the reins to stop, and the better and more experienced you become, the more you will find you are refining the signals you give in order to achieve greater refinement of control over and performance from the horse.

Keep practising all the movements outlined on the preceding pages, interspersing school – or flat – work with rides out in the country (see Chapter Three). Always remember when you are working in a school or manège to be one hundred per cent in control of your own thoughts so that you know what you are going to ask of your horse and expect of it at any given moment. If you are unsure of what to do next, you will quickly communicate this and your horse's performance will be correspondingly imprecise. And it won't be its fault.

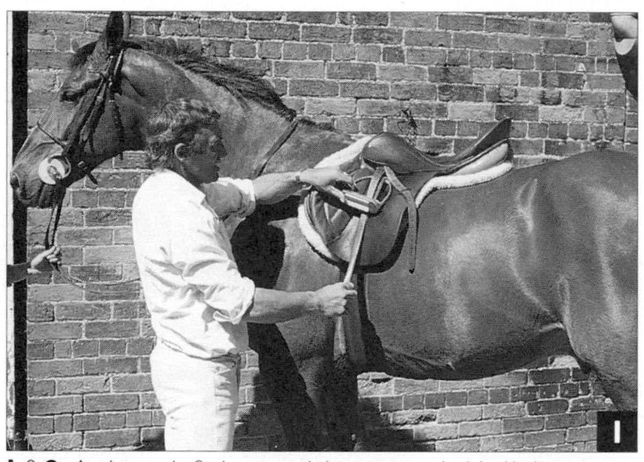

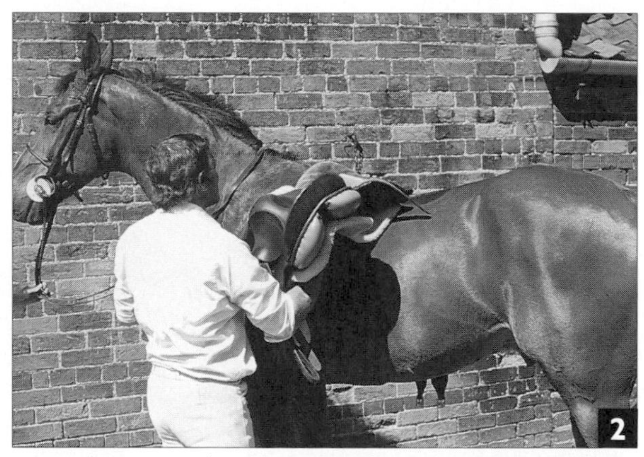

1 & **2** *At the end of a lesson, while someone holds the horse, run the stirrup irons up the saddle on either side, then (**2**) from the nearside unbuckle the girth and lift off the saddle. With a nervous horse, it is advisable to place the girth across the saddle before taking it off, so that the girth does not frighten the horse as it brushes against its side.*

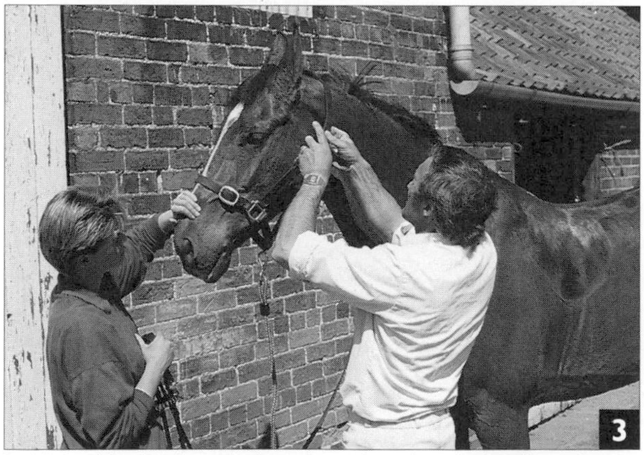

3 *Unbuckle the throatlash and noseband on the bridle and, with the reins still around the horse's neck, slip the bridle forward over its ears and off its face.*

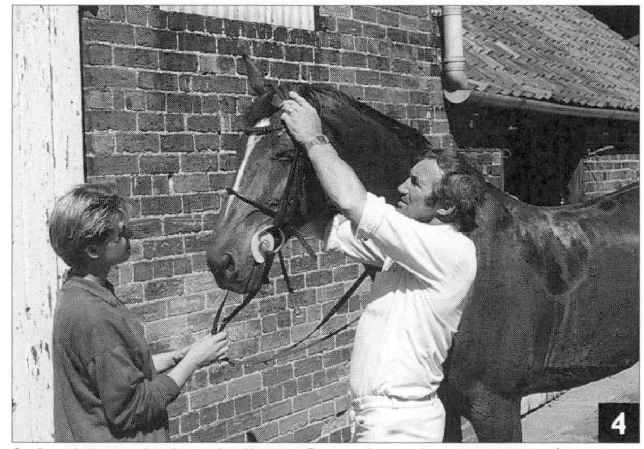

4 *Buckle on the headcollar before taking the reins over the neck so that you always have some form of control.*

5, 6 & **7** *Tie up the horse, so that you can wash it down. A horse should always be tied up with a quick release knot, which can be done in various ways but can always be undone in an instant if necessary. Begin the knot by threading the rope from right to left through a loop of string tied to a chain or ring in the wall.* (**6**) *Twist the loose end up and round to form a circle as shown.* (**7**) *Take it right round to the back of the rope and back to the left side.*

8 *Catch hold of the rope and bring a loop through the circle.*

9 *Pull the loop through.*

10 *Tighten the knot by pulling down on the end attached to the headcollar. To release it, simply pull sharply on the loose end.*

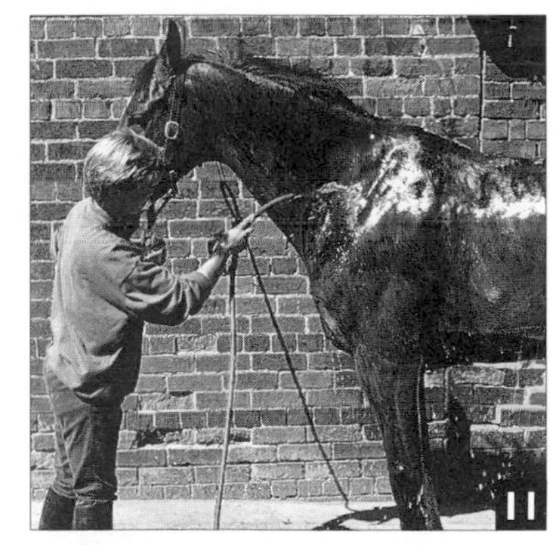

11 *To freshen a horse after riding on a hot day, hose it down with clean water on the neck, back and legs.*

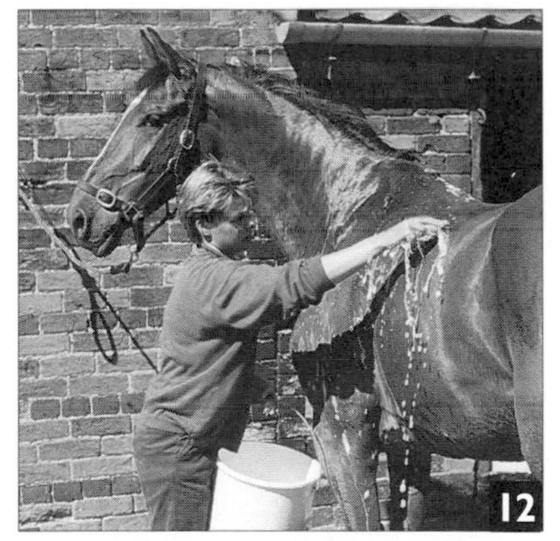

12 & **13** *Then wash off the coat with a horse body wash – like a shampoo – to remove any dirt and minerals that would have come to the surface in the sweat.* (**13**) *Remove the excess water with the rubber side of a sweat scraper. On a hot day like this the horse could be turned out in the paddock to have a good roll or put on the exercise machine to walk round calmly until it has cooled off. Never wash a horse off on a cold, wintry day, or it's likely to get a cold in its kidneys. Instead, rub it down well, getting it as dry as possible and then put it in the stable with an anti-sweat rug under its day rug.*

3

OUT FOR A RIDE

All horses and riders need to go out of the school to exercise every now and then. Continual school work will soon turn into a dull routine, and everyone will get bored and stale. A change of surroundings and a bit of free forward movement, unrestricted by the confines of the manège, will help to charge the batteries and make you both work better when you come back into the school. Later on, you will find that the best way to get a horse really fit, for whatever reason it might be necessary, is by giving it hard, regular exercise outside the school.

Before you leave the security of the school or manège, however, do make sure you really feel that you are a good enough rider to go out and enjoy the wide open spaces that lie beyond. How do you know this? Well, quite simply, you will know. You are the one that must have confidence in yourself. If you can do the things we discussed in the last chapter – coming to a halt in a straight line, then moving off into a canter on the correct leg, cantering with collected and extended strides and coming back to a halt again when you want to – then you are certainly competent enough to go out for a ride without being on a lead rein, and you should also feel confidence in yourself.

It is a good idea, if possible, to have ridden a number of different horses by this time and felt the differences in their responses to you and a given situation. Having experienced first-hand the fact that not all horses react to you and their surroundings in the same way will help you to be a bit more prepared for the unexpected.

As you will be the only person who really knows how confident you feel this is not the time to push yourself. If you do get on a horse and find you do not feel confident on its back, get off it again. There's no ignominy in that. In the Sudan a few years ago, I had to give a demonstration of jumping in front of a huge crowd. There were supposed to be other riders demonstrating as well, but none had been able to get there, so I had to ride all the horses, and there were forty-three of them. I rode forty-two happily, but the minute I got on the last one's back, I didn't feel happy. I felt it was not really sound. Its owner disagreed with me, got on the horse to show me I was wrong and had an accident with it. I know I am an experienced rider, but I promise that you will know, too, if you do or don't want to ride a particular horse. And your first ride out of the school, controlling the horse yourself, should certainly be on an animal you know well and enjoy riding.

This is one of my pupils, Hannah Etherington, taking her horse for a hack in the country. Here she is having a quiet trot along a pretty track. As the ground is quite hard here, going any faster than a steady trot could cause damage to the horse's legs.

THE PADDOCK

At the moment we are considering riding out of the school in the countryside as a recreational activity. Many riders are content to progress no further with riding than this, loving the companionship of their horse and the beauty and peace of the rural surroundings. Such people, if they own their own horses, will generally keep them at grass, or primarily at grass, so now we will consider a few aspects of the management of horses kept at grass.

The paddock – a sizeable area of good grass – is of course the first essential. It should be well and safely fenced, with a wide gate that latches securely without having to be tied up with bits of string or wire. There should be a padlock on the gate; there are always horse thieves about. It is best to fasten the padlock with a combination lock. You are only human and are bound to forget the key on some occasion or other! Make sure, too that a few responsible friends know the combination in case of accidents when you can't be contacted quickly.

Within the paddock there must be a good clean water supply. This is best provided in a watering trough with a ballcock system. Even if there is a stream running through the paddock, it is best to provide a water supply; if a horse drinks from a stream, it may well take sand or grit into its system which could cause colic – a severe stomach pain. Also the ground around the stream can get very wet and boggy in winter or bad weather.

In addition, if the horse is to be out all, or even most of the time, there should be some sort of shelter in the field. A high, thick hedge or line of trees could provide this, but better would be a wooden or brick building which is open on one side (not the side of the prevailing wind) so that the horse can go in and out as it likes. Put down a thick layer of straw to provide a soft bed for the horse to lie down on.

In the northern hemisphere it is really only hardy ponies that can survive the winter – and keep reasonably fleshy and well – out of doors. Most horses, particularly if they have any breeding, will benefit from being brought into the stable at least at night.

An ideal field shelter. This is not an expensive construction, but nevertheless serves the purpose admirably. The front side has a large opening, so the horse can wander in and out as it likes. Such a shelter should always face south – away from north – or north-easterly winds. The purpose of a field shelter is to keep a horse dry, rather than warm. As long as its back is warm, the rest of its body will create its own warmth.

If a horse is to be turned out in a field for a major part of the time, it is a good idea to freeze-brand it as here. This is a positive deterrent to horse thieves as it makes the horse easy to identify. In addition, if it were to be taken for slaughter, there would have to be a check on ownership before the animal was killed. If you are buying a horse that is already freeze-branded, you can check up for certain on its previous ownership.

Above *A horse wearing a modern type of New Zealand rug – a warm, waterproof rug for horses out at grass. This one is done up with cross-over understraps, as opposed to the old-fashioned type which were done up with a surcingle and leg straps. As you can see, the horse can enjoy a canter without the rug slipping and without being restricted in any way.*

Left *This sturdy post-and-rail fencing is suitable for fencing paddocks to contain horses and is infinitely preferable to wire fencing. However, if the fencing is to be between two paddocks in which horses are turned out simultaneously, you should use the type of fencing pictured* ***below****. In this the two fences are approximately 1.5 to 2 m (5 to 6ft 6in) high, thereby making it impossible for the horses to sniff one another over the fence. Should they disagree, horses may either paw at the fence or turn round and kick out – possibly damaging the fence or, worse still, ending up with broken legs.*

GRASS MANAGEMENT

Keeping a horse at grass is a comparatively easy system, but there is more to it than just putting the animal in the paddock from one year's end to the next. By "managing" the area, you will get considerably more value out of the grass.

It is important first of all to check there are no poisonous plants growing in the field. If there are they must be dealt with, preferably by pulling up by the roots. If treated with weedkiller, let them die completely and remove them before putting horses back in the paddock; dying plants often seem to be very palatable, but they are just as deadly.

The best way to conserve grass and get the best out of it is to divide up the area you have, into three if possible, two if you feel the area is too small for three. This can be done with electric fencing – use two or three strands or the special stud electric fencing available now. If the divisions are likely to be permanent, a more long-term type of fencing can be erected. Graze each of these areas in a three-week rotation so that the grass that is being rested has time to recover. Besides giving the grass a chance to grow, this will also help with the control of worms in the horse.

All horses – both those kept in the stable and those out at grass – suffer from worms, but it is generally more of a problem and danger with those kept primarily at grass. Here they are more susceptible to the worm life cycle which goes from horse to pasture and then back to horse as it grazes. Fifty per cent of worm control relies on pasture control.

Dividing the grazing area as described is one way to help, as nature will kill off the worm larvae living in the pasture during the resting period. Another is to go round with a wheelbarrow picking up droppings from the pasture every day, or, if time really does not allow this frequency, then twice a week – *without fail.* Horses always do their droppings in one area, so they are easy to find. They don't eat this grass, so it is a good idea to top it when it gets very long, then chain harrow the area and apply lime to it.

Worms are harmful and dangerous to a horse, and they will also feed off the food the animal eats. Whatever sort of food you are giving to a horse – concentrated feed, hay or just grass – it is far too expensive to be giving to worms! Horses at grass should be given a worming course in November, then wormed every two to three months according to the individual horse and the management of the paddock. A vet will recommend the correct wormer to give, and also advise on frequency.

Sensible and diligent grass management will pay dividends; if a pasture does get horse sick, it will need a good twelve months' rest, and it may be necessary to plough and reseed it if it has got into really bad condition.

Poisonous plants must be eliminated from any field in which horses are grazing. From top left: ragwort, yew, deadly nightshade and privet.

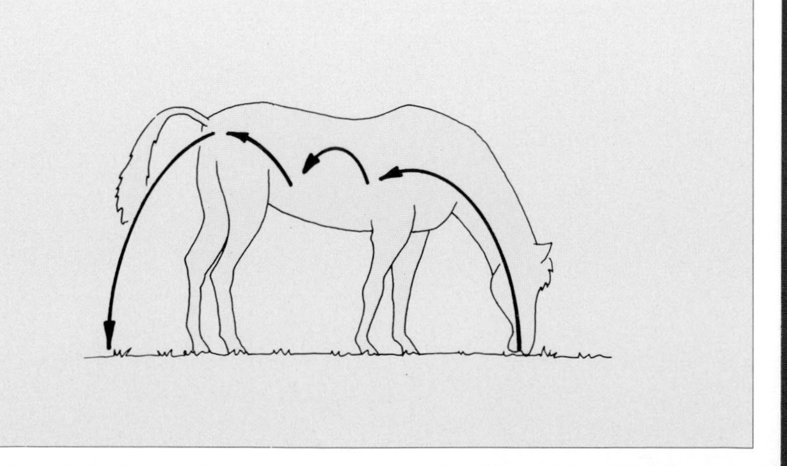

The other danger to a horse in pasture is worms. A horse eats the pastures which the larvae infest; the larvae pass through the horse's gut and develop into egg-laying worms. The eggs are passed out in the droppings, to thrive once more on the pasture.

FEEDING

Through the summer, providing the grass is good and the rotation system recommended is followed, it will probably not be necessary to give a horse at grass any supplementary feeding. During the winter, however, there is not sufficient goodness in the grass to sustain horses or ponies, however little exercise is expected of them.

The feeding of horses is an art, not a science, and it is impossible to give specific rules on what sort of food and how much to give to any horse. It depends on what sort of animal your horse is, the conditions in which it is kept, the work that is expected of it, whether it is easy to keep flesh on, whether it is a fussy feeder, and countless other "whethers". As a general rule, it is not a good idea to give quantities of oats, or heating feed, to horses and ponies at grass, particularly if they are only being exercised at the weekends.

All horses and ponies at grass should be given hay or horsehage (partly dried grass with a higher nutrient content than hay) when there is not sufficient goodness in the grass. This can mean in the summer, too, if the grass is very poor. Hay should be fed in a hay net or rack and it should be provided more or less all the time so that the animal can nibble away at it whenever it wants to during the day. Tie the hay net or position a hay rack in a sheltered place, preferably in the field shelter.

If you are giving supplementary feeds, give them at regular times, but not just before you are going out for a ride. Horses don't enjoy exercising on a full stomach any more than people do.

Shake the hay well before pushing it into the hay net so that any dust falls out of it. Buy only good quality hay and store it in a dry, covered place.
Fill the hay net well, then pull the string round the top to close it. Hay nets are usually made of nylon, though old-fashioned ones may be made of string. Make sure your hay net is in good repair and not riddled with holes or the hay will fall out and be wasted.

SHOEING

All horses and ponies need regular attention to their feet,and if they are to be ridden, they must also be fitted with shoes. The horn of the hoof grows like finger and toe nails in humans, and it has to be cut back to be kept healthy. A horse's feet should never be allowed to get too long or the horn will begin to split and break; also the horse is likely to stumble as it wanders around the field. Every six to eight weeks, the blacksmith should cut back a horse's feet. If the horse is only being exercised in a school and across fields, it may well be that its feet will need cutting back before it has worn out the shoes. In this case, the blacksmith will cut back the feet, reshape the shoes and reapply them. He will generally try to hammer the nails into the foot at slightly different points from the previous set of nails so as to avoid weakening the horn too much.

When the horn is being trimmed, the blacksmith will also pare down the frog, cutting away any dead skin and keeping it away from the bars of the feet (the corners on either side of the top of the frog). This allows the foot room to expand – a healthy foot is one that looks wide – and also makes it easier to get the hoofpick right up into this area to clean around the frog.

This shoe is fitted with a plastic gasket, used when the feet have very thin soles or, when wedge shaped, to "tip" the horse forward slightly when it has, for example, damaged its tendons.

If a horse has injured the sole of its foot a piece of rubber; leather or plastic may be fitted between the sole and the shoe.

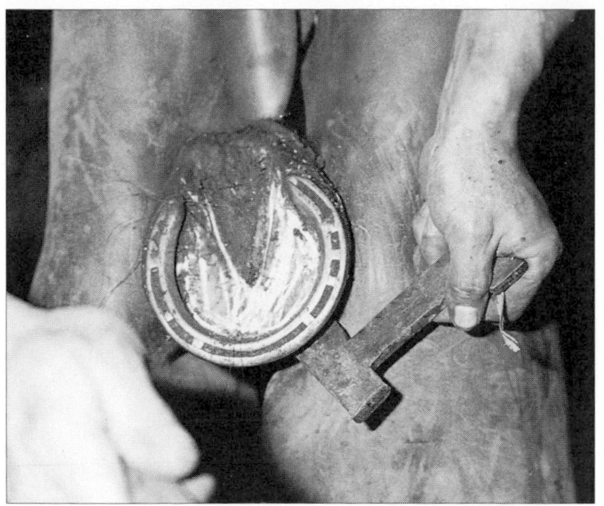

1 The farrier begins to remove the old shoe from the horse's foot.

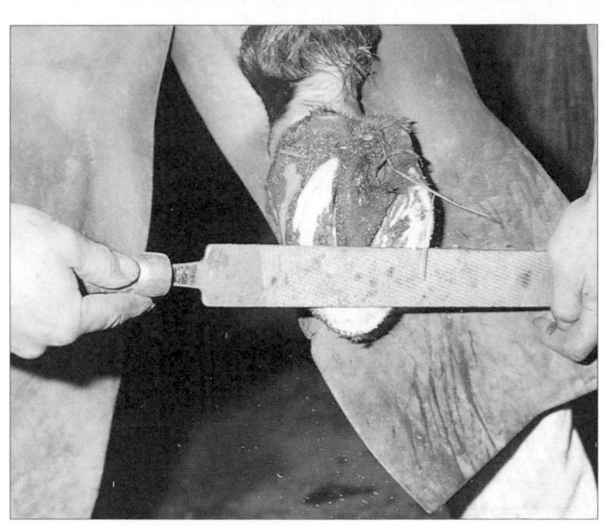

2 The hoof shows wear around the edges; the farrier files it with a rasp to make it smooth.

3 The hot shoe can now be fitted to the horse's foot.

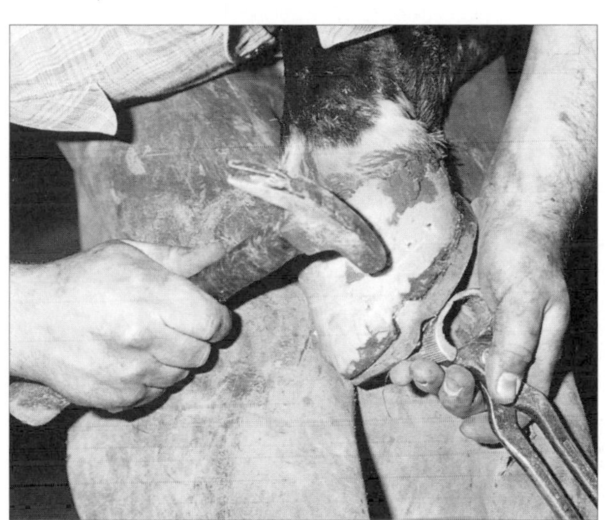

4 The shoe is "clinched up", the ends of the nails being knocked up over the foot.

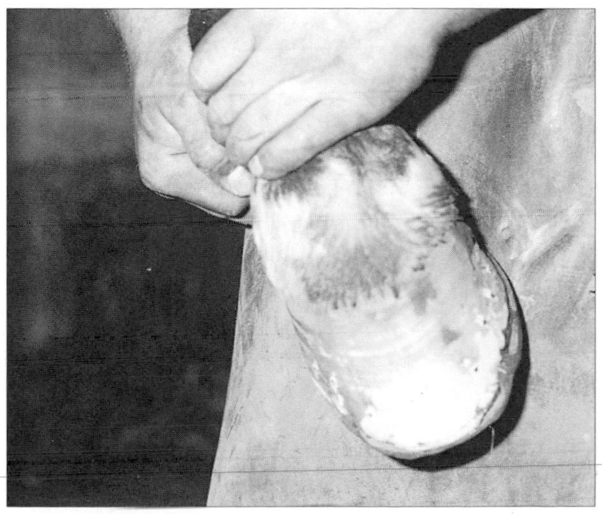

5 The shod foot is inspected. The other feet will now be shod.

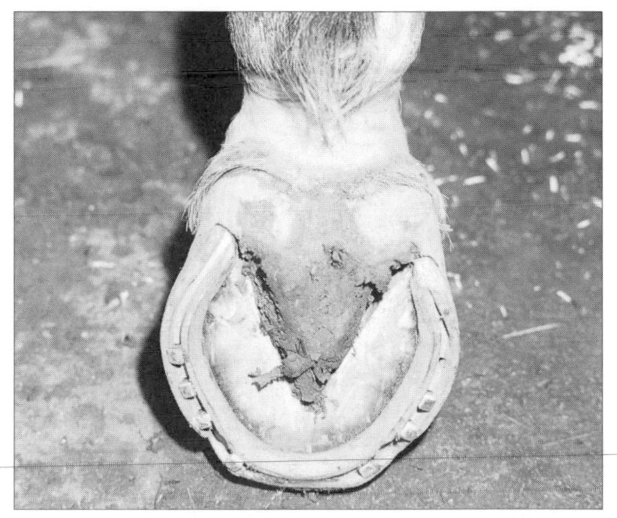

6 A clean, healthy foot with a wide frog and a perfectly-fitting shoe.

CATCHING A HORSE AT GRASS

Back to going out for a ride. If the horse is kept out at grass, the first thing that has to be done is to catch it and bring it into the stable area.

To catch a horse at grass you will need a small bucket of feed and a *headcollar.* If a horse is known to be difficult to catch, it may be turned out in a headcollar, in which case you would only need the feed and perhaps a rope to attach to the headcollar to make leading easier.

Remember when you have entered in the field to shut the gate behind you. Horses, and ponies in particular, are attracted to an open gate like bees to a honey pot, and you would feel pretty silly watching the pony you have come to catch disappear to freedom through the open gate! And shut the gate behind you when you lead the animal out of the field. Even if there are no other horses turned out in the paddock, an open gate looks slovenly and is something of an invitation for people to walk into the field.

A horse at grass needs to be caught up every day, even if it's not going to be ridden. It should then be checked over, especially its legs, for any injuries – cuts, lumps or bumps – it might have sustained in the field. This also gets it used to being caught and handled. A horse left endlessly on its own in a field will soon be pretty unwilling to be caught and subject itself to human company!

1 *Take a bucket of feed and a headcollar into the paddock and call to the horse.*

2 *Let it have a bite or two of the feed in the bucket; don't cheat and take an empty bucket with you – the horse will soon get to know and won't trust you.*

3 *Put the bucket on the ground and buckle on the headcollar.*

4 *Lead the horse from the field and remember to take the bucket with you and to shut the gate securely behind you, particularly if there are other horses turned out.*

PREPARING FOR THE RIDE

Once in the stable yard or similar area, the horse must be tied up while it is prepared for the ride. There should be a conveniently placed ring or small loop of chain for this and it is best to tie a small loop of string to the ring or chain and then tie the rope to the string. Should the horse pull back, it is only the string that will break, not the rope or headcollar. Horses should always be tied up with a quick release knot.

Horses at grass will need a little grooming before they are taken out. As living in the open air, and rolling on the ground, helps to keep the coat in a healthy condition, they don't need the full grooming – or strapping – that a stabled horse needs. However, any dried sweat or mud should be brushed off the coat and legs, the mane and tail should be combed so they look neat and tidy, the eyes and nostrils should be sponged so they are clean and, most important of all, the feet should be picked out and oiled. The horse is then ready to be tacked-up and ridden.

I Whether you are preparing a horse for a gentle ride in the country or to go to a show, the first thing you must always do is pick out the underside of each hoof using a hoof pick.

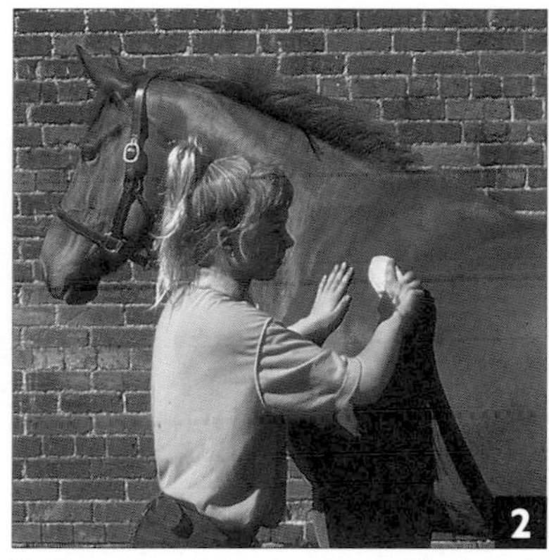

2 For a casual ride, brush over the horse's coat, under its belly and down its legs to remove any mud, dirt or dried sweat. If it is very dirty, it is best to go over the coat using a rubber curry comb first, before brushing, to loosen the dirt and bring it to the surface. Pay particular attention to areas under the saddle and girth.

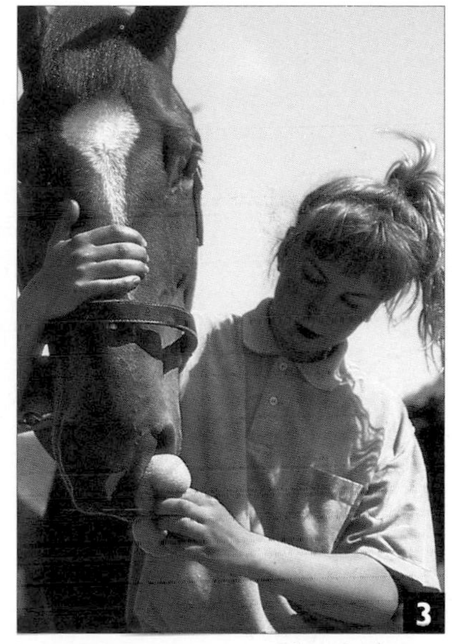

3 With a sponge squeezed out in clean water, sponge round the eyes and nostrils.

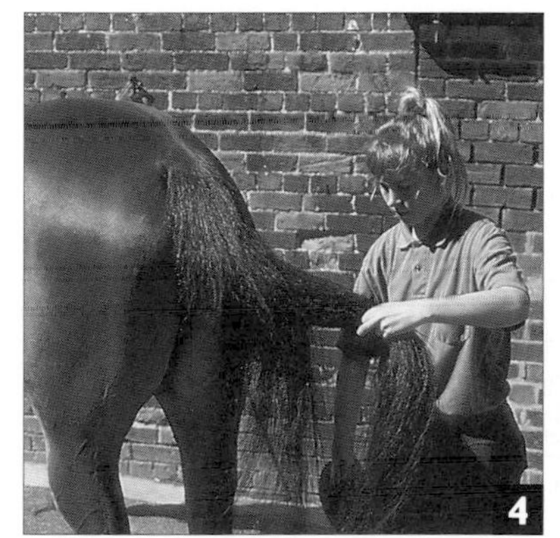

4 Using a body brush, brush any tangles from the mane and tail. Brush the tail by holding it in one hand and brushing down a few strands at a time. Don't use a dandy brush on the mane and tail – it is too harsh and breaks the hairs.

5 & 6 Oil the underside of the hoofs and round the horns to protect them from drying and cracking and to keep them supple. In very, very hot weather, it is best not to use hoof oil on the hooves, as the hot sun will cause a "frying" effect. Instead wash the horse's feet in a mixture of water and soda.

GOING RIDING – THE HAZARDS

Just as I recommended preparing yourself for the possibility of falling off at the beginning of this book, I would recommend, too, that you at least think about some of the things that can happen when you go out for a ride in the country so that you are as prepared as it is possible to be at this stage. And learn the correct way to hold and use a stick as this can be a useful adjunct when riding out of the school if the horse needs a positive reminder about who is boss.

A very real possibility is that your horse will shy – perhaps at a bird fluttering in a tree, at someone moving in a garden as you ride by – in fact at any sudden and unexpected movement that occurs. There is no way of avoiding this, or even anticipating when it might happen. But if you are riding correctly and *in balance with your horse*, it is less likely that its sudden movement will unseat you. I would urge you very strongly, though, not to ride along the road in traffic until you have experienced a horse shying in a field or on a bridle path. If a horse shies on the road, you really can be in big trouble if you are not confident of staying aboard. And, of course, the implications of your horse being loose in the traffic if you do fall off and can't hold on to it are quite horrifying.

A horse stumbling is another potentially unseating experience. As the rider you have more control over this not happening than you do with a horse shying. If you maintain a steady contact with the horse's mouth, and ride in an alert and aware manner, the chances of stumbling are lessened. Be particularly careful when riding on a very stony track or any uneven surface, and keep to a controlled and collected pace.

Another possible danger is when, frightened by something, the horse bolts with you and takes off into the sunset. The advice is, keep calm! It is terribly hard to put into practice, I know, but it is the best chance you have of the animal slowing down. The most natural response of an inexperienced rider is to panic. You tend to sit tight in the saddle gripping like crazy with your seat and legs and pulling hard on the reins. The response will be wholly negative; the seat muscles are actually pushing the horse forward, and in addition it will automatically push its head forward, thrusting its nose in the air in order to avoid the constant pressure from the bit. Its mouth, the nerve centre, actually becomes deadened, the bit meaningless, and the horse will go and go.

In fact, if you are in open country, the best thing is to let the horse do just that, go and go, keeping as relaxed a position as you can in the saddle. Then you can do one of two things; either begin slowly to pull the horse up, working off the knees and sitting over the centre of balance – not behind it as is the tendency – with your bottom off the saddle. Instead of

It is a good idea to know how to hold and use a stick when going out for a ride, just in case there are times and places when you want to give the horse a quick reminder about who is boss. You can hold a stick in either hand; which hand you find the easiest will probably depend on whether you are left- or right-handed.

1 *This is the correct way to hold a stick; the stop just protruding out of the top of the hand, and the length of the stick resting across the rider's thigh.*

a constant pull on the reins, keep gently pulling and relaxing, so that the pressure is not continuous and the horse doesn't set its mouth against you.

The other thing you can do is to let your horse go until it begins to tire. Again, this does depend on your surroundings, but if you are in open country and there is not a great danger from uneven ground, you simply wait until it starts to slow down. At that point, kick it on – now it's your turn to make it go – until it is really exhausted. Running-off can be a habit with a horse, something that it regards as a bit of a joke; if so, the joke must be turned on the horse. What you are saying is, "If you want to gallop, Mister, you just keep on galloping!"

2 *This is the incorrect or "Harvey Smith" way to hold a stick. To a novice rider, it would be distracting held in this position, and would affect your seat in the saddle.*

3 *A stick should never be used in this position – on the lesk of a horse – particularly a mare. It is a very tender spot and it could be harmful to hit a horse there with the whip.*

4 *If you need to give a horse a good hard hit to let it know you are thoroughly displeased with it, just turn the stick in your hand and give a strong tap across the hind quarters as shown here.*

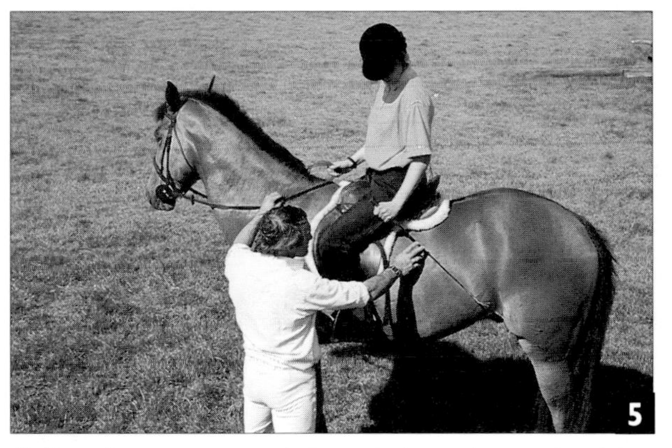

5 *For a sharp tap as a reminder to the horse, just use the stick smartly against the rib cage behind you leg.*

6 *A smart tap down the neck – say as you are approaching a jump – also provides an adequate reminder for most horses.*

THE COUNTRY CODE

Your first ride out of the school should contain as little road work as possible; aim if possible to do no more than just cross a road. For at least the first ten minutes of a ride do nothing other than an ordinary walk. Hold the horse on a steady rein; don't let it slop along, but give it at least this amount of time to loosen up and get its legs and adrenalin working. After that do some steady trotting before starting to canter.

Remember that by no means is the whole of the countryside available to you as a rider. All land belongs to someone, including woodland, so make sure that you have permission from the owner before you ride over it. Then be considerate: never ride over growing crops, and be particularly careful in spring when crops have only just been planted and may hardly be showing. At this tender age, a horse's feet will completely destroy them. Later on, bear in mind that not everything that looks like grass actually is. Take the trouble to learn about crops, what the different ones are and what they look like, but always keep to the outside of the field if you are unsure.

When corn and silage have been cut and you are confronted with a field of stubble, here is a good – and often a quite rare – opportunity to have a speedy gallop; there's no reason why you shouldn't, so long as you have permission. You'll ruin it for all horse riders if you ride over a farmer's land without first asking if you can.

As a horse rider, you are allowed to ride on bridle-paths, but not footpaths. Don't wander off bridle-paths into tempting fields or along other paths that are not bridle-paths. Although there is no reason why you shouldn't have a good canter along a bridle-path, be governed by the conditions. If the ground is very hard and stony, or very wet and boggy, it would be far more sensible to go at a steady trot. If there are a lot of overhanging branches, bear in mind that it is far harder to control a horse, not to mention to see where you are going, if you are having to lean forward on its neck to avoid being swept off. And if you come across people walking, don't charge past them, frightening the life out of them and spattering them with mud. Just ease up a little, so that you go past them at a reasonable pace. If they are walking a dog, remember that it might bark at you as you go by, making the horse jump and shy. If you are walking or trotting collectedly, again, you will have a better chance of staying in the saddle.

Remember to shut all gates in the countryside whether it appears as if the field contains livestock or not – they may be hiding over the crest of a hill. If you do ride through a field of cows, having obtained permission to do so, do so at a walk so as not to excite them to riot.

The softer verges by the edge of a track or bridle-path provide an opportunity for a canter.

This field has a crop of beet, so Hannah is wisely keeping right to the edge, riding along the hedgerow. You should only ride in fields of this type if you have permission, and be sure never to ride over growing crops of any type.

THE HIGHWAY CODE

Riders are not exempt from the Highway Code, and you should make sure you are completely familiar with it. Ride on the same side of the road as the traffic, going with it, so that cars come up on the same side of the road behind you, rather than meeting you head on. Always give hand signals to warn motorists of your movements, particularly if you are going to cross to the other side of the road. Warn motorists to slow down if there are hazards ahead they can't see or if your horse is nervous. Then wave them on when the way ahead is clear, and remember to thank them for their courtesy.

If you have to ride much on the roads, wear all the luminous gear recommended for riding (available at shops selling riding clothes) so that you are clearly visible. Stirrup iron lights are a good idea on murky days or in the late afternoon.

Everything to do with riding on the roads is a matter of common sense, but remember that you may have to contend with motorists who may view you as little more than a nuisance.

Riding in the dark or dusk should be avoided whenever possible; however, if it is absolutely essential – the only time you can exercise your horse, for example – both horse and rider must wear conspicuous clothing so that they can easily be seen by motorists. Here the horse has fluorescent bands around two of its legs (ideally it should have these on all four) and the rider has similar bands around the top of her boots and on her hat. Her "vest" is also fluorescent.

Hand signals used by riders, from left to right: "Stop"; "I am turning right"; "I am turning left"; "Please pass".

RIDING ON THE ROADS

Riding on the road today is simply a fact of life, something that if you are venturing out of the school frequently is almost unavoidable. Hopefully, as suggested, your first ride at least will involve as little road work as possible, but the chances are that if you want and are able to ride in different and varied places you will have to ride along the road.

When I first started riding out on the roads, with my father beside me on a bicycle, there were some nineteen million fewer cars using them with us! Those that there were tended to be much more horse-aware and considerate than they are today. Many motorists now seem to have no feeling for, or knowledge of, horses and will not slow down when they go past you. However, the attitude of recreational riders does not always help matters. If, as a motorist, you do slow right down to overtake a horse, giving it as wide a berth as you can, there is nothing more infuriating than to have the rider ignore the gesture and merely look down his or her nose as if you were some low form of animal life. Remember this, and always do thank motorists who are considerate to you; it could influence the way they act towards other riders. If you feel a motorist really drives irresponsibly as far as riders and horses are concerned, take the registration number and have a word with the local police, asking if they can do anything about it.

Keep in mind when riding on the road that horses and fast cars or big lorries are really not a happy combination. This way you are more likely to keep alert and aware than if you think you are riding a one hundred per cent traffic-proof horse. In fact, I would say no horse can ever be this; I certainly will never sell a horse with this sort of guarantee, even if I have never had a bad experience with it. You can never be completely sure of how it will react in every situation and it is better always to be aware of this.

Remember, too, that a horse always goes head first towards danger rather than backing away from it. If it is being skittish and a car approaches, it is likely to continue towards it. Always turn your horse to have a good look at the problem, whatever it may be, but if you think it is playing up, give it a tap with the stick and let it know who is boss. The road is simply too potentially dangerous a place to let your horse indulge in a fit of high spirits at whim.

Always ride in a collected way on the roads, making sure you are well in control. When you want to trot, make it a nice sensible pace, not flat out. The first thing you will learn if you do ride fast on the road is that it is very slippery, particularly if it carries much heavy traffic. When a horse slips on the road, it will begin to panic, and the chances are that you will too. If you are doing a good deal of road work, have shoes fitted with road studs, or shoes with holes for studs which you can screw in. Never canter along the road, road studs or not.

However tempting it may be, don't canter down grass verges. You will find most of them have water gulleys placed at regular intervals and your horse could easily trip if it came across one of these at speed. Also, if the grass is long, it could well hide old bottles, tin cans and other dangerous litter that passing motorists have tossed out of their cars.

If you are riding in an environment where there is heavy traffic, particularly many farm vehicles – tractors seem to upset most horses – you really must have a quiet horse. It is no good riding a highly-strung, thoroughbred type of horse in such conditions. It will be a nightmare for everyone.

The blacksmith hammering a road stud into a hind shoe before fitting the shoe on to a horse. The road stud, which is a permanent feature of the shoe, helps to prevent a horse slipping on the road surface.

1 *Hannah is demonstrating how to open, go through and shut a gate without dismounting. With this gate, she first has to lift the heavy latch over the gate post.*

2 *Next she pulls the gate towards her, making her horse walk backwards to get out of the way.*

3 *Now she is able to walk through. Always open a gate wide enough to give yourself plenty of room. Hitting a knee on a gatepost is very painful, and if the horse knocks itself going through, it might easily jump forward or sideways.*

4 *Once through the gate, Hannah turns her horse round to face the gate and pulls it back towards her.*

5 *Finally she latches it. Remember to shut all gates you need to go through when out riding, especially if you found them shut.*

6 *Out for a ride on the roads, Hannah stops as she comes up to a T-junction, to check on the traffic before crossing.*

COMING HOME

All your rides out in the countryside, although pleasurable, should, at least in the early days, also be furthering your learning programme, helping you to gain confidence and experience. Try to coordinate and practise what you learned in the school. Enjoy the surroundings – that is what you are there for – but don't just slop along on a long rein, almost unaware of how the horse is moving. Instead practise your collected and extended walks and trots as well as the ordinary paces. If there is somewhere where you can have a good long canter, on an even bridle-path, try a collected canter, then push into an extended one for a few strides before pulling back to a collected pace.

Be aware of the ground so that you make your own decisions about how fast to go. On the road, or a gravelly, stony or hard surface, walk or trot only. Canter only on earthy ground or grass, not on a stony track, where there is a good chance that both of you will end up on the ground. Remember that earthy ground can be as hard as rock if there hasn't been any rain for some time. If there is a sudden fall of rain, the surface will be dangerously slippery.

Just as you walked for the first ten minutes or so at the beginning of the ride, so walk for at least this length of time before your return to the yard. Bringing in a horse that is wet and sweating will be regarded as the height of bad and inconsiderate management. A horse should not be put back in a stable hot and sweaty, and it is not a good idea to turn it out in the field in this condition either, particularly in cold weather. It is a sure way of making it catch a cold.

Before turning out the horse in the field, remove the tack, put on the headcollar and tie the horse up. Then pick out the feet again – there may well be a stone lodged in the sole of the foot from the ride, and check down the legs for any injury.

If the horse is being given supplementary feeding in the field, now is the time to give it.

1 *When you return from a ride, take off the saddle and bridle, put on a headcollar and tie the horse up. Then pick out the feet again to remove any mud and stones they might have picked up during the ride.*

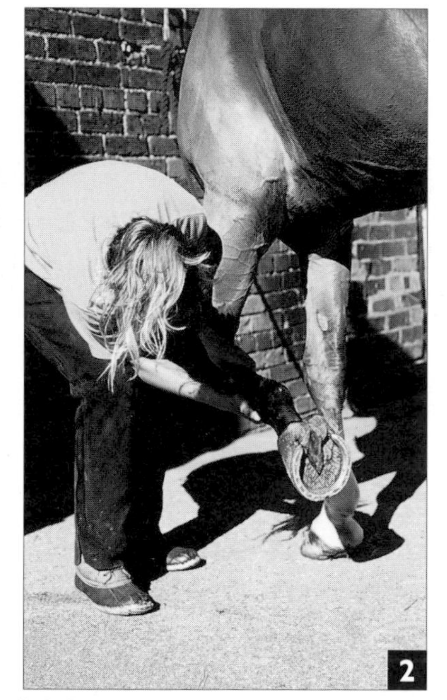

2 *While you are holding up the legs to pick out the feet, feel around the fetlock joint for any lumps, bumps or cuts and to feel if the horse has picked up any thorns.*

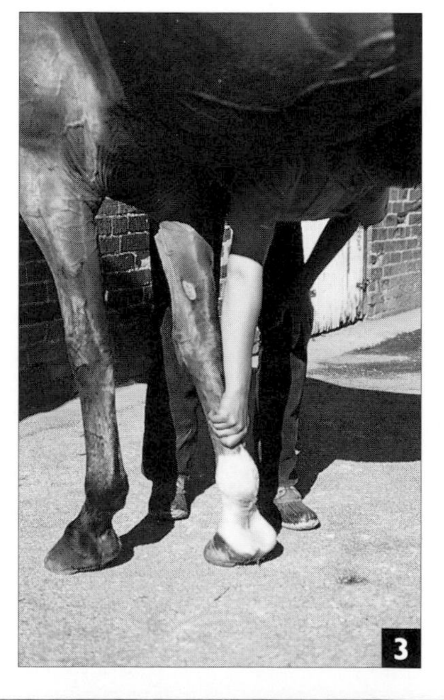

3 *Feel down the back of the leg for injury, too. Run your hands down both legs, so that you can compare them.*

4, 5 & **6** *Providing you have walked the horse for the last fifteen minutes or so of the ride so that it is not hot and sweaty, sponge it down if necessary – there is no need to hose it in this instance – and then turn it back out in the field. Lead it right into the field, closing the gate behind you so that it and any other horses or ponies in the field can't escape, before unbuckling the headcollar and letting him free.*

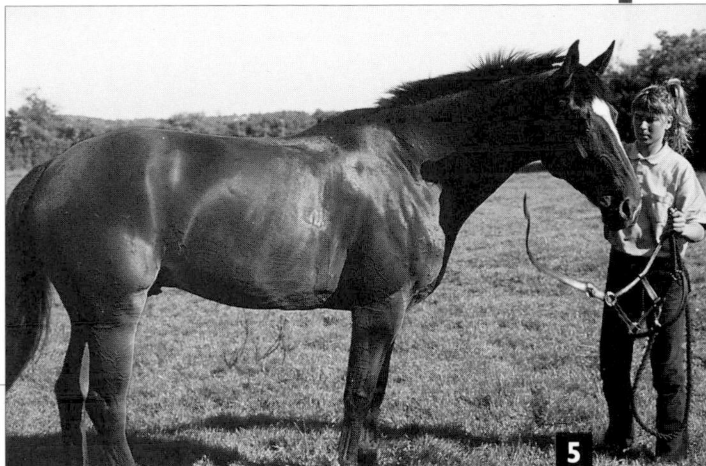

CLEANING TACK

Now that you have attended to the horse after your ride, the saddle and bridle should also have some attention before they are put away.

Hang the bridle up on a hook within easy reach, and unbuckle the reins and cheek pieces at the bit, so that the bit is released. Soak it in a bucket of water while cleaning the rest of the tack.

Clean all the leather on the bridle with a sponge that has been well squeezed out in a bucket of water with a little disinfectant or washing-up liquid added. Rub hard at the leather to remove any bits of dried sweat; if these are left to harden they could cause rubbing on the horse's face. Make sure you move all straps out of their keepers, as well as the stoppers on the reins, so as to give the underneath pieces a good washing.

When the leather has dried completely rub saddle soap into it, again using a sponge that is only just damp. If the sponge is too wet, the soap will go lathery and the leather will dry hard.

Scrub the bit until it is completely clean, and dry it well. Buckle it back on to the cheek pieces and attach the reins.

Remove the girth, leathers and stirrup irons from the saddle, then wash and soap the saddle in the same way as the bridle including the leather underside (even though you use a numnah). Wash and soap the stirrup leathers, checking again to make sure the stitching is intact and safe. Soak the stirrup irons in soapy water to remove all the dirt. Wash and soap the girth if it is leather; scrub webbing or nylon girths and hang them up to dry.

If tack is used every day, it should be cleaned in this way each time you have finished riding. Then once a week the bridle should be taken apart and each piece cleaned as described above, but individually. Take this opportunity to check all the stitching around buckles to make sure they are safe. If you like, you can polish stirrup irons and bit rings with metal polish to make them shiny and smart.

Once a month the leather will benefit from being stripped right down and given a good oiling with saddlery oil. Don't do it more often than this because the oil could cause the stitching around buckles to go soft if applied too frequently. The saddle can be oiled, too, except for the seat and flaps; never oil these parts as the oil will stain breeches or jodhpurs.

The seat of the saddle should be rubbed with a duster, or given only the lightest application of saddle soap, otherwise this will rub off and stain the breeches.

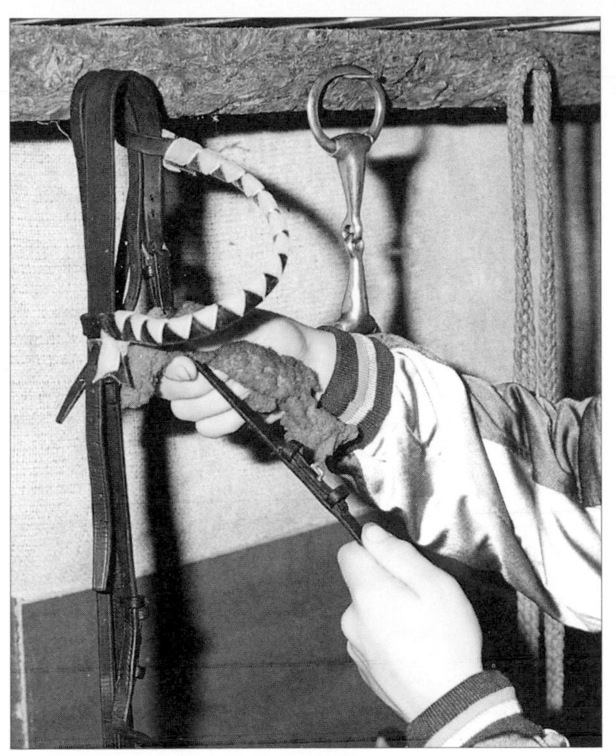

The bit, reins and noseband have been taken off the bridle, which is then washed with a damp sponge before being rubbed hard with saddle soap. Once a week at least, the bridle should be disassembled completely for cleaning.

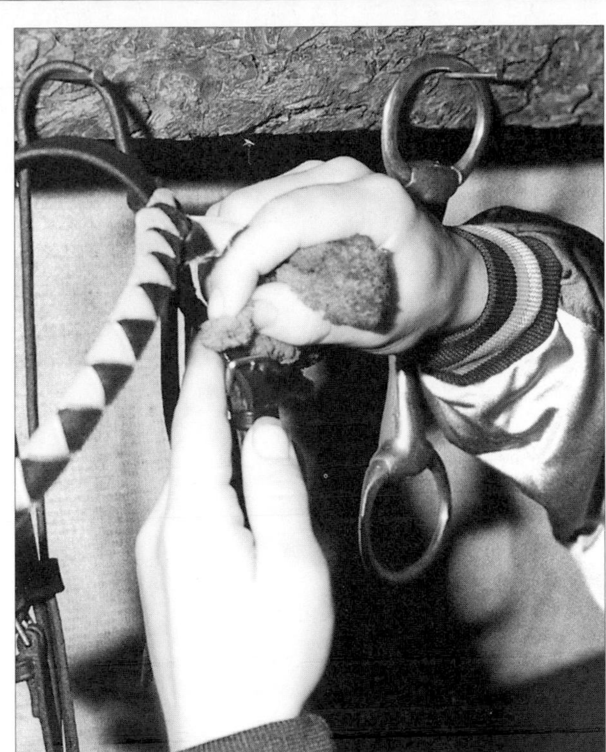

Particular attention is paid to the area around the buckles, to check the stitching is in good order and not about to give way.

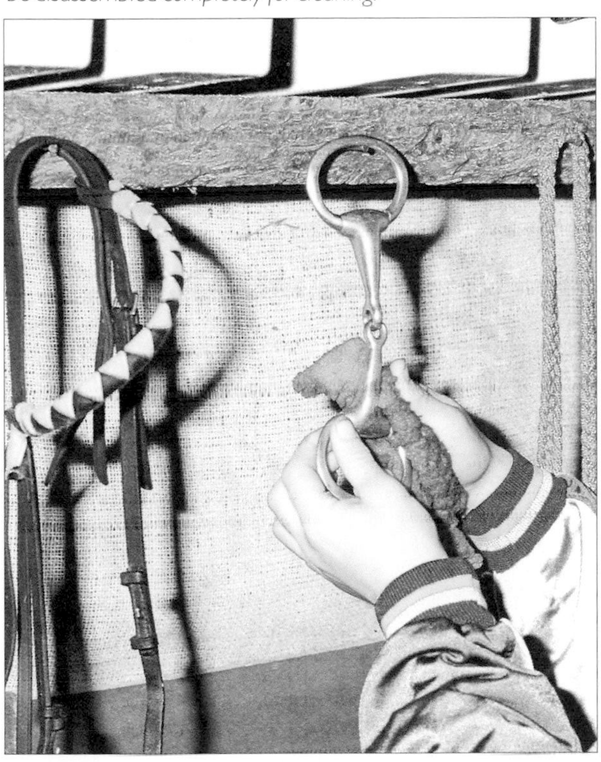

Here the bit is being cleaned. Generally, I would advise soaking it in a bucket of warm water while the tack is being cleaned, rather than washing it with the same sponge as used for the leather work, as here!

The leather underside of the saddle is being lightly sprayed with water before again being sponged off and soaped.

COUNTRY SPORTS

There are many riding pursuits that lead on from the simple activity of going out for a ride. Riding across country opens the way to many sports like hunting, as well as competitive hunter trials, team chases, eventing and long-distance riding.For any of these a horse must be trained to some level of fitness. A horse cannot be turned out in a field during the week, then ridden hard at weekends and be expected to give of its best. To hunt, or to take part in any competitive activities, a horse must be ridden at least every other day. To achieve a level of real fitness it needs to be walked and trotted for a good 6.5 km (4 mi) a day, which is roughly one hour's exercise. The horse will also need careful feeding in the winter, and watching in the spring, to ensure it doesn't get too fat on the rich spring grass. The topic of getting a horse fit is discussed in greater detail in Chapter Six.

Eventing is a competitive sport involving the disciplines of dressage, cross-country riding and jumping, and show-jumping. It had its origins in the hunting field.

HUNTING

Hunting is one of the oldest of all equestrian sports and it has no competitive element. For those who are squeamish about following a fox or stag hunt, there is always drag hunting. Here hounds follow a predetermined line laid with a bag of aniseed, and riders are guaranteed a fast ride across country with several natural jumps on the way.

To go hunting a horse has to be fit; to go drag hunting, both it and the rider have to be very fit. The horse must also be a good jumper; out fox-hunting, I know people who will never jump a fence and still manage to keep up with hounds, but out drag hunting it would be impossible to do this and stay with the field.

To prepare a horse for hunting, it should be brought up from grass two to three months beforehand with a bit of excess flesh on it. Then it needs steady, regular exercise – the 6.5 km (4 mi) mentioned above – with a lot of this done on the road to harden the legs. Steady trotting up and down hills will help improve fitness.

When choosing a horse for hunting, it is important to buy one that is used to the sort of country in which it will be ridden. There is no such thing as an all-round perfect hunter, because hunting country varies so much. To keep up with some hunts, you would need a horse that can gallop all day and take walls and banks in its stride, while for others, the need would be for a big, bold jumper. For hunts that go across country surrounded by fairly built-up areas you would need a horse that is prepared to stand still and wait when hounds have checked or if there is a queue to go over a jump. The best advice is always to buy a horse from the area in which you want to hunt it. And don't imagine a horse that jumps show-jumps will be a good hunter; my experienced show-jumper fell at the first two fences the first time I took him hunting!

Ready for a good day's sport in the autumn sunshine, the huntsman moves off with his pack of hounds to the first covert.

HUNTER TRIALS AND TEAM CHASES

These are two of the sports that have come directly out of the hunting field, the other being point-to-point racing, which is generally far more professionally competitive now than hunter trialling and team chasing.

The hunter trial was the first of the sports to emerge; it comprises a speed and jumping test across country, with fences similar to those found in the hunting field. Some hunter trials have obstacles, such as a gate which must be opened and shut and a heavy ploughed field to be negotiated, making them a truer test of the hunter.

Hunter trials are run on a very local basis, either put on by the hunt as a way of making money and having a get-together, or by local riding schools and clubs. It's unlikely that someone would ever buy a horse specifically to compete in hunter trials; it would be first and foremost a hunter, and hunter trials would simply be a way of enjoying a good competitive ride. Many people see them as a good training ground for a hunter: the horse has to jump fences on its own initiative without the benefit of some other member of the hunt giving it a lead or the thrill of the chase whipping up its adrenalin. Again, it must be emphasized that a horse could not be expected to be caught up from the field and jump well and fast round a hunter trial course – which might be 3 km (2 mi) or more long – without regular exercise beforehand.

Team chasing is a relative newcomer among equestrian sports and another that is generally for competitive enjoyment at the end of the hunting season. Four competitors ride round a hunter trial-type course together. At the end of it, three have to be *left standing* – that is, the three best times will count.

Since its introduction in the early 1970s team chasing has evolved and now has various refinements. For example, most courses now have what is known as a *dressing fence*, sometimes more than one. A dressing fence is a fence on the course which all members of the team must jump together, and there will be a judge stationed there to award marks, or penalty points, for this.

Usually team chase partnerships are formed in the hunting field between people who find their horses seem to get on well together, and who, with their horses, enjoy a good ride across country. However, there is no need to hunt to form a team chase team; it is simply that this is the most natural way of arriving at one.

If team chasing is a sport that interests you, take trouble to look into it properly. It has come quite a long way since its early, "mad-cap-ride-across-country" days, and there are all sorts of rules and regulations of which to take note. These may be subject to local variation, but must always be strictly adhered to.

The three members of a team-chasing team follow one another over one of the natural fences. There will be one or two fences around the course that they should jump together.

Riders in a team chase ride sensibly through the stream that is part of the course. Instead of splashing through it at speed, they have slowed down to a steady trot, so that their horses do not hurt their legs and feet on the stones. They can quickly pick up speed again after the event.

A rider taking a natural obstacle with confidence. It looks as if the organizers of the competition have turned storm damage to their advantage, using a fallen tree as part of the course. Note that the rider is wearing a steel crash helmet; it is essential to wear one of these for eventing, and sensible to wear one for hunter trials and team chases too.

EVENTING

This is the competitive sport to evolve from hunting that is probably the best known – and most professional – of all. Eventing at all levels, from a novice event to an internationally contested one, consists of dressage, a cross-country phase, and show-jumping. At three-day events, the cross-country phase is usually further divided to include a section of roads and tracks, a steeplechase course and a cross-country jumping course.

Eventing is a sport that can be enjoyed by all. There are even events held for really young riders – the under-tens – in which competitors will still have to perform in the three different disciplines.

At the top echelons of eventing great dedication is required; it is not a weekend sport. A horse that is to be trained for eventing needs a tremendous amount of time and work spent on it and there can be no short cuts and compromises. We recently sent a potential show-jumping horse of ours that was having trouble with cornering to the event and dressage rider Judy Bradwell, who rode for some of the photographs later on in this book, and one day she telephoned us after she had been riding it for five hours!

An event horse really has to be quite special – quiet and coordinated enough for dressage, a bold and big jumper for cross-country with a lot of stamina as well, then sensible and calm enough to jump a show-jumping course. Not one of these disciplines can be neglected at the expense of the others. There was a time when the main test was the cross-country jumping, but now a very high standard of dressage is required, and the event itself is often won or lost in the show-jumping ring.

Much is required of the rider, too. He or she has to be extremely proficient in each of the disciplines, and very brave, for the cross-country courses at big events are often daunting. If you watch event riders you will be able to see the ones who really know what they are doing. It is not merely a matter of galloping fast round those cross-country fences, hoping that the momentum will carry you round – and over. Top riders will have assessed each fence, knowing exactly at what angle they will jump it. In addition, they must be aware of the timing – there is a minimum as well as a maximum time limit – and they must know how to nurse a tired horse over the last few fences so as to be sure it doesn't hurt itself.

Another good demonstration of jumping a natural obstacle – at speed – with confidence and style. Note how the legs of this horse have been covered with grease. Most event riders do this nowadays, so that if a horse does get tangled up on a jump it is more likely to slip off easily.

Above *An unfortunate tumble during an event, but a very good example of how to fall off! The rider will take the brunt of the fall on her shoulders, enabling her to curl up the rest of her body, both protecting herself and cushioning the blow. She may be a bit bruised, but should otherwise escape any serious injury.*

Right *Eventing excellence – Lucinda Green demonstrates the right way to do it. She is in perfect harmony with her horse, and her hands are completely relaxed.*

LONG DISTANCE RIDING

This is a cross-country sport, but one perhaps that owes as much to the famous American trail rides as it does to hunting. Trail riding has long been a favourite sport in the USA, and it is becoming ever more popular in other parts of the world.

The essence of long distance riding is just that – to ride long distances – anything from 32 km (20 mi) to 160 km (100 mi). The very long ones are known as endurance rides, and they are aptly named; they really are the ultimate test of endurance and fitness for both horse and rider.

As a general rule, a long distance ride contains no jumping. That is not to say that riders wouldn't jump over a log that might have fallen across the track, but jumping does not form part of the competitive requirement. In fact the whole competitive element is a little different from that in other competitive sports. In many rides, the competition is against oneself: there are no winners except insofar as everyone who finishes the ride is deemed a winner. In rides that are judged, the condition of the horse counts at the end as a major factor; it is not simply a case of the rider who covers the distance in the quickest time being proclaimed the winner.

The type of horse for serious long distance riding is all important; first and foremost, it has to be an athlete. Arabian horses or those with arab blood are particularly good as they are hardy and have always been renowned for their endurance and stamina. As they tend not to carry much excess flesh, they are also easier to make fitter than some other types of horse.

Fitness really is the key to this sport and the horses that take part will have become accustomed to being ridden those long distances over quite a period of time. Serious long distance riders will take their horses to different parts of the country, so that they can experience different types of terrain – rolling hills, moorland, forests and so on. It is another sport that requires huge dedication; no horse or rider can go on even the shortest of an organized long distance ride without being well prepared for it.

Anyone who is interested in the sport should go and talk to people experienced in it, and find out what will be expected of him and his horse. However much you read about it, this is one sport you really want to hear about from those who participate regularly.

A competitor in a long distance ride pauses at one of the permitted stops and the horse is sponged off by an assistant to cool and refresh it. Note that the rider is using a good thick, cotton nummah under the saddle – the natural fibre absorbs sweat more readily than synthetic fibre – and has also fitted the horse with a breast-plate which reduces the chance of the saddle slipping. She is also using a bitless bridle, popular among long distance riders. The sheepskin around the noseband will help prevent the horse being chafed by the leather.

Long distance riders during the Golden Horseshoe Ride, and all three here are riding their horses in bitless bridles. You can see that all sorts of terrain has to be covered, some of it steep and rough, so it is essential that the horse is tough and fit.

4 LEARNING TO JUMP

To participate in any of the sports discussed in the last chapter – hunting, hunter trials, team chases and one- or three-day events – you will need to learn to jump. Even people happy to be no more than recreational riders usually learn how to jump so they can pop over the odd small fence they come across when out riding.

Learning to jump will also improve your riding by helping greatly with balance and preparing you for the moment when you are riding a skittish horse that is inclined to dance around and jump into the air. But above all it is a hugely enjoyable and exhilarating aspect of horsemanship.

Learning to jump should be fun – not frightening! Here, one of my pupils, Nicholas, demonstrates an exercise to help achieve good balance. This is an excellent way to ensure you do not use the reins as lifelines.

HORSE AND RIDER

It is most important to learn to jump on a horse that enjoys jumping. The horse must be prepared to take you up to a fence and over it without you having to think about whether it might or might not. There is quite enough to think about and do without having to push on a reluctant plodder: not only is this very disheartening; it will be a positive hindrance to you as you try to feel the correct movement and action. It's also important, if at all possible, to learn to jump somewhere which has good facilities – an all-weather surface school, poles and cavalletti of some sort, and a selection of jumps.

It is the rider keen to learn to jump who will progress the fastest. I frequently teach people who have never jumped a fence in their lives and yet here they are, enthusiastic enough to come to a show-jumping clinic. Because they are ready and willing to learn they progress quickly.

There is no need for any rider to be apprehensive about learning to jump, particularly in the early stages. All you need is the confidence in your riding ability that you have already gained. In any case, you will find that for the first few lessons your horse will hardly leave the ground.

It is a good idea now to ride in long boots rather than jodhpur boots as they will offer some protection if you should knock your leg against the side of a fence.

A horse's legs should be protected by tendon boots during jumping to prevent injury to the tendons through knocks. Various types are available; those shown here are a perfectly serviceable but very inexpensive pair made of synthetic material. They are fastened with clips and provided they don't get ripped they should last for a long time.

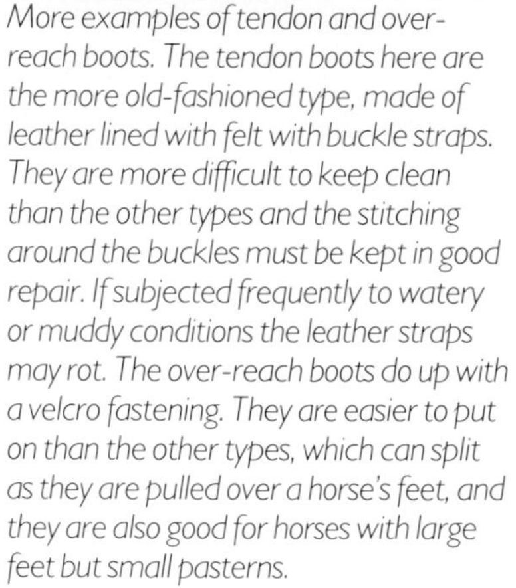

More examples of tendon and over-reach boots. The tendon boots here are the more old-fashioned type, made of leather lined with felt with buckle straps. They are more difficult to keep clean than the other types and the stitching around the buckles must be kept in good repair. If subjected frequently to watery or muddy conditions the leather straps may rot. The over-reach boots do up with a velcro fastening. They are easier to put on than the other types, which can split as they are pulled over a horse's feet, and they are also good for horses with large feet but small pasterns.

These tendon boots are better quality and excellent for competition work. They are made of sheepskin-lined leather and are particularly comfortable for the horse. They are fastened with elastic clips. The horse is also wearing over-reach boots in case it should clip the back of its front feet with its hind feet. This pair is Italian and of a high quality, and should last for many years where cheaper varieties would start to perish and rip. They slip on over the horse's feet. Keep over-reach boots like these in a warm place; if they are very cold when pulled over a horse's feet they may split.

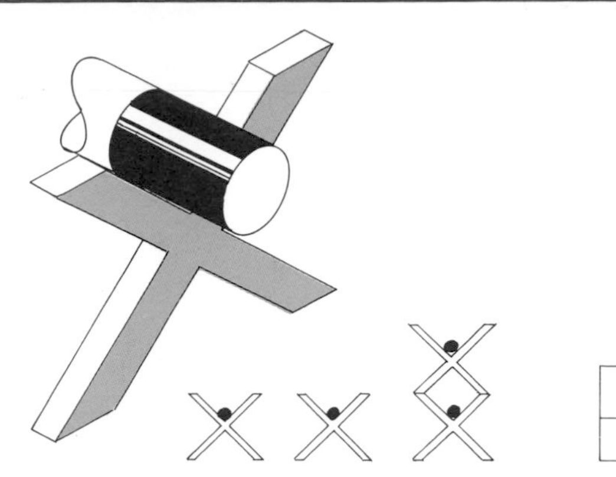

Old-fashioned cavalletti (**left**), in which the pole is bolted to two crossed strips of wood, could be positioned to give three different heights, but if a horse knocked them it could get its legs caught in them. A safer way to set up a grid is to use independent blocks (**right**) which can also be used at a variety of heights. If a horse knocks the pole with its legs, it will fall harmlessly to the ground.

Learning to jump should be done in easy stages and should always be fun. These youngsters ***(right, below right)*** *are having a good time – undoubtedly the best and quickest way to learn.*

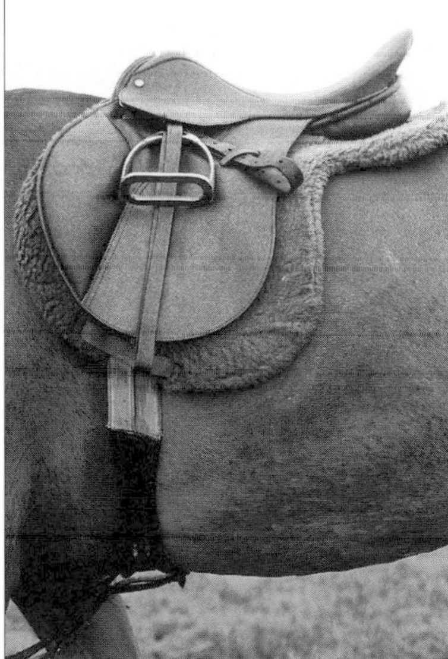

If you are going to do a good deal of jumping, you should use a proper deep-seated jumping saddle, which has padded knee rolls to support the knees. This one has an elasticated girth which is ideal for jumping – it stretches as the horse stretches its body over a fence. However, the elastic must be replaced when it loses its elasticity.

THE GRID

The aim of every competitive jumper now is to ride his horse round the course in an even, easy canter pace, arriving at the jumps in such a balanced rhythm that he almost seems to continue over the fence in this bouncy stride. This is what you are aiming for, but of course it is not something you can achieve straight away. As ever there are certain steps to follow and the first exercises in learning to jump for both horse and rider are the grid exercises I talked about in Chapter One.

A *grid* in jumping parlance is a series of poles or *cavalletti* placed at regular intervals on the ground. To begin with, the distance between them should coincide with a horse's trotting stride, so will be about 1.8 m (2 yd). Begin by placing five poles on the ground, spacing them evenly this distance apart. If you are in a manège, position them down one long side of the school.

Begin by doing no more than walking round the school or field in a lively walk and maintain that pace as you walk down the poles. Once you are happy doing this, come round at a good, balanced trot and keep this pace going down the poles. The horse should trot over a pole with each step of the stride.

At this stage, many books about learning to jump will talk at length about the "jumping position". Like the aids, I would rather you didn't think about this at the moment, but let it develop naturally. Sit upright in the saddle doing a rising trot over the poles and looking straight between the horse's ears.

The next stage is to raise the poles no more than about 22 cm (9 in) off the ground and trot through them again. Then raise the final pole about 45 cm (1 ft 6 in) off the ground so that the horse has to make a small jump. It is quite possible that it may jump unnecessarily high over this one; simply lean your body forward with your bottom just out of the saddle and your weight supported on your knees, still looking straight ahead. Don't worry about anything else.

What tends to happen to many people, even if they have been told all about the jumping position, is that as a horse lifts its front legs off the ground and jumps forward over a fence they are left behind the movement and thrown back in the

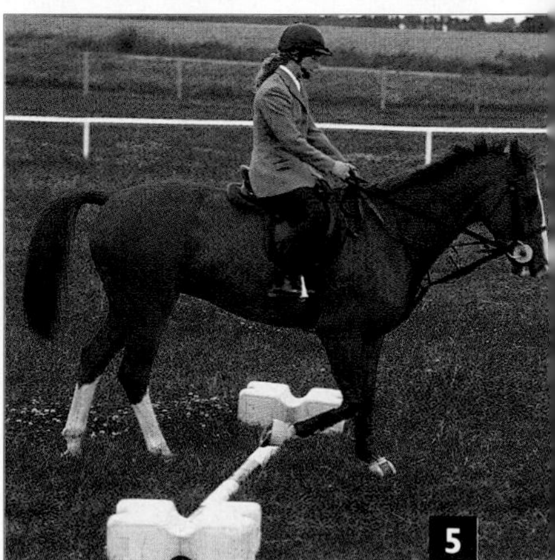

This is the very first stage of learning to jump for horse and rider. Here Diane is walking her horse through a series of five poles laid on the ground. The horse, a novice jumper, is being ridden in draw reins as it has a tendency to poke its nose forward. You can see how it is looking down at the poles. Diane sits quite calmly using a little leg pressure as it takes each step, her hands relaxed at its wither.

saddle, losing all balance. If you find that this tends to happen to you, what I say to my novice pupils will help you: aim to get over the jump before the horse – that is, imagine you are almost throwing yourself over the jump ahead of it. You'll never actually do it, so don't worry; as the horse rises over the jump it matches your movement and you will become coordinated with each other as you go.

Try to keep your hands as near the wither as possible. You will be holding the reins in the correct position for an ordinary trot, which means they are at the right length to enable the horse to stretch its head slightly forward as it jumps. Relax your fingers a little if you feel you are gripping too tightly and using them as lifelines. Remember that tension and fear travel down the reins and are communicated to the horse.

Here another novice horse attempts to trot through the grid which is now raised just off the ground. It negotiates the first two poles, but becomes unbalanced and knocks down the third. Although it does negotiate the fourth, it has become unsettled and runs out at the fifth. The rider is rather too crouched in the saddle, with her leg too far back and turned out so that she is not really in a position to control her horse and keep it straight.

You can see in the third picture that the horse is already thinking about running out and has moved to the right-hand end of the pole. It needs strong pressure from the right leg to steer it back to the centre of the pole. However this is an inexperienced horse that had done no grid work at all until we took these pictures.

You can see that a horse will sometimes take a disproportionately big jump over a small fence. In fact, this rider is leaning too far forward and her legs are right back, so that she is basically out of balance with the horse and likely to be thrown back into the saddle on landing. In her favour, however, is the fact that she is not interfering with the horse's head as it jumps.

GRID EXERCISES

You will find that as the horse jumps over the fence, even though it took off from a trot, it will move away at a canter. I have only ever known one horse who would trot away from a jump; the jumping movement is akin to the canter stride, so naturally a horse will begin to canter after landing. Knowing this, however, prepares you for it, and you will find that if you were leaning forward very slightly while going over the jump the horse's action of landing will naturally bring you back into the saddle. You will find the position I recommended for the canter (see page 42) – with your bottom 2 to 4 cm (1 to 1½ in) out of the saddle – is the right position to adopt when cantering round a jumping course.

If your horse bangs the fence with its legs don't look back to see what happened to the pole. Get into the habit *now* of never looking back at a fence once you've jumped it; if it has fallen, you won't put it back by looking at it. In show-jumping, the riders who look back at their fences are the ones who are unprepared for the approach to the next fence, and that could mean disaster.

Let the horse canter for a few strides, then bring it back to a trot and go round the arena to do the exercise again. Think about riding correctly around the arena; often, because the novice is thinking hard about the grid exercise, he lets the horse cut the corners.

Set the grid up going in two directions to make sure you are equally confident going in both. Then set it up in a figure-of-eight, with the grid going across the central diagonals. Let the horse canter the circle loops at either end, but bring it back to a trot to go through the grid. This is a good exercise for both of you – you will have to think and ride more positively than you did when the grid was merely

The same rider brings her horse round again at the grid which now has a small jump at the end. The horse negotiates the first pole, although already she has it on too tight a rein. You can see it is resisting over the second pole and the rider is behind the movement, her reins far too short. From there things go from bad to worse, until – completely unbalanced – the horse not unnaturally refuses to jump the small fence at the end of the grid.

This is a much better effort by horse and rider. As you can see, the rider is now more relaxed and by the second pole the horse is beginning to drop its head and relax too. In the third picture, the rider has completely relaxed her hands and the horse jumps the final fence quite happily. The rider's position here is not at all bad, although her legs are too far back. Her body is inclined gently forward, she is looking forward between the horse's ears and she is giving the horse the freedom of its head.

placed down one long side of the arena, and it provides a good suppling exercise for the horse.

Next increase the number of poles, putting them in correct trotting sequences at different places round the arena. Then increase the number of poles in one sequence, moving up to eight, then up to twelve. In America, where these grid exercises are a standard part of many jumping schooling arenas, they work up to 32 poles. The more poles you place, the more difficult it is to keep the rhythm, for a horse's natural inclination as it goes down a line of poles is to go faster and faster. Your aim is to keep it at the same speed and rhythm constantly.

You may find the horse rushes down the poles whatever you do, so rather than having to concentrate too much on control at this point, try putting the poles at slightly differing heights. The horse will then have to think a little as it goes over them. The poles, not just the rider, act as the controlling factor.

Keep changing the height of the poles of the grid just slightly to keep both horse and rider alert. Raise just one end of the pole before putting it up to full height so that you can choose where to jump it.

CANTERING AND RIDING IN A STRAIGHT LINE

Now try the simple grid exercise at a canter. You will need to place the poles a little further apart – a pony canters on a stride of approximately 3.2 m (3½ yd) and a horse on a stride of 3.6 m (4 yd). Keep to four poles followed by the 30 cm (1 ft) high jump; approach the grid at a trot, but as the horse goes over the first pole squeeze a bit harder with your legs to ask for a canter. With each canter stride the horse will go over a pole, and it will soon sense that as it goes over each pole it is correctly placed for the next one.

What you are doing here, more than jumping, is emphasizing the canter stride and feeling the rhythm you want to establish and maintain around a course of jumps.

A good exercise is to position a pole after the final jump of the grid and for the trainer to stand by this, facing dead centre down the grid. In this position the trainer can see which leg the rider needs to apply more strongly to keep the horse straight and can give instructions accordingly.

The poles are placed so that they come in the middle of the canter stride; rather than acting as jumps themselves, they help to set the rhythm of the canter pace. Your concentration at this stage should be on maintaining the rhythm of the canter – nothing else.

Make sure, too, whether you are trotting or cantering down the grid, that you maintain a perfectly straight line. If you use coloured poles, like the ones we have used in the pictures, you can use the central strip as a marker. If you are using plain white poles, it is a good idea to mark the centres with a dab of paint or some coloured paper or plastic as a guide.

The way to keep a horse straight as it moves, whatever the manoeuvre required at the time, is to use your legs correctly, nudging against its side with one or other leg as you feel the horse beginning to stray. However, where you look and how you sit in the saddle will also greatly affect its movement. If you look straight ahead, between its ears, that is the direction it is likely to take. Look to the left or right and it is likely to move to the left or right as the movement you make with your head will automatically bring about some corresponding movement in your body which will quickly be transmitted to the horse. Your hands, incidentally, should be the last of the aids you use to influence movement. As long as you sit straight, look straight ahead and use your legs as necessary, your hands should remain still and sympathetic at the withers.

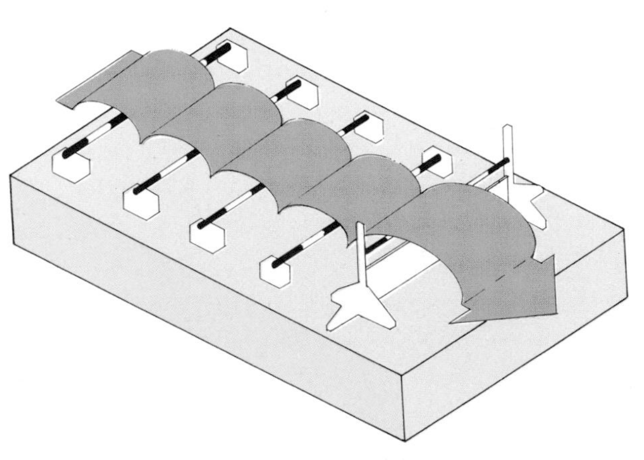

The grid of four poles set at intervals of 3.6 m (4 yd) helps the horse and rider to establish an even rhythm in cantering towards the fence. The poles should be marked to help the rider keep the horse in a straight line over the grid.

Here the horse is executing the grid very well. Coming in at a trot, it trots over the first and second pole, moves up to a canter over the third and fourth and stretches well over the small jump. The rider is sitting quietly in the saddle for the first two poles, just inclining her body slightly forward, but as the horse begins to canter, she lets her legs go back too far. In the next picture she has corrected this, but as the horse takes off over the jump she throws herself too far forward, with the result that her legs slide back again.

From my position at the end of the grid I have instructed the rider to try to keep her horse absolutely straight, negotiating the central red stripe each time. The result is not bad at all, but you can see that she is using her right leg more strongly, which is making the horse move very slightly to the left.

Here our other novice rider tries the same exercise of coming down the grid in a dead straight line. However, you can see in the first picture that she is going wrong; by looking to the right she will automatically be steering the horse in that direction. As a result it moves further and further to the right until it finally runs out of the grid altogether. You can see that she is no longer using her right leg against the horse's side which would steer it back over to the left.

PULLING UP AFTER THE GRID

If you have moved the grid, placing it on a diagonal, put it back in a straight line down one side of the school, or where you first had it in the field. The aim now is to pull up in a straight line three strides after landing over the small jump. This is an excellent exercise for learning control in a show-jumping ring; remember to use your legs to steer the horse, to keep it straight and to get its hocks under it. Then pull gently on the reins, just as you did when you learned to pull up in a straight line (page 52).

Of all the grid exercises we have so far discussed, this is probably the most difficult of all, so don't be despondent if you find it very hard to do. It is more important to achieve a smooth stop, with the horse balanced and happy, its head down and not fighting the action of the bit, than it is to pull up in a really straight line.

As you get comfortable with the grid exercises, think more positively of the aids you are giving the horse. I recommend that you concentrate on lateral aids now, as these are the best for jumping. As the horse goes over the jump squeeze your leg against its side to indicate that you want it to lead in the canter with the leg on that side as it lands after the jump. If, for example, you want it to canter right-handed after the jump to go in a circle to the right, squeeze with your right leg. We will come back to this later with some more positive exercises, but if you feel confident enough you can begin thinking and practising now.

And if you feel happy doing this, then try squeezing very slightly just before the take-off, again with the leg on the same side as you want the horse to lead in the canter. By doing this you are beginning to anticipate the movement, giving the horse an indication of what is expected of it as it lands.

Here I have told the rider to pull up in a straight line as she reaches me. In her first attempt she comes to a halt at an angle, as you can see.

In this picture she is approaching me in a completely straight line and by correct use of her legs should be able to maintain that position as she comes to a stop.

Here the rider has been instructed to pull up three strides after the jump without me standing there as a guide – and the results are not good! She jumps the fence well, but immediately on landing she is exerting more pressure on her right rein, bringing the horse's head round to the right. Unsupported by leg aids – note how the rider's legs are pushed forward in the final picture – the horse stops with its head in the air, its hindquarters trailing behind it and totally unbalanced. Note the position of the rider's hands – they should be down by the withers, not pulled back into her body like this.

FUN EXERCISES

At a recent clinic, there was a group of young riders who really had difficulty in coordinating their balance during the grid exercises, so we devised a few other exercises to help them. Try these exercises yourself; even if you think you are fairly coordinated, they will show you how balanced you really are, and after doing them a few times your balance will undoubtedly improve.

First of all, take your feet out of the stirrup irons and cross the leathers over in front of the saddle, or take them off the saddle altogether. Now try doing any of the grid exercises at a trot and a canter (remember the poles will need placing further apart for the canter). Keep your legs in the correct position, wrapped closely round the horse's sides, with your toes up and pointing forwards.

When you feel confident about this, do the exercise again, but this time pull up after the jump. Have a look at your feet; are your toes pointing upwards – or downwards?

It is essential that you do the next exercises in an enclosed manège. Put the leathers and irons back on the saddle and your feet back in the irons. Now knot your reins so that they are shortened by a third (or use shorter reins). Hang on to the ends as you come into the grid, then drop them and stretch your arms out in front of you at shoulder level. This will encourage your head to go forward and so help you balance correctly. As you land over the jump, pick up your reins straight away and control the horse.

Next, try placing your hands on your hips as you do the exercise, then one hand in front of you and one behind you. Both of these are harder than the previous exercise because your arms are not helping you to balance or position yourself correctly. Consequently, they are highly valuable!

Another exercise you can do is to place the first pole on the ground, the next one 15 cm (6 in) higher, the next 30 cm (1 ft) high and the fourth 45 cm (1 ft 6 in) high. Again these should be set at a canter stride so that each pole comes in the middle of the stride and helps to exaggerate the bouncy rhythm. Try going down the poles without stirrups and without holding the reins.

Jumping over small jumps without your feet in the stirrups can greatly help to improve your balance and confidence, and it ensures that you do not use your stirrup irons to support your legs. Cross the stirrup leathers over in front of the saddle so that they do not bang the horse's sides. You can see in the first picture how off balance the rider is – her right hip has collapsed so that her leg is just hanging straight down by the horse's side. As she moves down the grid, she has rectified her position.

Here the rider is going down the grid without reins either – again, a great exercise for improving balance and confidence and ensuring you do not use the reins as lifelines. Knot them to make them shorter so that they do not hang down by the horse's legs. Holding arms out sideways like this helps to balance the rider. Although the rider's legs here are a little far back as she goes over the jump, her body position is very good.

Now the rider puts her hands on her hips which makes balancing that little bit more difficult. A very good exercise to try.

Here our rider is coming down the grid without stirrups or reins. Although she starts off a little lopsided, she corrects this and really maintains very good balance whilst using her legs well to keep the horse straight and balanced. Both horse and rider appear to be enjoying themselves, and this is certainly the best way to learn.

Here our young riders are having fun, with both riders and ponies enjoying their jumping. Eight-year-old Philippa is giving it her all in effort and concentration as she lets go of the reins over the final jump of the grid. I think we can forgive the pointing-down toes on this occasion! Robert follows on doing the same exercise on his pony – a very keen jumping pair! Finally Nicholas demonstrates good balance, although his legs are a little far back.

POSITION

What riding the grid without stirrups will have done for you is to really make you use your leg muscles to help you balance and move in coordination with the horse's movement. You may find that when you put your feet back into the stirrup irons the leathers seem too long.

Many people advise riders to shorten their leathers a hole or two when they start to jump. I would recommend that you begin with them at the length you find comfortable for normal riding, and progress to shortening them after you have begun to feel the jumping movement. Certainly you should not try to jump with the leathers at a length that makes you fight to keep your feet in the stirrups, but then you should never ride with them as long as this anyway. If they are slightly too long you will find that as you wrap your legs around the horse's belly and move forward over the jump your feet will probably come out of the stirrups; that is unseating for you and it is unsettling for the horse to have the irons flapping against its sides.

If you find that you are losing your irons, or you feel your legs are banging against the horse's sides, try shortening the leathers by a few holes. This may feel slightly uncomfortable, but it will make you push your heels down and this will strengthen your leg muscles. Your legs will become stronger and more effective. After doing the grid exercises like this for a while put the leathers back to a length that feels comfortable – this may still be a hole or two shorter than your normal riding length.

What shortening the leathers does is compress the angle of the knee so that it can act as a pivot to support the rest of your body more effectively. As you jump higher fences, you will find you want to get further forward, and shorter stirrup leathers assist you in doing so.

An example of a near-perfect jumping position. The rider is looking straight ahead between his horse's ears, he has slight, relaxed contact through the reins to the horse's mouth and he is in perfect balance, positioned absolutely over the horse's centre of balance. He is jumping at speed, which may be why it looks as if the saddle has slipped back just very slightly.

These two pictures show typical positions of a novice rider learning to jump. In both, the rider is way behind the movement and the horse's centre of balance. As she comes over the jump her whole body position is far too far back and she has had to hold her arms straight out in front of her in order not to interfere with the horse's mouth. As she lands over the jump she is using her reins as lifelines to support her. In fact, if she did not do so she would fall backwards, she is so far behind the centre of balance.

Here is another example of a typical novice position. The rider is far too far forward, so much so that her body and right shoulder are leaning on the horse's neck. Her head has disappeared almost from view over the other side, but it is obvious she is looking down at the ground, and her legs are way up in the air behind her. The only good thing to say is that she is not interfering with the horse's mouth.

SEEING A DISTANCE

"Seeing a stride" is a term you may well have heard or read about in connection with jumping. It means knowing exactly how many strides you are away from a jump, so that you are able to judge when there are four – three – two – one normal canter strides before take-off.

Because it is the distance that one is assessing, I prefer to talk in terms of *seeing a distance*. If, for example, you have judged there to be four normal canter strides between jumps, and your horse lands short over the jump, making it necessary to ask it to shorten its stride and put in five before take-off, it can be hard to make this mental switch if you have the idea of four strides established in your mind. Or your thinking can be upset if something distracts the horse and it puts in a short stride when you are not expecting it.

Trot into the grid as usual and then ask for a canter. As you canter over the poles count out loud, one – two – three – four – five. This way you will learn to feel the timing of the stride.

Now take away the fourth pole of the grid, so that you have three poles, a gap where the fourth pole was, then the jump. The horse will canter over the first three poles, then take one more canter stride – a *non-jumping stride* – before taking off. You'll find it takes off in exactly the same place as it did when the fourth pole was there; put a piece of paper half the length of the stride in front of the jump – about 1.8 m (2 yd) – and you'll find the horse takes off within a hair's breadth of this point every time. This is because the poles have established the rhythm of the canter and put the horse in the correct place for the jump.

By taking away the fourth pole and having one non-jumping stride before the jump, you'll begin to understand what is meant by "seeing a distance". Next take away the third pole, so that there are two non-jumping strides between the second pole and the jump. Keep the rhythm the same for two strides and then canter over the jump.

Finally take away the second pole, so that there are three non-jumping strides between landing over the pole and taking off over the jump. Providing you maintain the rhythm of the canter, the horse will still take off in exactly the same point for the jump. It is important to understand this, because it will help you in seeing the distance.

This exercise of taking away poles is invaluable for helping you see a distance, and being able to see a distance is the basis of successful jumping. However, it is extremely difficult and, I assure you, not something you are going to learn in one lesson.

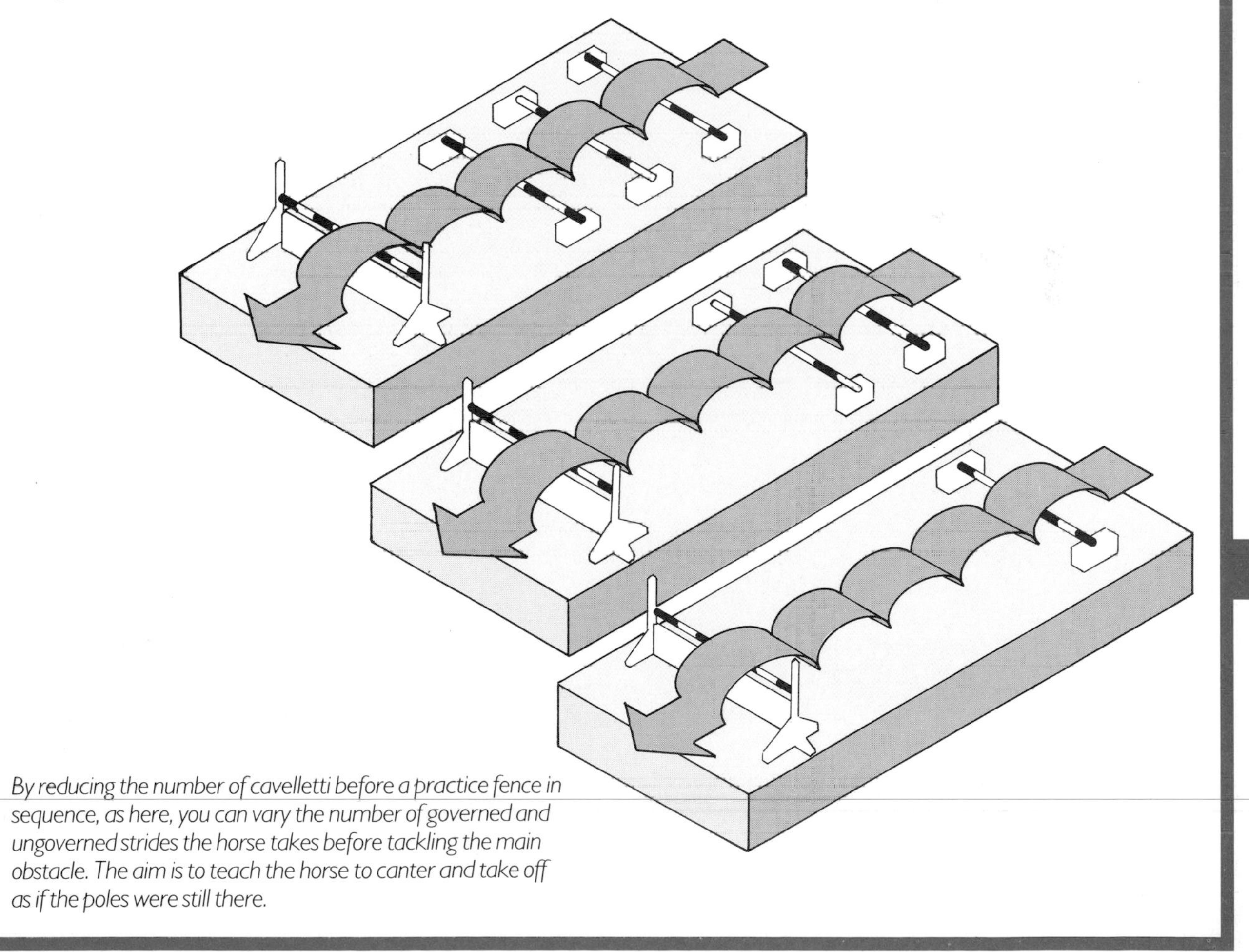

By reducing the number of cavelletti before a practice fence in sequence, as here, you can vary the number of governed and ungoverned strides the horse takes before tackling the main obstacle. The aim is to teach the horse to canter and take off as if the poles were still there.

GREATER CONTROL

As you do all these exercises with different numbers of poles placed in different positions still aim, every now and then, to come to a halt in a straight line three canter strides after landing. This will teach you to steer between hand and leg; it will help you in really understanding the horse's point of balance; and, particularly important in show-jumping, it will help you in learning to control your horse immediately after landing.

Nelson Pessoa taught me, way back in the early 1960s, the importance of getting control of a horse as soon as it lands over a jump. The very first stride it then takes will influence the way it approaches and jumps the next fence. As show-jumping courses become ever more twisted and complicated, with more and more jumps put at odd angles to one another in a small arena, this increases in importance. When you are jumping a course like this you have to know whether you want the horse to take a long or a short stride as it lands over a fence in order to put it right for the next one. Nearly everyone who rides is taught to jump; few are taught the importance of establishing control on landing.

Incorporate the following exercise into your routine, too. Have the grid, with all four poles and the jump at the end,

A good exercise for controlling a horse or pony when jumping. Following one another down the grid, each rider must exercise control to keep an even distance behind the one in front. You can see here that the leader, Hannah, is relaxed and happy, while Louise has become tense because she is trying so hard to stay in position. Further back, Philippa is quite relaxed moving forward gently to take her turn.

By riding down the grid in pairs, the riders again have to exercise great control to ensure they keep together. You can see the concentration on our young riders' faces!

placed down one long side of the school. Canter round the school in a collected canter with an even rhythm all the way. As you go round the corner before the grid, slow to a trot, trot over the first pole, then push forward into the collected canter again and continue all round the school in the same rhythm of pace. Remember to turn the grid round so that you can do the exercise on both reins.

Then change the grid to a 7.3 m (8 yd) sequence with six poles, so that the horse canters over a pole and takes one non-jumping stride before going over the next pole. Canter all the way round the school and through the grid at a collected pace, the rhythm of which never alters. It can be hard to maintain the rhythm around the corners of the school, so pay particular attention when going round them.

The important thing with all these exercises is to keep varying them, so that you and your horse are being exercised mentally as well as physically. Your horse is not able to anticipate what you are going to do at any given time, and neither of you gets bored!

Here the two boys have managed very well, particularly as they are on very keen ponies! They begin the exercise with the poles on the ground, asking the ponies to trot through quietly. Once that has been achieved, we have left all the poles on the ground except for the last one which we have raised to make a small jump. As you can see, the boys have controlled their ponies well, so that they take off at the final pole together. Next time, I shall ask Nicholas (on the right) to think more carefully about the position of his hands. In fact, you can see from his horse's ears and general demeanour that the rider has caused tension through his concentration; the rider on the left, however, is beautifully relaxed.

JUMPING INDIVIDUAL FENCES

I cannot emphasize enough how important it is to spend time doing these grid exercises. They are absolutely invaluable in helping you to see a distance, to understand the importance of establishing and maintaining a rhythm, and in gaining your confidence for jumping. They will stand you in much better stead than if you were to spend your time at this stage seeing how high you could jump before you scared yourself silly. And remember that these are the exercises top show-jumpers do with their horses *all the time*.

The next step is to learn to jump fences individually. The best way to do this is to build a small jump about 75 cm (2 ft 6 in) high on the long side of the arena. Place a pole on the ground 6.4 m (7 yd) in front of it (assuming that your horse canters on a 3.6 m (4 yd) sequence). The aim is to have the pole about 90 cm (3 ft) short of the distance of two strides; it will then act as an accelerator or a braking pole, whichever you need. If you are coming in towards the jump too fast or too slowly, either of which are likely at this stage, the pole will correct the stride and put the horse in the right position for take-off.

A horse measures the height of a fence from top to bottom, rather than the other way round, which we tend to do. Its eye begins at the top of the jump and travels down to the ground; the pole on the ground therefore helps the horse to judge its take-off point. If you measured the distance between the take-off point and the jump, you would find that, roughly speaking, it would be the same as the height of the jump.

As always, the aim is to approach the pole and then the fence at an even rhythm which does not vary as the horse jumps and moves away. At one time you would always see a rider come towards a fence, check his horse a few strides away and then push it on to make a tremendous effort in the last few strides. This simply does not work in the technical world of show-jumping today. The courses are too big and twisty with too many fences positioned in a small space. The only hope is to go round the course in that easy canter rhythm, taking the fences almost in the stride.

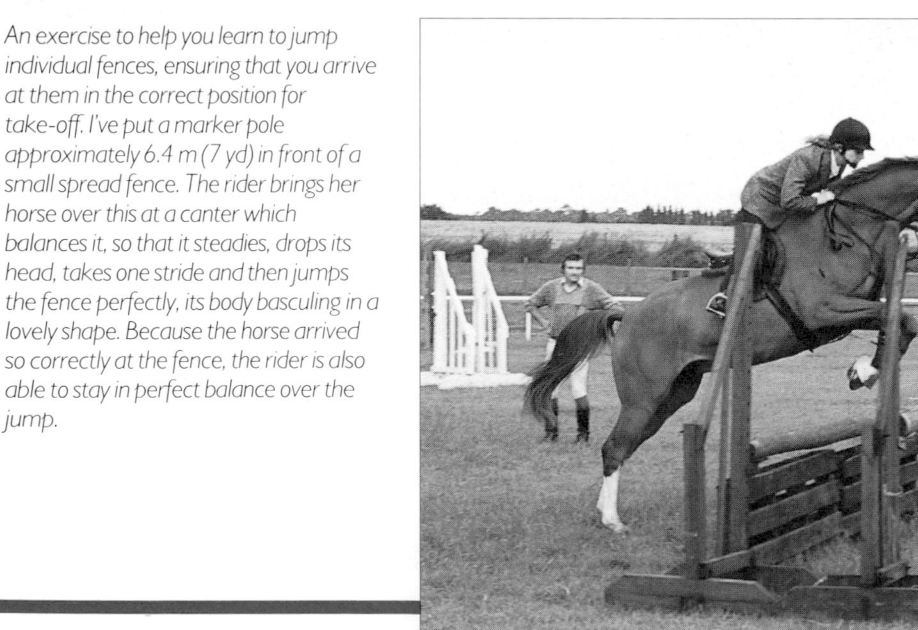

An exercise to help you learn to jump individual fences, ensuring that you arrive at them in the correct position for take-off. I've put a marker pole approximately 6.4 m (7 yd) in front of a small spread fence. The rider brings her horse over this at a canter which balances it, so that it steadies, drops its head, takes one stride and then jumps the fence perfectly, its body basculing in a lovely shape. Because the horse arrived so correctly at the fence, the rider is also able to stay in perfect balance over the jump.

DIFFERENT TYPES OF JUMP

When you are confident about jumping a jump like this, put fences up all over the school – in fact build a mini-course. Vary the types of fences so that you have uprights, parallel bars, gates, oxers and even small walls, and still place a pole on the ground 6.4 m (7 yd) in front of all of them unless you are building a triple bar; for this the horse needs to take off a bit further away in order to make the spread, so a pole would position it incorrectly.

None of these fences should be more than 90 cm (3 ft) high. Your aim is to jump in an even rhythm, not to see how high you can jump. You will inevitably end up frightening yourself and quite possibly putting the horse off jumping because you have ridden it badly.

Jump the fences in different sequences, so that your horse is not able to anticipate where it is to go next. This way it is up to you to ride the horse properly.

Now start thinking about jumping a combination – that is, two fences with one or two non-jumping strides between them. Place these across the school on the diagonal, and come into them on a left-handed canter. As you jump the second jump squeeze with your right leg so that the horse canters off on its right leg, and continue round in the circle this way.

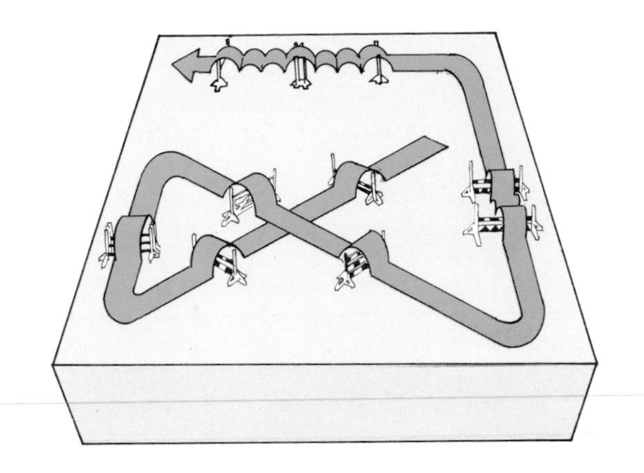

A simple course that you can set up at home, with no fence higher than 90 cm (3 ft). This course begins with a small vertical jump, with three canter strides – 14.5 m (16 yd) – to the next fence, also a vertical. Next there is a triple bar, then a vertical, after which there are four strides – 18 m (20 yd) – to another vertical. Next there is a sharp left-hand turn over a couple of uprights just one stride – 7.3 m (8 yd) – apart. Finally, down at the far end of the arena, there is a combination of three jumps consisting of a vertical followed by three strides, a parallel followed by three strides, and another vertical.

Learning to jump water should come early in a rider's training over jumps. Here Robert demonstrates a perfect jump over water. We've placed a pole just 30 cm (1 ft) above the surface, in the centre, to make the pony bascule correctly.

If your horse is frightened of jumping ditches, let it have a good look at it first, so it realizes there is nothing nasty lurking down there. But be prepared for a big jump when it does finally go over!

Another example of a water jump and the horse jumps it beautifully. The rider, however, is looking down at the water instead of straight ahead to the next jump -- remember that this is a very bad habit to get into.

Include a small wall in your jump training, so that the horse gets used to jumping fences that it can't see through. If you compare these two jumps, you will see that one horse and rider are throwing themselves over the fence, whereas the others are jumping in balanced harmony.

Jumping up on to and then off a bank. This is probably not an obstacle you can easily construct at home! However, it is a good one to include in your learning programme. As you can see, our rider is now feeling much more at ease and confident in herself and her horse as she jumps.

1

2

3

SUMMING UP

By now you will have come a long way in these jumping sessions. Remember that you should always be confident that you are in control of your thoughts and the movement. Stick to one horse when you are learning to jump, really getting to know it well. Then when you get a little more confident you can try the exercises on different horses.

As you start to jump individual fences, which are going to be higher than the poles in the grid exercises, the one thing that should be at the back of your mind is the thought of your legs being ready to squeeze the horse's sides, both to balance it and to give it the confidence to go over the obstacle. The horse will know you are telling it you believe it can do it and it will be eager to demonstrate its trust in you.

Remember that the horse gets its knowledge of what you want it to do from the movement of your legs, arms and body. If you always make the same mistakes, the horse will begin to counteract them. This is why it is important to keep varying the exercises; that way you will find you are correcting your mistakes and the horse will not be able to anticipate your next move.

Whenever you approach a fence, think about the way you are moving towards it. You should be in that easy, constant rhythm, whether you are trotting or cantering, but if you find you are slightly behind and are going to arrive at the jump awkwardly be ready to squeeze a little harder with your legs so that the horse lengthens its stride. If you are coming in too quickly keep the leg pressure on so that the horse knows it has to think, but just slightly tighten your fingers round the reins so that it backs off a little and negotiates the obstacle comfortably. In the grid exercise the poles would make this adjustment for you; when you are jumping individual fences you have to recognize the need for the adjustment and make it yourself, so you must think about what you are doing.

You should never be just sitting on a horse like a lump of dough; always be creative. In jumping, the one static object is the fence – you and the horse are either moving towards it or away from it, always in perfect balance. You must always be ready to keep up the leg pressure when moving towards fences as this helps to balance the horse and put it right for the jump. Even if you are coming in too fast you must maintain contact with the horse through hand and leg so as to give it confidence. If you don't it is likely to jump into the middle of the jump and frighten itself, or it will refuse because it will know it is out of balance.

Being able to jump natural obstacles which you encounter out on a ride can make your riding a more enjoyable and complete experience. From here, you can decide if you want to jump competitively.

5 ADVANCED RIDING AND SCHOOLING

By now you are undoubtedly a competent rider, able to control your horse in any foreseeable situation – secure in the knowledge that it will obey you – and able to jump happily most obstacles that you encounter, either out in the countryside, or set up in the school.

From here, you have various options. You can remain as you are, happy to be a recreational rider, perhaps taking part in the odd local competition. Or, if you prefer, you can begin to specialize, concentrating mainly on jumping for example, and competing in show-jumping competitions. Whatever your decision, however, all riders at this stage will benefit from learning a little about the movements of dressage, or advanced school work, and how to execute them. Very often this means teaching – or schooling – your horse in the art, as well. And art it undoubtedly is.

Such schooling, sometimes referred to as *flat work*, is something that we in the UK all too often tend to neglect. All riding horses – hunters, show-jumpers, eventers, even recreational riding horses – benefit from this sort of schooling, and feeling them respond to the refinements of your commands is one of the great joys of riding. You do need plenty of patience here, however; results are not achieved overnight.

Advanced riding and schooling mean learning greater refinements of movement and control. Skill needs to be combined with patience; this kind of work cannot be hurried and perfection will not be achieved in a day.

THE STABLE

If you find you want to progress beyond simply going out for pleasant countryside rides in which you feel confident about popping over the odd obstacle that stands in your way, one of the things you are going to have to think about is keeping your horse stabled rather than out at grass. A horse kept wholly at grass is only really ever fit enough for general hacking, and perhaps light riding club activity. Keeping a horse at grass is less trouble than keeping it in a stable. But it does mean that it is not having the full programme of care, exercise and diet that it needs to keep it really fit.

There must be enough room in the stable for the horse to be able to move around comfortably and lie down and get up easily. The stable should be light and airy, with good ventilation but no draughts. The bottom half of the stable door should bolt securely from the outside (top and bottom – horses often learn how to undo top bolts) and the top half should open right back against the wall where it can be secured so that it doesn't continually swing open and shut. The floor should be solid with good drainage.

You must provide a deep, comfortable bed of straw, shavings or shredded paper on the floor of the stable. Use wheat straw rather than barley: if a horse eats barley it becomes bloated whereas wheat straw does less harm. A horse that gets into the habit of eating straw, however, should be kept on shavings or paper, and so should a horse with an allergy to dust.

The bedding has to be kept clean. This is achieved through a daily activity known as *mucking-out*. All soiled bedding should be removed, the clean bedding piled up and the floor swept. The new bedding may be left piled up during the day, or through the morning at least, being put down for the horse later in the day; however, I prefer our horses to have a good comfortable bed, 15 to 20 cm (6 to 8 in) deep, throughout the day in case they want to lie down. A horse can very easily chip the bone of a hock if it lies down on a concrete floor with no protection.

Either way, all soiled bedding is replaced with fresh after mucking-out, and the bed is banked up around the walls so that the horse does not bang its legs as it goes to lie down or get up. At regular times during the day droppings are removed so that the task of mucking-out is made as easy and light as possible.

Very smart stabling for a number of horses. This is the American system of stabling at large equestrian establishments: several compartments are contained within one large barn-like building. Metal bars, rather than solid walls, help to keep the compartments light and airy.

Establishing and sticking to a routine for looking after horses in the stable is the best way of doing things. At this well-run establishment, there are as many helpers as horses, but everyone is busy and getting on with their particular job, working as a team to ensure that the yard is clean and tidy and runs smoothly at all times.

A typical example of stabling suitable for someone with a couple of horses they want to keep in. Two separate loose boxes are contained in the building; the roof overhangs the front of the stable so that the horse is kept dry even if it is looking out over the stable door. Immediately outside the door the ground has been concreted to stop it getting wet and muddy.

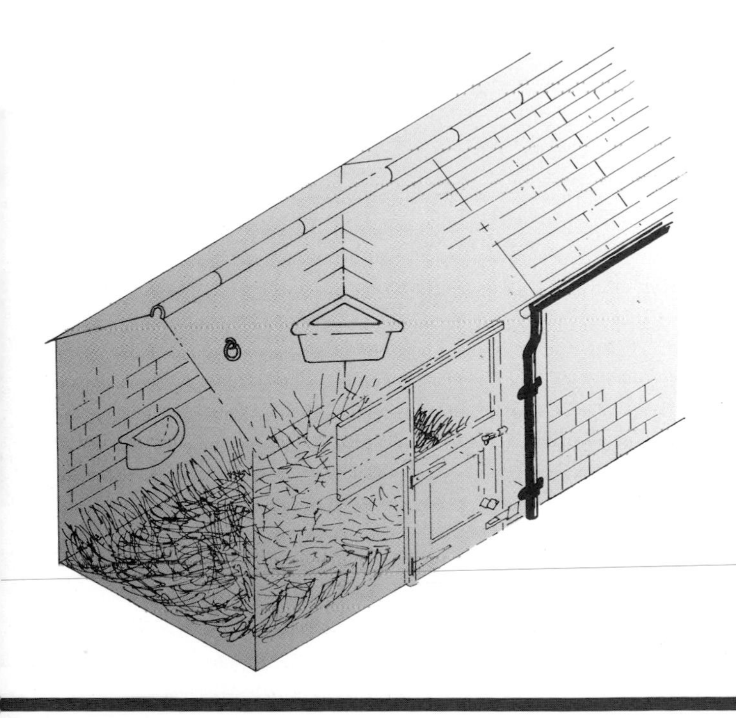

A traditional English loose box, with drinking bowl, ring and corner manger. The straw is banked up against the walls so that the horse does not bang its legs as it lies down or gets up, and the top of the stable door is left open as much as possible to provide good ventilation.

FEEDING

Feeding a stabled horse is more complicated than feeding a horse kept primarily at grass. When we talked about feeding grass-kept horses on page 61, I explained that feeding horses is an art and not a science, and this applies even more when you are feeding a stabled horse. Your aim is to keep its weight stable, feeding for fitness rather than fatness, and to keep it interested in its feed.

In fact, the hardest thing of all is to keep a horse at a peak of fitness for nine to ten months of the year, and in practice you will find you have to let it down a bit every now and then, feeding a warm mash with a dose of Epsom salts, or any other recognized laxative, once a week to give it a bit of a clean-out, before bringing it back up again.

There are no strict rules for feeding a horse, in terms of what sort of feedstuffs to give or how much. It depends on a number of factors – the type of horse, how much work it is doing and whether it is a good or a fussy feeder. A horse in heavy work needs a balanced diet of protein, carbohydrate and fibre just as we do and you can provide this in different ways. Bear in mind that the tendency is generally to overfeed rather than underfeed.

Until recently, we have always fed our horses on a basic diet of bran and chaff (or, as bran has become so hard to obtain, a feedstuff known as *molichop* – chopped-up hay and straw mixed with molasses – which has the same effect as bran), oats, and barley, with mineral and vitamin additives to give a balanced diet. In addition, of course, we feed hay, or hay mixed with *horsehage* – a dried grass feedstuff with a little more nutritional value than hay, and we also feed a laxative mash at regular intervals to horses in work. There are complete mixes of food available but they tend to vary slightly from bag to bag; each will always contain the same percentages of protein, fibre, etc. but the manufacturers may use different ingredients to make up these percentages, and not all of them may suit all horses.

Having said all this, however, I am now about to embark on a system of feeding that is new for me and comparatively new on the market, although the principle is as old as time. It is a system of feeding grass grown in a six-day cycle in a machine in our own yard. The grass – a barley grass – is grown quite naturally, but under completely controlled conditions, so that it always has the same balanced content of vitamins, minerals, fibre and protein. Grass is of course the horse's natural food, and this "perfect grass" is exactly right for the horse. You can feed stabled horses on it alone, or you can use it as a supplement to any other feedstuffs that you like to give.

We feed our horses three times a day, at 7.30 a.m., at midday and at 5.00 p.m. If I have a horse who is a difficult feeder and is in heavy competition work, I will spread its daily rations out over four smaller feeds as horses like this fare better on a "little and often" feeding regime. Every horse has a hay net in its stable which it can pull away at as it likes.

Feed at the same time each day – a horse will soon know when to expect its meals. In a yard with several people helping they can all give a hand with feeding so that the horses don't have to wait anxiously while their stable mates are fed before them.

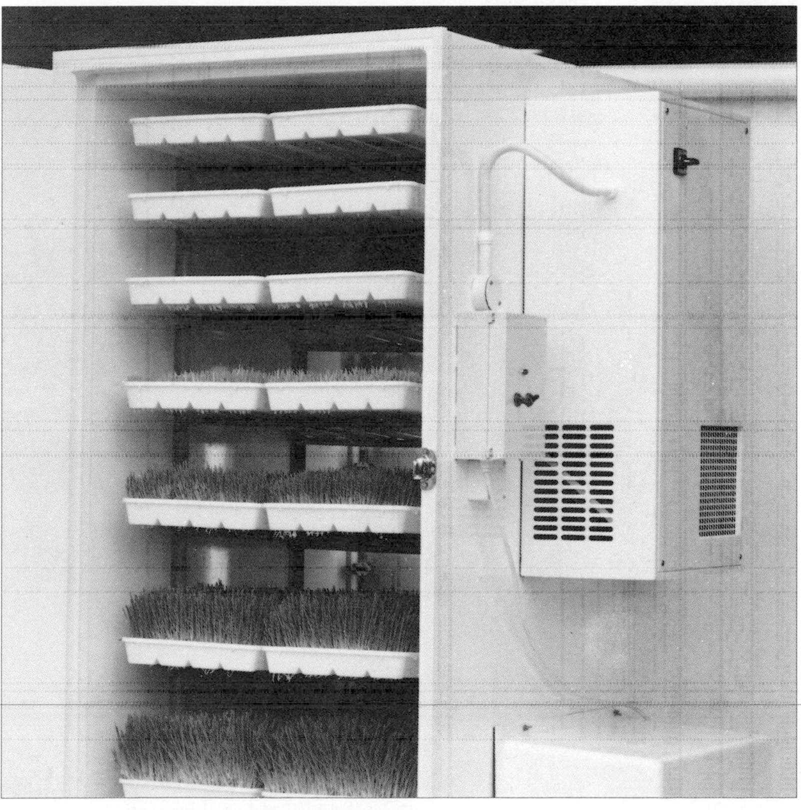

Above *The ultimate in convenience food: grass served up on a tray!*

Left *With this system of feeding, barley grass seed is 'planted' on day one and is ready for cropping and feeding six days later. A comparatively small machine yields an amazing amount of extremely 'pure' and nutritious food.*

STABLE ROUTINE

The way to look after horses in the stable is to establish a routine and stick to it. Horses are creatures of habit and they stay contented if they know what to expect of their stabled lives.

Our day in the yard starts at about 7.00 a.m. and the first job is to wash out the water buckets and refill them. I prefer water buckets to automatic stable watering devices as I can see how much each horse is drinking: any change tells me that there may be something wrong with a particular horse. Also, automatic watering devices can easily go wrong, either getting blocked so the horse gets no water, or getting stuck so the water keeps running and floods the bedding. The best water you can give your horse to drink is rainwater, so set up a water butt near your stable if you can.

Next the rugs and blankets are checked. If they have slipped we take them right off and put them back on rather than trying to straighten them. Then the horses are fed and left in peace to eat and digest their meal before we begin mucking-out. If possible, we move horses to other stables or put them on the exercise machine (see page 136) while mucking-out is going on.

After mucking-out the horses are given a thorough grooming or strapping, the stages of which are shown in the pictures. This grooming is more extensive than that given to the grass-kept horse (see page 65) and is an important part of keeping a stabled horse clean and healthy. A good grooming massages the skin and helps the circulation as well as improving appearance. Exercise, a reduced session of grooming – brushing the coat, washing the eyes, nose, dock and round the sheath, and the midday feed follow, and then the horses are left in peace. In a busy yard, each will have had to wait its turn for exercise. At the evening feed, we also skip out the stables (that is, fork up all the droppings), and wash out and refill the water buckets.

Keep all your grooming kit together in a box so that you know where it is and it is easy to take from place to place. In the top of the box, pictured, there is a sponge, two mane combs, a hoof oil brush and rubber bands for plaiting the mane. In the bottom there are curry combs, body and dandy brushes, hoof oil and baby oil (for wiping round the eyes and nostrils to give the horse a smart appearance).

Mucking-out – removing droppings and soiled bedding from the stable – is a daily chore. Here a barrow-load of dirty shavings is being wheeled off to the muck heap.

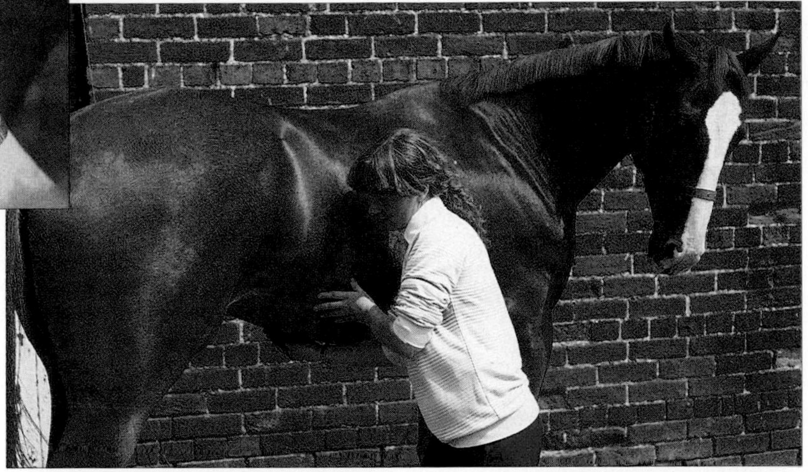

Close-up of a rubber curry comb, used for the first stage of grooming a horse. It massages the skin and brings the dust to the surface of the coat. Use it all over the body in a circular motion, particularly under the belly and between the front legs.

This is a nylon curry comb, which can be used instead of the rubber curry comb to do the same job. It can also be used to brush the mane.

After curry combing for a good ten minutes, the horse is brushed all over, again in a circular motion, with a body brush. This brushes away all the dirt and scurf loosened by the curry comb.

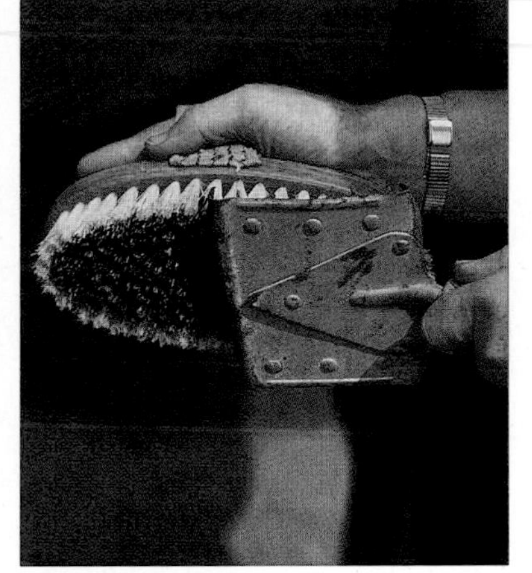

After each brush stroke, the body brush is drawn across a metal curry comb to remove the dirt. The curry comb is banged lightly on the ground every so often to get rid of this dirt.

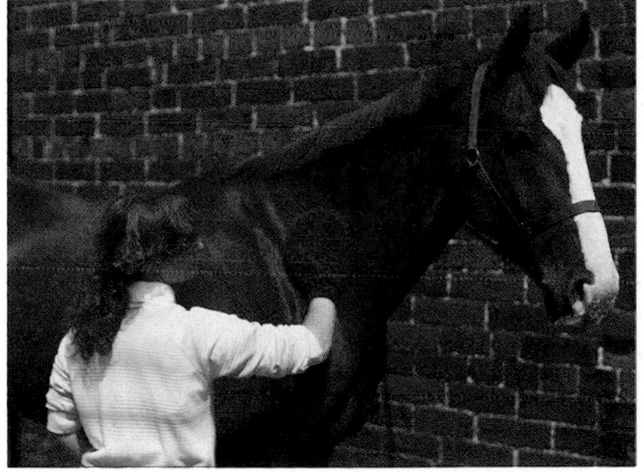

The final attention to the coat, to lay it down and make it shine, is to rub it over in the direction of the hair with a grooming mit or pad. Years ago, grooms would twist straw into a wisp to do this job, spending perhaps fifteen minutes on it. This helped to muscle the horse as well.

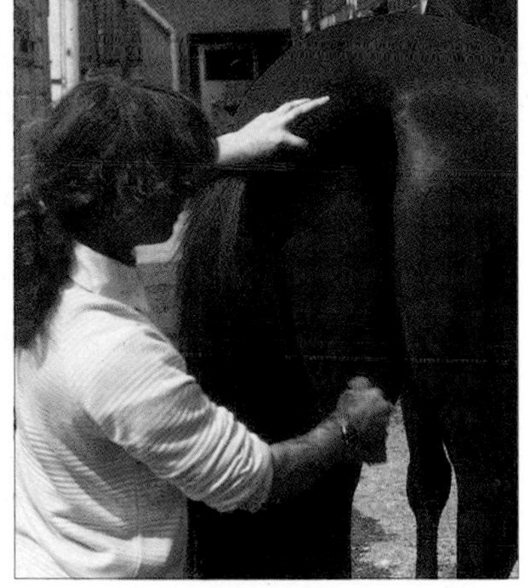

At the end of grooming, sponge out the eyes and nostrils with a clean sponge squeezed out in cold water. With a separate sponge clean the dock and under the tail; a weak antiseptic solution can be used for this.

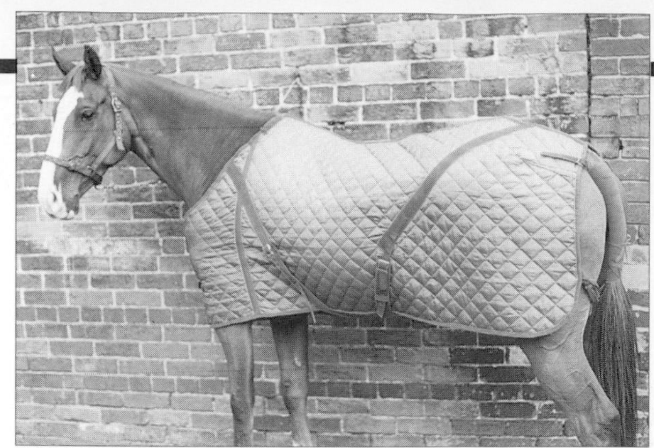

This is an American night rug made of an easy-care synthetic material. The cross-over strap system, which originated in America, has largely replaced the old-fashioned arrangement of a jute rug held in place with a surcingle or roller that fastened round the horse's belly. The tendency was for the rug to move if the horse rolled or even lay down, and the roller could also rub, causing sore withers.

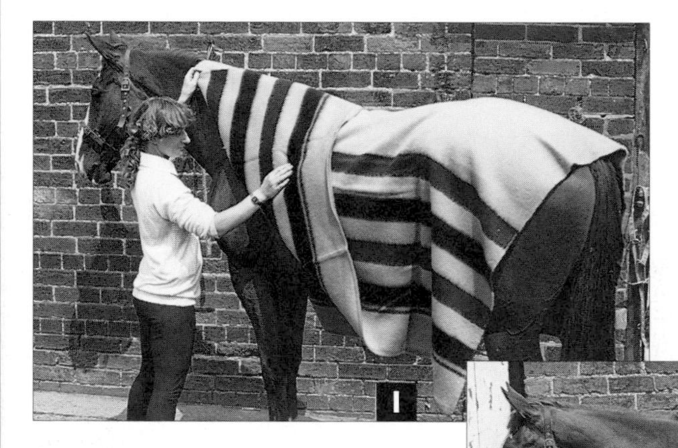

Rugging-up the old-fashioned way

This was the way to rug a stabled horse for the night before the more sophisticated rugs started coming on the market. Many people will still use rugs and blankets like these. First a Witney blanket is put over the horse's back, well up on the neck. The sides are folded as shown and the jute rug placed on top and the front buckle done up. Then the blanket is folded back over the rug and an iron-arch roller placed on top. This one has a breastplate which helps to prevent it from slipping.

2

3

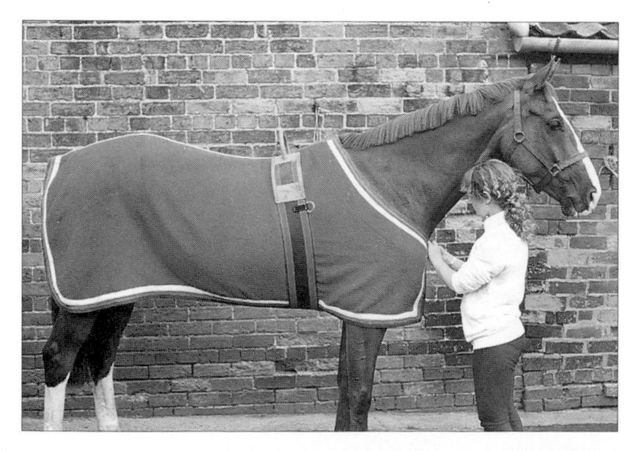

A smart woollen day rug worn with an iron-arch roller. Such rugs are usually used when travelling to shows rather than for everyday wear in the stable where they would soon get dirty.

GENERAL HEALTH

Being aware of your horse's condition and noticing if it is feeling off-colour are your responsibility, and depend on knowing your horse. All the books in the world can tell you the signs of good health – bright eyes, shiny coat, firm droppings and so on – but you must know your own horse's demeanour and its idiosyncrasies to judge whether it is well or not. This is far more reliable than checking whether its coat is dull or shiny.

If a horse leaves its feed, or drinks more or less water than usual, it can be a sign of something amiss. For instance, a horse will be reluctant to eat if its teeth have been allowed to become too sharp and they are hurting. If they do grow to a point – and they grow quickly and need frequent checking – they must be filed down. There is a way of checking that a horse's teeth are not causing trouble: while it is feeding you approach it and take hold of its tongue; food that is not being chewed properly will have gathered between the horse's back teeth and its cheeks and will fall out. In our yard we carry out this check as a matter of routine every four to six weeks. Or your horse may be leaving its feed because you are giving it too much or because the feed buckets are dirty: make a habit of scrubbing them out each time.

You should run your hands over a horse's body and legs every day, whether it is kept at grass or stabled, to see if there are any injuries. Again, you are checking to see if anything is different from usual, whether there are bumps or swelling on the legs that are not there normally. Check the condition of the feet and shoes when you pick out the hooves.

If you do think there is something wrong with your horse, consult the vet for advice.

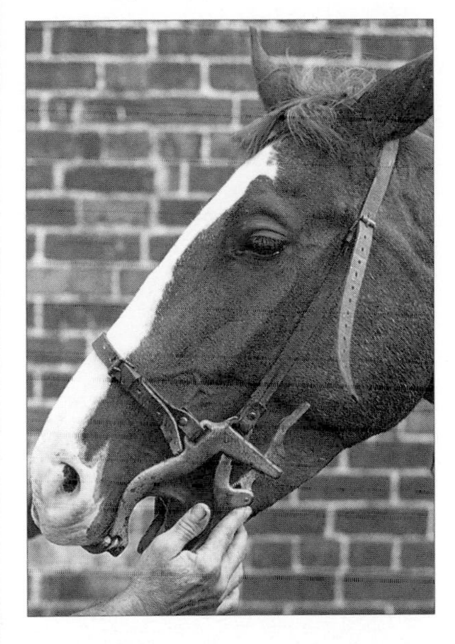

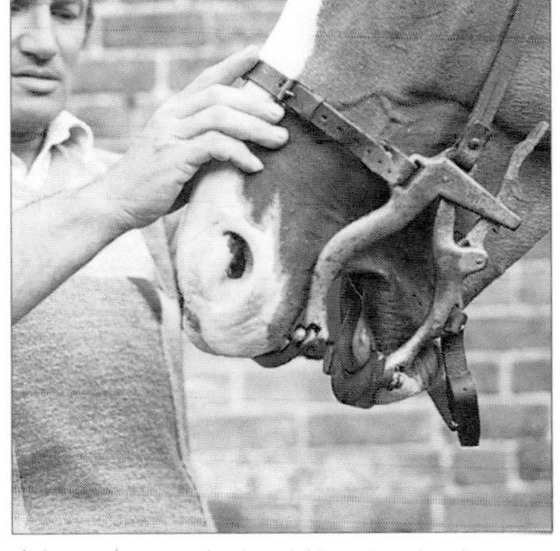

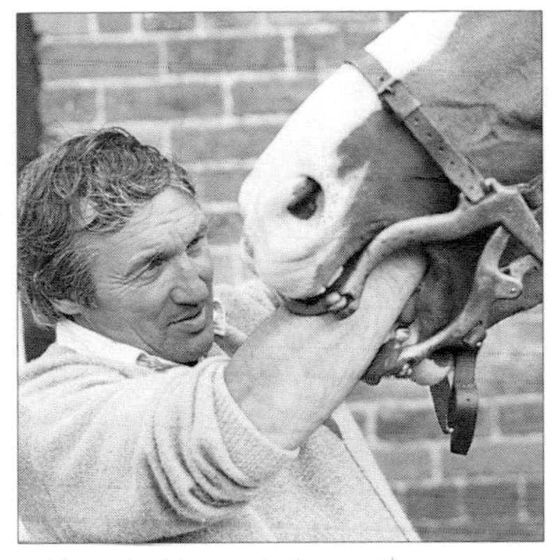

A horse's mouth should be checked regularly to make sure there are no very sharp teeth causing sores or making the horse reluctant to eat. Horses' teeth do grow quite fast. To some extent they will wear them down as they eat, but they seldom do this evenly; hence the appearance of sharp edges and points. In this picture, I have fitted a special gag which automatically opens the horse's mouth and allows you to reach right to the back where problems occur.

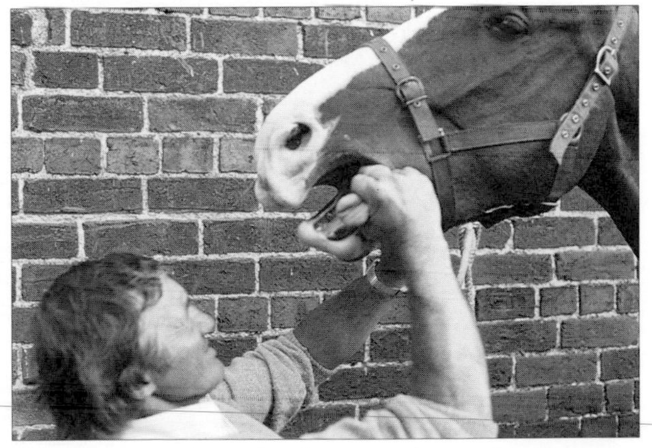

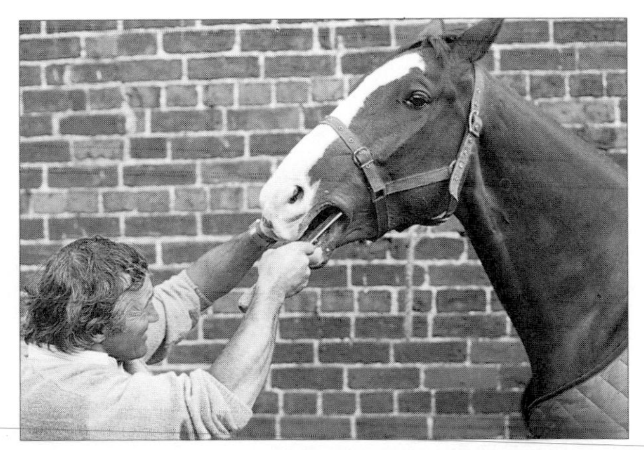

You can examine the teeth without a gag by opening the mouth and holding on to the tongue as I am doing here. Having found a sharp tooth at the back of the mouth, I am filing it down with a special rasp. Get the vet or a horse dentist to do this at least twice a year.

PACES AND BENDS

Having got your horse into condition through a programme of good stable management and exercise, you can think about tackling more advanced movements and paces.

The elements we will discuss in the following pages are *refinements* of pace and movement, so horses have to be taught them, just as riders have to be taught how to execute them. They are basic dressage movements, and although this is not a book about dressage itself, there could be no better person to demonstrate them than an expert on dressage like Judy Bradwell, who is the rider in the pictures on this and the next few pages.

The thing to think about first is the execution of the paces and how the horse is moving. In working towards greater refinements in the paces, you should begin with the trot as this has greater natural impulsion than the walk. Initially you will be aiming at a *working trot* in which the horse moves forward with active, swinging steps – the "activity" coming mainly from its hind legs, its back swinging gently in rhythm with the movement. The hind feet touch the ground in the prints of the front feet. It should be an unhurried pace, so, having asked for a trot, control the forward impulsion with your reins and move your body in rhythm with the movement. You will feel if the horse is balanced; if not you can help to balance it by riding in 20 m (22 yd) and 10 m (11 yd) circles.

From the trot you can go back to the walk, and the pace you are looking to establish now is the *medium walk*. This is a comparatively unconstrained pace; the horse should move forward with lively, active steps, its outline slightly compressed from a long-rein walk (see picture). Its hind feet just over-track the front feet. You must allow your horse to use its head and neck, but control the pace with your seat and legs as well as the reins so as to make the hindquarters work. Using your legs alternately, your left leg as the

After working at the trot, let your horse walk forward on a long rein for five minutes or so to reward it for its efforts and to make it relax. You should begin, end and intersperse all schooling sessions with periods of walking on the long rein, initially to loosen the horse and to get it ready for work and then to reward and relax it. Here Judy demonstrates the correct length of rein for a good stretchy long-rein walk.

A working trot in which the horse is showing balanced movement with good engagement of its hind legs and the correct bend in the hock. Its head carriage and bend in the neck are also good. More time is spent schooling a horse at a trot than at any other pace, so it is important to perfect the different movements. Each one should be perfectly balanced with the energy for the steps coming from the hindquarters. The hind legs take the weight of the horse as well as propelling it forward.

Here the horse is demonstrating a medium trot, in which a little more impulsion is asked for from the hindquarters and the steps are correspondingly a little longer. Although this horse is only a novice, it is demonstrating a very good outline.

horse's left foreleg goes forward and your right leg as its right foreleg goes forward, helps to establish a good swinging rhythm.

You must concentrate more now on how the horse executes turns and bends, to make sure it is moving the whole of its body correctly. In any turn, the degree to which the horse is bent along its body will depend on the sharpness of the angle in the turn. The front and hind legs should remain on one track so that the horse is bent evenly down the length of its body – from nose to tail – and the speed or momentum of the pace should not vary. Because the tendency is often to slow down at turns, keep up the pressure with your seat and legs, flexing with your rein in the direction of the turn to bend the horse round your inside leg – exerting pressure with the calf on the girth – and keeping the quarters in line by using your outside leg just behind the girth. The more acute the turn the more pronounced should be the diagonal positioning of the legs in this way. The outside hand determines the degree of the bend by its restraining action, preventing the horse from bending its head towards the inside hand.

*In both these pictures the horse is doing a medium walk. In the first (**1**) it is showing a good outline for a young horse; its head and neck are a little low which would be expected in a horse of this age and experience. In the second picture (**2**) the horse's outline is a little more advanced. Its carriage is better and, being better balanced, it is taking more weight on its hind legs.*

*Here the horse is taking the corner correctly in a trot, bending evenly along the length of its body. (**1**)*

*This is not such a good corner. As you can see the quarters have fallen in slightly and the bend is uneven. (**2**)*

*Cornering in trot seen from head-on. The first picture (**1**) shows a good bend, while in the second (**2**) there is too much bend in the neck and the outside shoulder is consequently falling away. You should exert equal pressure with both legs during a turn or going round a corner so as to maintain the even bend. However, if the horse tends to cut its corners use the inside leg more strongly; if, on the other hand, it tends to throw its hindquarters out off the track, use the outside leg more strongly.*

HALF-HALT AND LEG-YIELDING

In advanced riding and schooling, a *half-halt* is a much-used technique and an important one for horse and rider to learn. It is, in effect, a momentary check that can be used at any pace. The slight slowing down has the effect of balancing the horse, and warning it that you will be giving it a new instruction so it must be on the alert and ready to respond. All changes of pace or movement should be preceded by a half-halt.

The aids for a half-halt are the same as those for a halt. Close your lower legs against the horse to keep it straight and push it forward into a restraining hand. The restraining hand is perhaps stronger than it would be for a halt, but as soon as you feel the check in pace, you should immediately relax your hands and give the aids for the movement you require.

Teach a horse to half-halt and get to know the feel of it, by riding up and down the arena asking for a half-halt at the same place twenty or thirty times. The horse will begin to anticipate it and will slow down automatically, and at that point you can push it forward again.

In the more advanced movements another important principle is "leg obedience", that is, for the horse to move away from pressure from your leg. Leg-yielding is an exercise which teaches this. It is an elementary two-track movement generally introduced quite early in a horse's training.

Half-halt: *you can see the check in pace and how the horse is listening to its rider, ready to respond to her next commands. Its hind legs are well under it, so it is collected up, ready for the next movement.*

In this sequence, you can see Judy is trotting forward freely in the first picture. In the second, she begins to apply the aids for a half-halt, and in the third the horse is responding, its hind legs well engaged and its concentration good.

In *leg-yielding* the horse moves forwards and sideways, its inside leg crossing over and in front of the outside leg. In most two-track work (see page 132) the horse is bent around the rider's inside leg, but in leg-yielding its body stays almost straight, with only a slight inclination away from the direction in which it is moving.

To leg-yield to the left, ride at a walk along the side of the manège on the left rein, then use your right leg against the horse's side to push it to the right. Flex your right rein fractionally to ask for slight flexion to the right, i.e. away from the direction of movement, and support this with your left rein to prevent the horse falling away to the right. Keep your left leg against its side to keep it moving forward.

Practise leg-yielding to left and right at a walk and a trot to make the horse supple and obedient.

Leg-yielding: *this comes early in the training of any horse to teach it "leg obedience", that is, to move away from a leg aid. In this picture, you can see the start of the movement in which Judy is asking the horse to bring its hindquarters off the track and bend very slightly away from the direction in which it is moving. A little further into the exercise and you can see how the horse crosses its front legs as it moves away from the pressure of Judy's right leg.*

Here the horse is leg-yielding on a diagonal line in the arena, again moving away from Judy's right leg. Its body is almost straight, its head just slightly bent away from the direction of the movement.

A good hind view of leg-yielding. Again you can see the legs crossing over.

COLLECTION AND EXTENSION

Towards the end of Chapter Two, and also to some extent in the last chapter, we discussed the shortening and lengthening of a horse's stride. This is something you should be concentrating on more now in your schooling sessions, looking for *collection* and *extension*.

A horse can achieve collection and extension at a walk, a trot and a canter. To become truly collected can take years of training and, without a great measure of collection, a horse cannot really achieve full extension; the power for the extension comes from the contained collection. Indeed, collection forms the basis of all dressage.

When a horse is properly collected it is light and relaxed and yet at its most active and agile. Because it is "collected" together its body becomes more compact, so that its outline (a term used frequently in dressage, referring to the overall shape of the horse's body) appears shorter and its carriage more erect. The horse must, of course, be completely balanced and its movements supple. The collection of its body results in its steps being springier – shorter but higher – and its pace "bouncier" than usual. All the power for this comes from the hind legs. Collection is achieved from the rear to the front of the horse; in fact its weight is transferred to its haunches so that the joints of its hind legs become more deeply bent, acting like springs. Its forehand is correspondingly lightened, its neck arches, the bend coming very definitely at the poll, but not so much that the line of its face comes "behind the vertical" – that is, an imaginary vertical line drawn from the front of the top of the forehead to the ground.

Aids for achieving collection are given below. Remember that there are degrees of collection and it can take very many years of patient training to arrive at the maximum. A horse takes time to develop the muscles in its hindquarters that allow for complete collection.

When a horse moves in extension it moves its whole body to achieve the greatest length of stride possible, again in all paces. Now the tracks of its hind feet come well in front of those made with the front feet, but the pace should still seem quite unhurried. The energy for the stride again comes from the hindquarters, so the forehand should be light and the steps look effortless. The horse's outline will be lengthened to allow for the greater length of stride, but the head should be held naturally, responding to the rider's hands but never leaning on them which would put too much weight on the forehand to achieve the required lightness of pace.

Collected walk: *compared with a medium walk, the steps here are a little shorter and more elevated.*

Collected trot: *again, you can see how springy and elevated the steps are compared with those of a medium and working trot. The lift comes from the impulsion created by the deeper bend in the hind legs. Collection at a trot is the easiest collected pace to ask for, but you use the same aids to ask for collection at any pace. First you must feel sure that the horse is listening well to your aids, that you have a contact with your legs and seat, and that you can feel the horse responding to the reins. Ask for a half-halt to get the horse's attention, then drive it forward into your hands by bracing your back to use your seat – this helps to engage the hindquarters – and using your legs by its sides. Repeat the aids, interspersed with a series of half-halts, the idea being to create pent-up energy which is released in lightness and shorter, more energetic steps.*

Extended walk: *the horse is taking longer steps here, but it should be stretching its neck a little more to reach into the contact of the rein. Because it is not doing this, its outline is not quite long enough.*

Extended trot: *you can see in the picture above that the horse is stretching forward and really covering a lot of ground with each step. Its outline is good and it is in perfect balance. Another view (right) of extended trot in which the horse is showing good activity; its hind legs are well engaged to give a strong, long step. Ask for extension in walk, trot or canter from the collected pace: give the aids for a half-halt, then push the horse forward using legs and seat quite strongly at the same time as yielding with the hands.*

Here the outline is correct for an extended walk, but there is not enough impulsion in the steps.

Transitions: *all transitions should be as smooth as possible whether you are asking for a change of pace either upwards or downwards or from collection to extension or vice versa. Be patient though; it will take time to achieve this. Here Judy is moving from walk to trot and is demonstrating a good transition with the horse propelling itself forward and up into the trot, the power coming from its hindquarters. Its outline is good.*

Here Judy has just asked the horse to extend the trot and you can see again how it is pushing itself forward from its hindquarters, ready to lengthen the stride.

A transition from trot to walk. *You can see the horse is listening to the command and is pulling, or collecting, itself in, ready to step forward into the transition. Never think of coming "back" to a walk from a trot or to a trot from a canter. In any downward transition, the movement should be forward into the pace, not back into it.*

COUNTER CANTER AND FLYING CHANGES

Collection and extension can be performed at a canter just as in the other paces. In addition there is a *medium canter*, in which the hind legs are active, the forehand light and the nose just in front of the vertical, and a *working canter*, which is a little more active with all legs.

A well schooled horse should also be able to perform a *counter canter*. This means it can canter left- or right-handed round an arena, in perfect balance, but with the outside leg leading and bent very slightly in the direction of the leading leg, i.e. to the outside. This is a more difficult manoeuvre than it sounds; the temptation for an inexperienced horse will be to canter *disunited* in order to balance itself. This means that in the second step of the canter, instead of diagonal front and hind legs working together, those on the same side move at the same time. Thus, for example, the horse canters in the sequence off-hind, near-fore and near-hind together, then off-fore, instead of the correct sequence of off-hind, off-fore and near-hind together, then near-fore.

A good example of a working canter on a young horse: it is well balanced, with its hind legs under it and its step elevated.

Don't ask a horse to perform counter canter until you are confident that it is able to shorten and lengthen its stride to command and that it has achieved quite a degree of collection in the pace. Its transitions from trot to canter and canter to trot should be smooth, and it should also go from walk to canter smoothly on request.

In a *flying change* the horse changes the leading fore and hind legs, and thus the whole sequence of the canter, in the air during the moment of suspension, without going back to the trot. It is quite an advanced and difficult movement for a horse, although those with a bouncy canter find it easier to learn.

Do not attempt to teach or perform a flying change on a horse until it is able to perform a good collected canter and a well balanced counter canter, and you are confident that it will lead with either leg on command from a walk as well as a trot. When cantering in a straight line, the aids are as follows: prepare the horse by asking for a half-halt, then apply the aids firmly for the canter on the opposite leg. Say your horse is cantering with the near-fore leading. As you feel it respond to the half-halt lighten your seat and brace your back to the right, move your right leg forward to the girth and your left leg a little further back. Support with the reins to keep the horse straight, but try to avoid making it flex its neck to the new inside lead – it should move in a straight line.

Intersperse training for a flying change with counter canter serpentine exercises. The horse will then not associate a change of leading leg at the canter with a change of direction. The ultimate aim is to get it to perform a series of flying changes while going down the centre or across the diagonal of the school.

In this transition to canter, the rider is not in a good position and the horse is showing its resistance to the aids. It has hollowed its back and lifted its head high at the poll which has made it unbalanced.

This is a better example of a transition from trot to canter, in which rider and horse are balanced and in harmony.

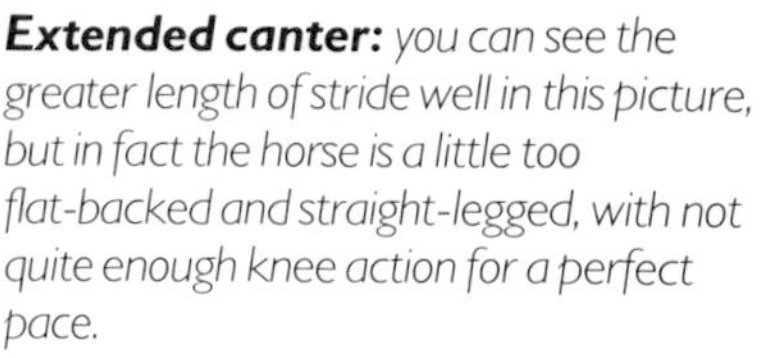

Extended canter: *you can see the greater length of stride well in this picture, but in fact the horse is a little too flat-backed and straight-legged, with not quite enough knee action for a perfect pace.*

Counter canter on the right rein, with the horse's near-fore leading. The horse remains bent in the direction it is going, in this case slightly to the left, round the rider's left leg. This is quite an advanced movement – above novice standard in dressage competitions. The horse must remain in perfect balance and harmony as it canters round a circle.

You can see the bend to the left in this picture. Judy's right leg – the outside leg of the canter pace – is positioned just behind the girth to keep the horse balanced.

Preparation for a flying change. *The horse is in a good collected canter, with its hind legs well engaged and bent, ready to make the necessary spring to change the leg. Good collection is essential before a flying change can be achieved, as considerable weight has to be taken on the hindquarters. A horse must thus be well established in its training in collection. The "jumping" movement required in a flying change can easily excite a horse, so don't start trying to teach or practise it on a day when it is feeling jumpy and excitable. Wait for a day when it is listening and responding well and quickly to your commands.*

THE HALT AND REIN-BACK

Although every horse should be taught to stand still at an early stage in its training, teaching a true halt comes a good deal later when the horse has learnt to accept the aids and has achieved a good degree of collection and extension. At this later stage, when you apply the aids for a halt – lightening the seat, closing the lower legs and pushing the horse into a restraining hand – the horse should come to a complete stop, its weight distributed evenly over its four legs, attentive to your next command. It should remain quite still, but alert, ready to move instantly either forwards or backwards.

If a horse tends to fight against the restraining hand action when you want it to halt, restrain with your hands, then relax them, and repeat this several times as you slow the horse down. Some horses will simply lean against a constant restraint or push their heads forward in an effort to counter the pressure on their mouths. Make sure that you give leg and body aids first: if you restrain the reins without the other aids, the horse will throw its head in the air.

Initially, a horse is unlikely to come to a halt with its legs squarely and evenly beneath it. Look down; if the forelegs are not together, nudge the horse to take a step forward. If the hind legs are not together, nudge with the leg on the side of the leg you want to move forward. Only make the horse stand like this for a short time before asking it to move again.

The *rein-back* should not be taught to a horse until the idea of forward movement has been thoroughly instilled in it. It will always be done from a halt, and unlike the walk it is a pace in two-time in which the horse moves diagonal pairs of legs. A rein-back in four-time is incorrect.

The aids are given opposite. Be sure to keep your hands low on the neck as you exert a gentle restraint on them. If you raise them and exert strong pressure while also giving leg aids, the horse may rear up. If you feel it beginning to do this, relax the reins and quickly urge it forwards with your legs.

This is an acceptable halt for a novice horse. Ideally its hind legs should be a little more together, so that it is standing square.

This is not a good halt at all. The horse is "above the bit" – that is, its poll is too high; it is not accepting the bit correctly. Therefore it does not have such a good outline as in the previous picture.

Here the outline is better again, but the horse is not standing completely square. *Judy is riding the horse here in a* double bridle *which is a bridle with two bits – a snaffle and a curb. This is excellent for advanced schooling as it gives the rider greater refinement and precision of control. However, it should only be used by riders who understand fully how it works on the horse's mouth and head and how to use it accordingly. Judy has also changed into a black coat, so that she and her horse are now correctly turned out for an advanced dressage test.*

Rein-back: *you can see the horse moves its legs in diagonal pairs in a correct rein-back, not individually as it does in a forward walk. A rein-back is always asked for from a walk; make sure the horse is well collected and ready to respond to a command. Push it forward into your hands by bracing your back and closing your lower legs. As the horse prepares to move forward restrain with your hands, so that the energy created by your seat and legs requires it to move backwards. Ask for no more than three or four backward steps and yield with your hands very slightly after each step so that the horse does not start rushing. After a maximum of four steps, halt and gently ride forward immediately, but again without rushing.*

LATERAL WORK

Lateral work is also known as work on two tracks. This is exactly what it is – the hind legs move on a different track from the forelegs. The horse moves sideways, or aslant, at an angle of about 30°, with one pair of legs crossing over in front of the other. Leg-yielding (page 124) is oneof the very early lateral movements, although it is generally used to teach leg obedience rather than as a two-track movement. The more advanced two-track movements are performed in dressage tests to show the precision with which a horse will respond to a rider's commands. The horse must be thoroughly supple, well balanced, responsive, and have a good idea of collection before being taught the movements. Lateral work can in fact help improve collection.

Principal lateral movements are the *shoulder-in, travers* and *renvers*, and *half-pass*.

In a shoulder-in, the shoulders are brought in from the track at an angle of about 30°. The outside foreleg and the inside hind leg remain on the same track with the other legs on two separate tracks, and the inside foreleg and hind leg step over or in front of the outside ones.

Travers and renvers are a little more demanding than shoulder-in, but extremely good for suppling the horse. In travers, the hindquarters are brought in off the track and the horse moves forwards and sideways, bent round the rider's inside leg, in the direction of the movement. In renvers, it is the shoulders that are brought in from the track and the horse is bent round the rider's outside leg, so that it is still bent in the direction of the movement. This bend is the difference between shoulder-in and renvers.

The half-pass is similar to the travers but whereas travers is executed along the school, the half-pass is done diagonally across the school. The lack of the fence or wall as a support makes it a slightly more difficult movement. In the half-pass the horse moves forwards and sideways in a diagonal line, its body parallel to the long sides of the school, but bent slightly in the direction of the movement. The forehand should very fractionally lead the hindquarters and the outside legs across in front of the inside ones.

Shoulder-in: *you can see clearly here that shoulder-in is a movement on three tracks. The horse is bent around the rider's inside leg (in this case the left leg) and is thus bent slightly away from the direction of the movement.*

The same movement, but Judy needs to exercise a little more control over the horse's inside shoulder.

Here the angle is more correct; you can see the bend looks easier and more natural.

Travers: *a movement that is a preparation for the half-pass; the bend required in each is the same. The hindquarters are brought in from the track, while the horse is bent round the rider's inside leg in the direction of the movement. You can see in both pictures how the outside legs have to cross over the inside ones.*

A sequence showing the half-pass. In the first picture the horse has just turned the corner of the school and is beginning the half-pass movement which is always performed across a diagonal of the school. The horse should be bent in the direction it is going, with the forehand fractionally in the lead. It is a bad fault if the quarters are leading. The horse's body should remain parallel to the sides of the school, except for the slight bend. Half-pass can be performed in walk, trot or canter, but it should always be in the collected pace. The speed should remain in exactly the same cadence as the forward pace with the stride neither shortening nor lengthening.

A close-up of half-pass to show clearly how the legs cross over. You can see here, too, how the body is almost parallel.

6 PREPARING FOR COMPETITION

There was a time when, for us, competitions were a complete way of life. We spent up to five days a week on the road in the summer, and perhaps three to four in the winter, so that the horsebox was more home than home. The horses, too, were so used to moving from one place to another that they really took no notice of it. You can always spot the horses of professional riders at shows; they look completely relaxed and at home. Often you'll find them just wandering around among the horseboxes. Harvey Smith, as soon as he gets to a show, looks for a piece of grass and simply turns his horses loose on it. They are so keen to have a mouthful of grass after several hours on the lorry that they just put their heads down and have a good graze.

The first rule of any competitive riding is that your horse must be fit and properly prepared for what it is you want it to do. And, whatever the type of show or event, the procedure for getting your horse and yourself ready and for travelling to the show, and your behaviour when you get there, are always very similar. You should try to become acquainted with as much of all this as you can beforehand; showgrounds can be daunting to the inexperienced and any nervousness or anxiety from the rider is soon transmitted to the horse.

Competing in horse shows – at all levels – can be great fun. Careful preparation is all-important, ensuring that you and your horse or pony arrive at the show calm and confident for what lies ahead.

GETTING A HORSE FIT

There is no magic about getting a horse fit, and keeping it that way; it entails nothing but hard, and often quite tedious, work. Yet it is of vital importance; just as an athlete must be fit in order to perform at his or her best, so must a horse.

If you are bringing a horse up from grass after a period of rest, it is going to take a good two to three months to get it to peak fitness. If it is in work, but not at the peak of fitness, it will take a little less time. Remember, however, that just as some people find it easier than others to get and stay fit, so horses will vary in the same way. This is when knowing your horse is important. You should have a thorough understanding of how much feed it needs to keep it in tip-top condition; over-feeding will be as much death to fitness as under-feeding. You also need to know what sort of exercise routine your horse needs to keep it alert and interested. There is no one programme that will suit every horse and you must experiment with the basic outline to find what suits yours.

If your horse is really unfit, you should begin the fitness programme by walking it at a steady pace for one hour a day. Yards with a lot of horses, like ours, tend to do this on an exercise machine. This is a very "20th century" device, designed to help us cope with the pace of modern life. If you've got a dozen horses or more to exercise every day an exercise machine doesn't solve all the problems of getting and keeping horses fit but it does at least help with the exercise. If you had, say, four or five horses to look after, you could well find it worth the investment; you know the horses are safe when they are on it, you know exactly how far they are doing, and you can time them exactly. Most of our horses walk 6 to 13 km (4 to 8 mi) a day on the exerciser.

Otherwise, just take your horse out for a good hour's walking a day to begin with. Keep off the roads as much as possible; not only are they dangerous, but the hard surface wears out the horse's shoes more quickly and can be very jarring on a horse's legs.

The exercise machine I made in 1972 to facilitate exercising horses in our busy yard. Four horses can be exercised at a time on this machine (Harvey Smith has a similar machine which takes twelve horses at a time!) The board you can see to the left of the picture moves round on a long arm and ensures that the horse moves forward at an even pace.

A horse on the exercise machine – just letting the camera know what it thinks of having its picture taken! The machine can be operated at different speeds, so that we can give horses a canter round if this is required. As you can see, they are exercised completely freely on this machine.

Another type of exercise machine that operates on a treadmill system, like a running machine used by an athlete. Here a groom stays with the horse to control the speed and make sure it does not panic.

FITNESS PROGRAMMES

Give a horse one hour of steady walking each day for ten days, then increase it to one and a half hours, including perhaps half an hour's trotting in three or four bursts during this time. From here, exercise programmes will vary according to what you want the horse to do.

A hunter, for example, really only needs about one and a half hour's exercise a day to get and keep it fit. Over the first few weeks, this will be walking, then walking and trotting, to get its legs hard. As the hunting season approaches the horse should also have a good stretch of fast cantering included in the routine. This is known as a "pipe opener", and helps to ensure that its wind and breathing are sound and up to coping with the work required of it. Pam aims to include a couple of sessions of fast canter with her horse for about 5 to 6.5 km (3 to 4 mi) each week.

A show-jumping horse will need more intensive exercise than a hunter. Once they are reasonably fit, say after two months of steady walking and trotting, our top show-jumpers will walk 3 km (2 mi) on the exerciser each morning, with twenty minutes of concentrated flat work with a rider (or on the lunge – see pages 140-1), including work over the grid (see page 142). This is the athletic part of the fitness programme, exercising mind and body together to keep the horses in tune and alert. After that they have another fifteen to thirty minutes of ordinary exercise with a rider, just going easily round the farm. Then they are brought back, washed down with a body wash if it is a warm day, and put back on the exerciser for another 3 km (2 mi) of walking to cool off. Thus their daily quota is one and a half to two hours of varied work.

If we are having any problems with a show-jumper, such as those outlined in Chapter Seven, we would work on those problems within the exercise routine. Most top-class show-jumpers get very little serious jumping at home. The grid exercise keeps them athletic, and we may jump them on the lunge every now and then for a change, but jumping over big show-jumps in the school is not part of the programme for most experienced show-jumpers. They know their job and the main thing is to keep them fresh between shows. A novice horse, however, will benefit from some regular practice jumping at home.

Event horses need a great deal of work in their daily programme; most would have at least two and a half hours a day. This would include probably one hour a day on dressage, as well as a lot of steady exercise to make them hard and sound in leg and wind. Jumping would be included in the exercise programme two or three times a week, but again it would be gymnastic-type exercises rather than jumping big jumps. Dressage horses need to be very muscled as well as fit. Besides steady exercise for one to one and a half hours a day, they would have a good hour's dressage work. Unlike show-jumpers, these horses need to be kept at their work all the time.

All aspects of horse management are prone to fads that come and go, and fitness programmes are no exception. At one time, "interval" training was popular, particularly with event riders. The idea of this was to push a horse very hard for a short time, then rest it until its pulse rate was back to normal, before pushing it again, thus increasing its stamina all the time. I'm not necessarily criticizing other methods, but I feel that the essence of getting a horse fit is a good diet that suits the horse combined with hard, steady and varied work. Whatever you call your fitness programme, and despite variations in the details of how you implement it, this is what it ultimately comes down to.

Every fitness routine should begin with a good hour's walk a day, preferably along firm tracks. A horse should be asked to walk out well during this, not be allowed to slop along on a loose rein, so that it really works its muscles.

Grid exercises are included in the fitness routine of all our jumpers. Two days before these pictures were taken, this horse had won the Scottish Young Riders Championship competition. Grid exercises keep a horse supple and athletic, and help to break up the routine. In Europe, particularly in Germany, dressage riders include grid work in the weekly exercise and training routine of their horses. It can be a help in teaching a horse to shorten and lengthen its stride.

3

2

1

A good fast canter included in the routine at least twice a week helps to keep a horse's lungs and breathing in good condition.

Jumping natural obstacles during a good ride in the countryside is far better than giving a horse twenty minutes' exhausting slog around a set of jumps in a school. It keeps it alert and interested as well as exercising the mind and body. The only time our show-jumpers get jumped around a set of jumps at home is if we are having specific problems with one of them.

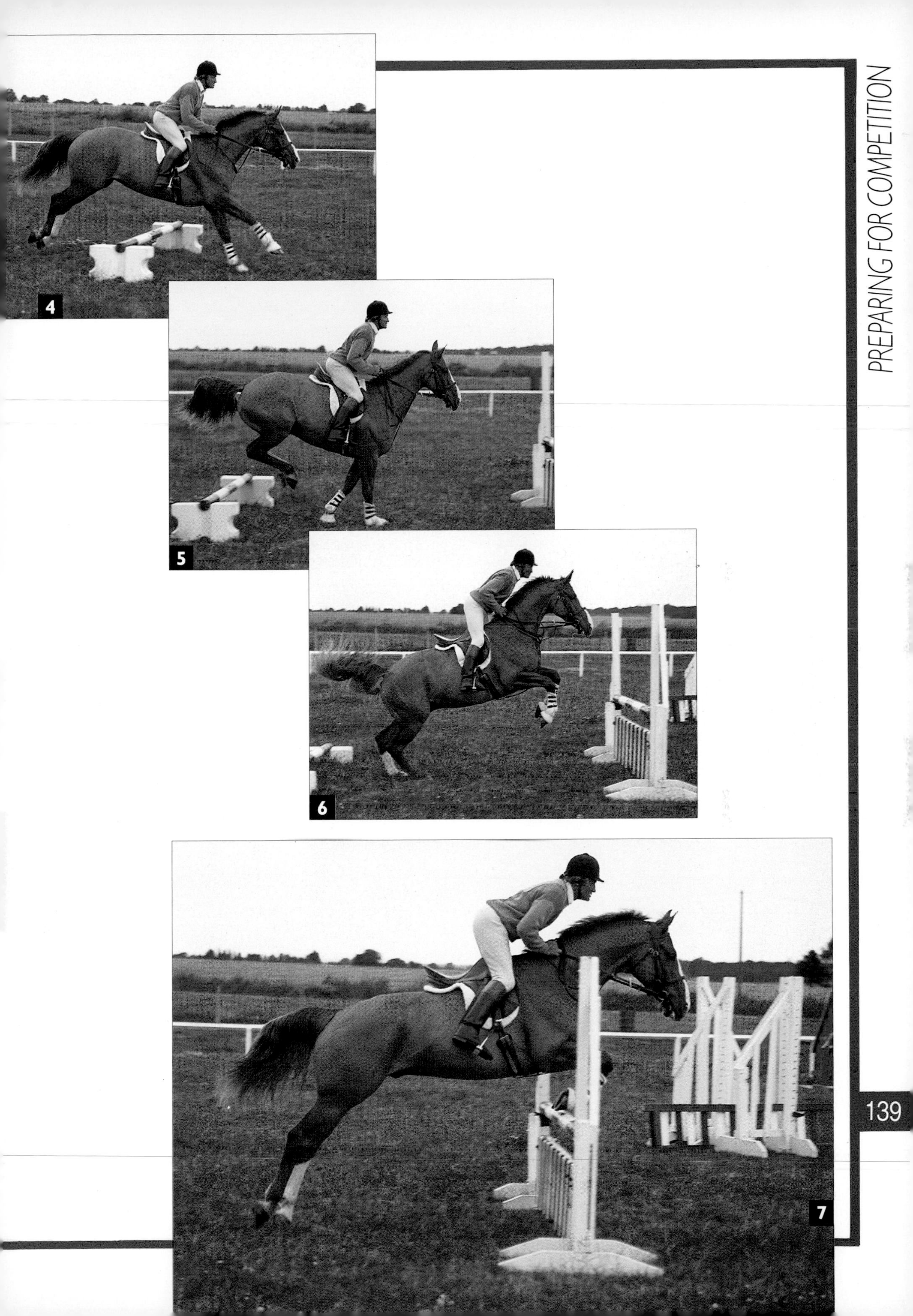
4
5
6
7

LUNGEING AND LONG-REINING

Lungeing and long-reining are both excellent ways of giving a horse general exercise, getting it fit and keeping it that way. Pam is a great believer in these forms of exercise. When she was leading point-to-point jockey in the 1970s, her racehorses were lunged regularly. Pam's father always maintained that half an hour's exercise on the lunge was as good as one hour's riding exercise. The fact that the horse is kept moving all the time means that you can really work it hard.

These forms of exercise are good for other reasons too. With a highly strung, somewhat scatty horse, you will often get on better if you lunge it rather than ride it. It is all too easy when you are riding to find yourself having a battle with each other and then you end up by falling out. It is much easier to relax a horse when it is on the other end of a lunge or long rein; the regular rhythm of the work helps to calm it down, until that calmness becomes the norm.

Working a horse on the lunge also helps it to think for itself. Show-jumpers, in particular, will often rely too much on their riders; if the two of you are not getting it right together it can help to revert to the lunge for a while. Recently, when I was having problems with a horse that just would not take off in the right place – stand off properly – when it took off at a jump (it would always pop in a short stride at the last minute before take-off), Pam took over and lunged it several times over jumps, until it began thinking for itself, learning to be independent and to jump freely. Inexperienced riders particularly tend to do too much thinking for their horses, especially when jumping. To include lungeing over jumps in the exercise routine can be a great help. You can see from the ground that the horse can think for itself perfectly well if only you will let it.

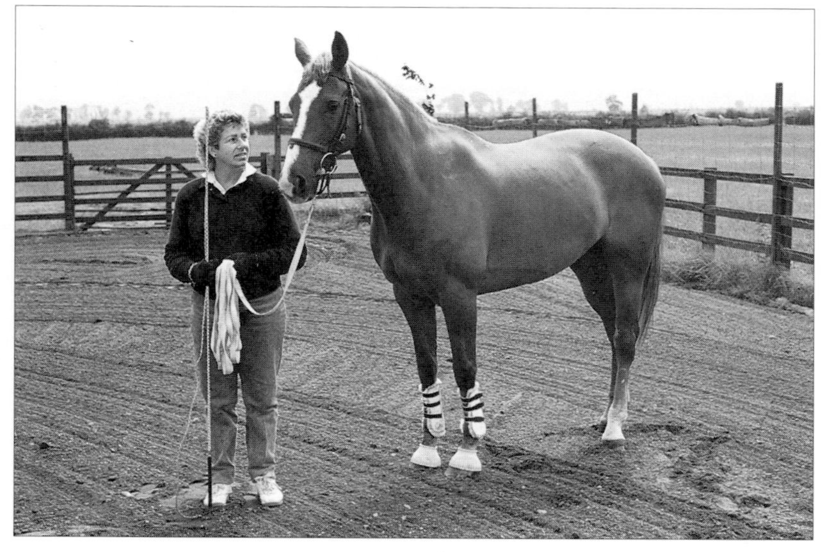

In these pictures, Pam is working her horse Durrow, a twelve-year-old thoroughbred and Grade A show-jumper. Lungeing is particularly good for him. You can perhaps see the scar he has on his near-hind; this was the result of a terrible accident we had some years ago when our lorry was in a head-on collision with a car. Lungeing helps him to stay supple and keeps the muscles in this leg working.

LUNGEING FOR FITNESS

For lungeing without a rider, you can attach the lunge rein to one or other bit-ring. However, as the purpose of lungeing now is to make the horse work correctly and build up its muscles, it is important to have some device to keep its head in the proper position. This can be done in various ways, for example with side reins – short reins attached to the bit at one end and the saddle or training roller at the other – or with an *Abbot Davis*.

Begin by lungeing the horse in a confined space until you feel confident. The ideal is an area about 15 m (17 yd) square; if necessary, make an enclosed area using the boundary fences at the corner of a manège or field as two sides with some jump wings and poles positioned to give the other two sides.

If the horse is very excitable and fresh at first, simply get it to canter round you for ten to fifteen minutes until it has calmed down. Then you can start to work it. Begin by asking it to walk in a circle around you, using your voice and a slight flick of the lunge whip if necessary. Lungeing is, as it happens, a great way of teaching a horse to respond to your voice and this is extremely important. If you listen to some of the top riders as they go round a show-jumping ring you will hear them talking to their horses all the time. When Harvey Smith won the Derby at Hickstead he was talking to his horse, Mattie Brown, who was still new to these types of courses, the whole way round. There is nothing like talking to a horse and feeling it respond – as long as you say the right things! I missed out on winning a car in a competition in Austria a few years ago when, after coming too fast into a gate after a triple bar, I said "Whoa" instead of "Steady" and the horse I was riding, Boysie, responded so well that he pulled up!

When you are confident that the horse is walking out well around you on the lunge, ask it to trot. Begin by saying "Trot on" and clicking your tongue. Flick with the whip, if necessary, but you'll find it soon won't be. (I have broken countless lunge whips by putting them down beside me and treading on them because I never need to use them.) Make sure the horse is really using its spine and shoulders, then ask it to canter. This it should do quite slowly; don't get it to go faster or it will just keep on increasing the speed. A slow canter is all that should ever be done on the lunge.

Work for about fifteen minutes in both directions – this is quite long enough to lunge a horse. The aim is always to try to get it to relax its neck and then use the whole of its body from ears to tail, moving in perfect coordination. Its head carriage affects the way a horse uses the rest of its body (which is why it is important to have some device to set the carriage), and so if its head is held correctly it will work the rest of its body correctly too. Remember that all the time you are looking for and aiming to establish a rhythm in movement at all paces. Keep the horse alert and interested, but calm.

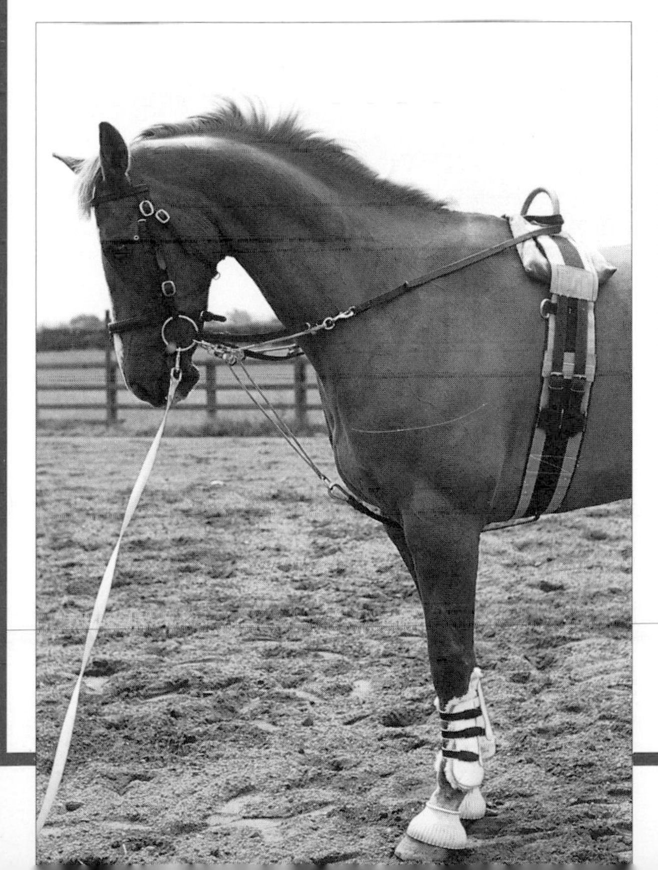

Here Durrow is ready for some serious work on the lunge. Because Pam now wants him to work all his muscles properly, she has fitted the Abbot Davis to the bridle. This hooks on to the bit-rings, is attached to the reins and passes down between the horse's front legs to the surcingle. It helps to keep the head in the correct position, and it is the head position that ensures a horse is working all its muscles correctly. Note that the reins, which have to be attached to the bridle here to support the Abbot Davis, are looped around the leather arch of the roller so that they do not trail downwards. A pad under the roller stops the roller rubbing the back.

JUMPING ON THE LUNGE

You can do grid exercises (see Chapter Four) and jump a horse on the lunge. The grid exercises help to make it athletic, while jumping on the lunge is good because the horse is free to manipulate its body over a jump without some tiresome person bumping around on its back.

Lungeing a young horse over a jump is a good way of determining how willing a jumper it is. If it moves forward freely and eagerly, you know it is enjoying it and is keen, which is vitally important in a potential show-jumper. A few years ago, I bought three geldings that were all out of the same mare, by the same stallion; they were five, six and seven years old but had not been broken. So I broke them in. Two did everything I wanted on the lunge and long reins, including jumping well and happily, and were sold to American riders. The third was simply not responsive in the same way and was eventually sold locally as a hunter.

When jumping on the lunge, I think you should dispense with any equipment to set the head carriage. Other people will disagree with me, but my feeling is that, for jumping, a horse's head should be free. Attach the lunge rein to the bit as before, or to a small leather strap clipped at either end on to the bit-rings.

Begin by trotting the horse down the grid, which you have spaced to correspond with its stride. It is easier if you build the grid on an arc of a circle so that you can remain virtually still and the horse can continue on around the circle. Then space the grid out a bit and ask the horse to canter round. You can raise the final part, if you like, to make the horse stretch more.

When you are jumping a horse on the lunge, the aim is to get it to *bascule* correctly, that is, to stand off and manipulate its body in a perfect arc, over the jumps. This you can do with the aid of poles placed on the ground to give guide lines for take-off. You must have low jump wings so that the rein doesn't get caught on them, or you can rest a pole down the wing from top to bottom so that the lunge line slips down it.

You can lunge over any type of jump; it is an excellent way to get a tricky horse to jump water, for example, avoiding that battle of wills that can take place between horse and rider at water jumps. A horse is often more willing to put its trust in you when it is being encouraged from the ground.

And do watch the horse carefully when you are lungeing it over jumps; you will be able to see just where it takes off naturally to jump a fence which will help you when you are riding it.

4

5

Now the final part of the grid has been raised to make a sizeable jump. Because Durrow is in perfect balance as a result of negotiating the rest of the grid, he is able to take the fence perfectly, springing off his hocks and stretching himself forward. You can see from his eye that he is looking at the fence and concentrating on what he is being asked to do. By lungeing a horse over fences like this you have an opportunity to study its movement during jumping, which should help when you are riding it.

Pam has built a grid on the circle to include in her lungeing programme. She has got Durrow cantering through it; in the first picture, you can see he has come in a little too fast and is having to brake on landing, really using his hocks. In the second picture, he has checked himself and dropped his speed right down, so that he completes the grid in perfect balance. This is a good illustration of how a horse has to think for itself when doing these exercises on the lunge. For a show-jumper in particular it is invaluable training; if, for example, in a jump-off, an over-enthusiastic rider goes too quickly into a combination, a horse that has had this kind of training will automatically slow itself down in time for the second part of the jump.

A beautiful jump over our water jump. The horse is completely relaxed and clearly enjoying what it is doing. Pam is holding the lunge rein up high so that there is no danger of it getting caught on the sides of the fence. The sloping pole at the front of the fence helps to ensure that the rein slides up the wing. If a horse shows reluctance at jumping water, training it to do so on the lunge can often help and it saves unpleasant battles between horse and rider!

LONG-REINING

With long-reining, instead of having one rein line as in lungeing, you have two, each attached to a bit-ring and threaded either through the rings of a training roller on either side or through the stirrup irons, which should be tied with a strap under the horse's belly to prevent them from flapping around. In long-reining you can either drive the horse forward, walking directly behind it, or you can get it to move in a circle around you as in lungeing.

I always include long periods of long-reining when I am breaking in a horse. It teaches it to walk into the bridle, moving forward freely and easily, using all of its body. Now the tendency, I think, is to break in horses too quickly; we always used to long-rein a horse for a month during breaking, taking it out on the roads every day for an hour or so, though I wouldn't do this any more as it's too dangerous. But we still long-rein around the fields of the farm. Long-reining is also a very important part of horse management, getting the horse used to being handled and to obeying commands from the voice.

I think it is a good idea to set the head carriage again with

For long-reining we use plough lines instead of lunge reins. These lines, still available from some saddlers, are the ones used years ago by people working horses on the land. They are thicker at one end – the end you should hold – tapering down to about 1 cm (½ in) at the other end. The narrower ends are tied on to the bit with a conventional knot and the lines are then led through the stirrup irons, which are held roughly in place by a leather strap passing under the horse's belly.

The correct position for your hands during long-reining. If your hands are held too high you will be interfering with the horse's mouth and will not have the same precision or sensitivity of control.

Pam demonstrates an incorrect position for long-reining. Her hands are far too high and she is leaning back pulling against the pony. As a result both Pam and the pony have tensed up; you can see how it has its mouth open and is "locking" its jaw. Its ears demonstrate that it is not happy and relaxed.

Another demonstration of how not to begin long-reining. Pam is now far too relaxed and has let the lunge lines drop right down on the ground. If the pony moved suddenly it could easily get tangled up in the lines.

an Abbot Davis or side reins, aside from the long reins, although this is not essential. You should walk 2.4 to 3 m (8 to 10 ft) behind the horse, holding your hands low. The reins should be fairly relaxed, although not dropping on the ground or you may find you are hanging on to the mouth and consequently restricting forward movement.

You can see from where you are behind the horse whether or not it is really using its spine. When you ask it to turn to left or right, it should be curving through the whole length of its body, not just turning its head.

Make the horse walk forward evenly and rhythmically; get it to bend round corners and move in circles. Because you are behind the horse and it can't see you, it has to work and think for itself. As with lungeing, you will find out which horses are really willing to learn. They have got to want to please you and be prepared to go forward on their own. From your position some 3 m (10 ft) behind, it is actually very hard to make a horse do anything it doesn't want to!

A very good exercise on the long rein. We have positioned a line of barrels by the side of the school and Pam is walking the pony through them. She can see from her position whether or not it is bending correctly through the length of its body. The exercise calls for far greater obedience than it would if the pony were being ridden; it must be more willing and more prepared to think for itself.

Another useful long-reining exercise: the pony is being asked to walk through a very narrow space. Begin this exercise with the barrels further apart, and gradually bring them closer together so that finally the pony or horse is walking through a gap that is only just wide enough for it to pass through.

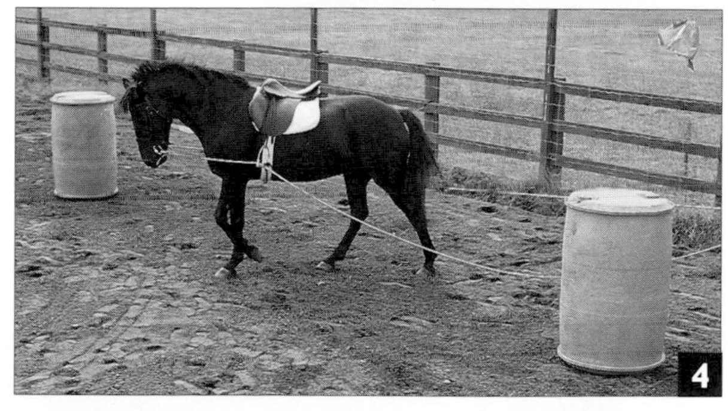

An excellent exercise for horses that are inclined to cut their corners. A grid of poles is placed in a fan-shape around the corner of the school and the pony is long-reined over them. You can see in the first and second pictures how it has dropped its head to look at them and is really working its body. It is so intent on the exercise that it negotiates the corner perfectly. The exercise is also having the effect of making the pony think for itself again. You can see by the knee action in the first picture that it has come into the grid a little too fast, and is having to shorten its stride. Balanced again, it stretches forward well over the remainder of the poles.

Here Pam is making the pony rein-back on the long reins. You can see it is about to take a backward step with its near-fore and off-hind together, and that it is really working the muscles of its back. When it has taken a few steps back, Pam will ask it to walk forward. A rein-back – ridden or performed on the long reins – should always be followed immediately by forward movement.

CONTINUING FITNESS

The secret of *keeping* a horse fit, is to give it a daily routine of general exercise but to vary it slightly all the time. Exercise it in different surroundings, sometimes lungeing it in the school, other times riding it out in the countryside. Vary the order in which you do things so that it doesn't know what to expect. It is essential to keep your horse interested, otherwise it will become bored and stale, at which point its performance will deteriorate too.

Always include a lot of walking and some trotting in the daily exercise as this, more than anything else, gets a horse's legs hard and thus less prone to strains or concussion injuries. Ted Edgar had a horse, Jacarpo, that was old when he got it; he then passed it on to the late Phil Oliver, and the horse, already successful, became one of the greatest money-winners in the country. Its exercise routine between shows consisted of a couple of hours a day walking round the farm. This was all the exercise it needed to keep it fit and it knew its job so well that it needed no jumping in between shows. Most horses will need more exercise, and more variety, than this, but don't underestimate the value of walking.

Even if your chosen field of sport is show-jumping, never neglect your flat work. Most European and American show-jumpers could easily do an elementary dressage test; not so the British. It seems as if they think that to compete in show-jumping they must be doing it all the time. Although it is probably during flat work that 99 per cent of all problems are cured, this is often the percentage of time some people think they should be jumping their horses. At international shows, while the British riders are working their way sleepily through breakfast, the American riders have already been out for an hour or more, working their horses on the flat!

The only essential jumping exercise to include in the routine is the grid exercise, and you really can't begin this too early in a horse's career. I had a horse not so long ago with a huge jump in it; it could jump 2 m (7 ft) high, but it had had no real ground work in its training and couldn't go round a show-jumping course really well because it couldn't cope with distances. In the end I gave it away as a hunter.

So, lungeing, long-reining, grid exercises either ridden or on the lunge, plenty of walking and trotting and a good "pipe opener" once or twice a week. This is the way to keep a horse fit and mentally prepared for competition.

This is a very dangerous situation; if a horse plays about on the road, all sorts of terrible accidents could ensue. If, as your fitness programme progresses, you feel your horse is a little bit too excitable and above itself when you plan to ride it out, give it ten minutes or so of active trotting on the lunge before taking it out of the yard. It is also a good idea to drop the protein level in its food a little; this may be contributing to its high spirits.

BOXING AND UNBOXING

Once your horse is fit, you can start to plan your competitive career in earnest. Stick to small classes of not too high a standard at first. Be a big fish in a little pond, not a minnow in the ocean. In any case, you may find yourself competing against the big names in small competitions; top riders are always bringing on new horses and they will jump them in novice and local competitions to begin with.

It is probable that you will go to a show with a horsebox or trailer, so make sure your horse is entirely happy about travelling. Take it for a few journeys before entering it for a show, perhaps somewhere where you can unload and have a ride. You certainly want to ensure that it is thoroughly used to this and to sort out any problems now; there's nothing worse than arriving at a show with a horse all sweated-up and anxious from its journey.

For travelling, a horse's legs should be protected with bandages or leg guards. If you are using bandages put foam, cotton wool or gamgee underneath them, extending this right up above the hock. We don't bother with knee or hock boots; they can often upset a horse not used to having them flapping around on its legs, and most boxes are fairly well padded so a horse is unlikely to hurt itself. It should wear a tail bandage to stop it rubbing its tail, and then whatever rugs you feel are necessary. For the first few trips, the fewer rugs you put on the horse the better, as there is less to bother it. Make sure any you do use are done up quite tightly, so that there is no danger of them slipping during travelling and frightening the horse.

The boxing and unboxing procedures for a horsebox and trailer are shown in the pictures. If a horse is difficult to load, tie long lunge reins to the box or trailer on either side of the ramp, quite high up, and get two people to hold them straight out from the ramp. Encourage the horse up to the ramp with a bucket of feed, but don't hurry it, let it take its time. Lead it into the trailer, and as it goes in the two people holding the lines should exchange sides of the ramp so that the reins cross over behind the horse, keeping it in place. What usually happens is that a horse will load into a box or trailer but then back out immediately; the aim is to restrict it by the lunge lines, so they should be kept tight until the strap is done up. Put up the ramp as gently as possible.

Spend time leading the horse in and out of the box or trailer, always keeping calm and relaxed. Try loading it at feeding time and giving it its feed so that the box becomes a place with pleasant associations. I often put a new horse into the box and let it stand there for several hours so that it quickly learns that the box is not something to fear.

To unload a difficult horse, the assistants should stand on either side of the ramp, holding the long reins out taut, so that the horse can't slip off the ramp and frighten itself still further.

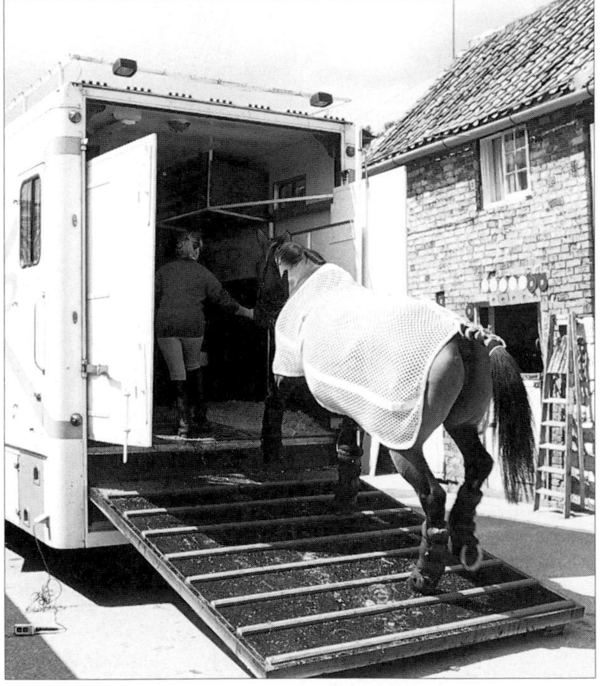

Loading the horse into the box. It is led straight up the ramp with no fuss. Note how its owner is leading it on a very short rope so that there is less scope for its stepping backwards.

Unboxing is undertaken with the same lack of fuss. The horse is led down the ramp, again on quite a short length of rope. Here its owner, Rachel, is holding the rope a little higher than usual; the horse can see what it is doing, but Rachel is ready to lift its head should it trip.

Bandaging the legs to protect the horse during travelling. First wrap a strip of gamgee, cotton wool or foam round the leg, and then wind a warm stockinette bandage over this starting well below the knee and going down over the pastern joint. Wind the bandage back up the leg to just below the knee and then down again to finish in the middle. Tie or fasten the tapes or velcro on the outside so that the horse cannot rub them free with the other leg.

1

2

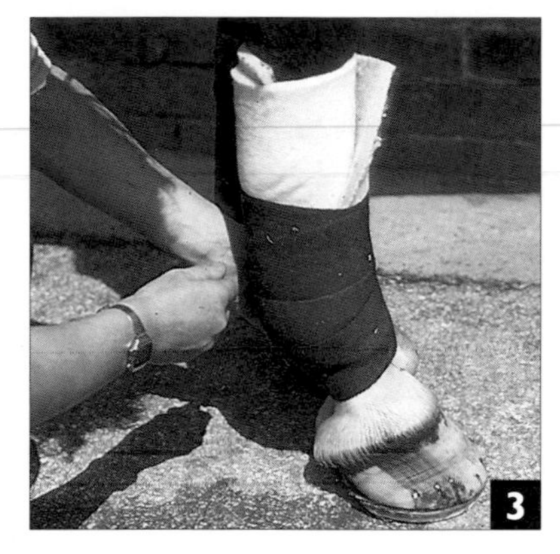
3

4

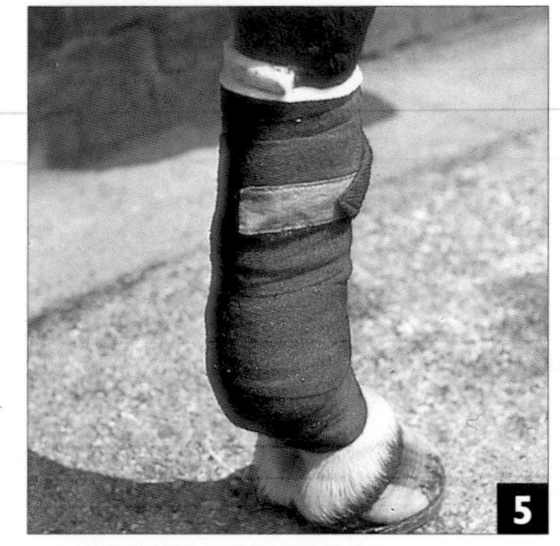
5

When the hind legs are bandaged the gamgee, foam etc. should come up to and preferably extend over the hock to protect it from any knocks or bangs. The bandage itself stops short of the hock.

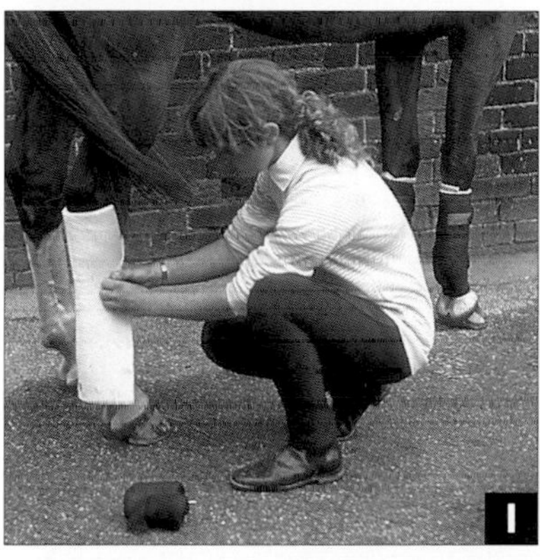
1

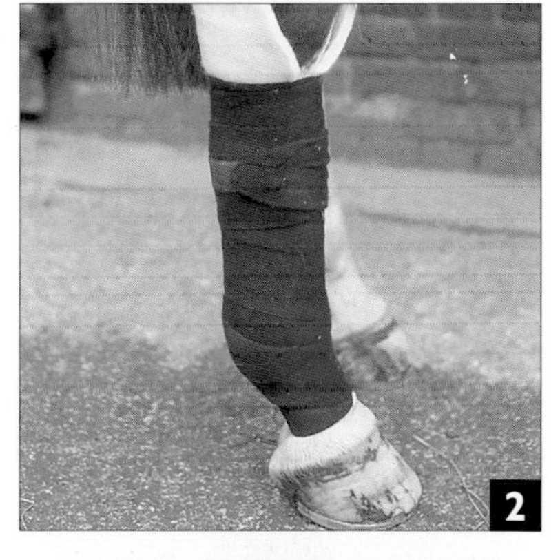
2

This horse has been got ready for travelling. It is wearing an anti-sweat sheet held in place by an elastic surcingle. This type of rug is used for travelling and for a horse when it is still hot after exercise. The mesh allows it to cool and dry off without getting cold, which an ordinary rug does not. The horse's legs are protected by specially designed padded travelling guards rather than bandages, and it is also wearing knee caps. Its tail is protected by a tail guard; it could also have been bandaged (see page 153).

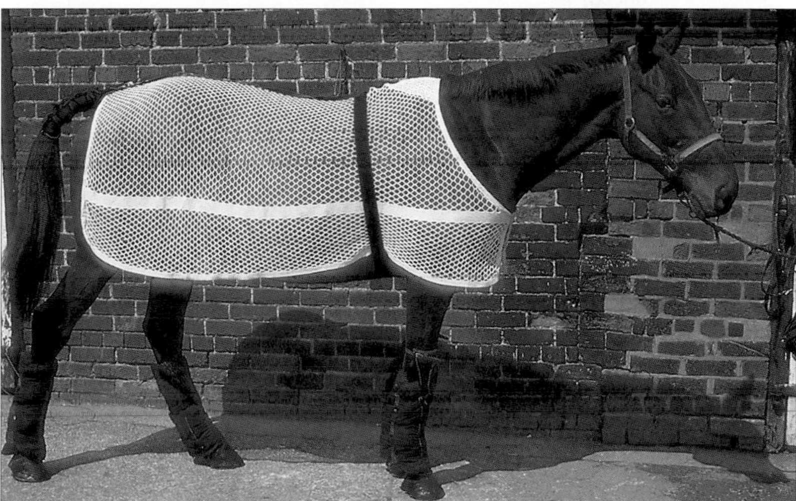

TRAILER OR HORSEBOX?

Whether you choose a trailer or horsebox will depend on a number of factors – how many horses you will be taking around with you, whether you want a place where you can live at shows, and how much money you can afford to spend.

If you are choosing a trailer, don't buy a single one unless you only have a tiny pony to move around. Single trailers are just too cramped for a horse. There should be a 75 cm (2 ft 6 in) space between the floor and the bottom of any partition, or if there is not an actual space this part should be made of flexible rubber, so that the horses can spread their feet and balance during travelling. You know what it is like on a crowded train or bus; if you have to stand with your feet tight together, it is very hard to balance. It's just the same for a horse, and if it is having trouble balancing, it will panic.

Whoever is driving the trailer or box should always remember that they are transporting horses, who are just as likely to feel the effect of bad driving as people are. Horses become bad travellers because of the way they are thrown about in a trailer or horsebox, for instance when the driver is going too fast then has to brake hard. I travelled in the back of a trailer recently with a horse whose owner had complained it didn't like travelling. I can only say I could well understand why! The box should be driven at a steady speed, so that the minimum of braking is necessary (except in unavoidable emergencies), and particular care should be taken to drive round corners smoothly.

If we are travelling horses over long distances – for example, I have driven horses to Vienna and Madrid without stopping *en route* for the night – we never go for more than eight hours without stopping to give them a drink. We stop and unload the horses, giving them fifteen or twenty minutes to walk around and stretch their legs and have a nibble of grass. As long as they are not asked to travel for a longer spell than this, they will be fine; a horse can sleep standing on its feet.

Here we have boxed a tricky horse with a pony that is used to going in and out of the trailer, and we will leave them standing side-by-side for a while just to get the horse used to being in the trailer. If we were going to transport them anywhere we would have the partition in place between them; leaving it out while they are standing here together enables the nervous horse to gain confidence from the proximity of its friend.

Unloading quietly through the front ramp of the trailer. Not all trailers have a front unloading ramp like this, but it is quite an advantage. Many horses prefer to come forwards out of the trailer rather than back down the ramp.

SHOWS AND STABLING

Plan which shows you intend to enter so that you have a sensible programme with plenty of time for recovery and for tackling at home any problems you encounter there. Most small shows take entries on the day, but check with the show secretary about this and enter in advance if necessary.

If you are going to compete far and wide, you will need to get your horse used to different stables and venues as it will need to stay in these overnight. If you take it to a strange place when it's always been used to its own secure loose box, your horse will walk around the strange stable all night wondering what is going on and be in no state to give of its best the next day.

If you've got more than one stable, particularly if one is round the corner or further up the yard, you can change your horse round from time to time. If you've only got one stable you could change with a friend nearby for the night every now and then so that your horse gets used to being in a different place.

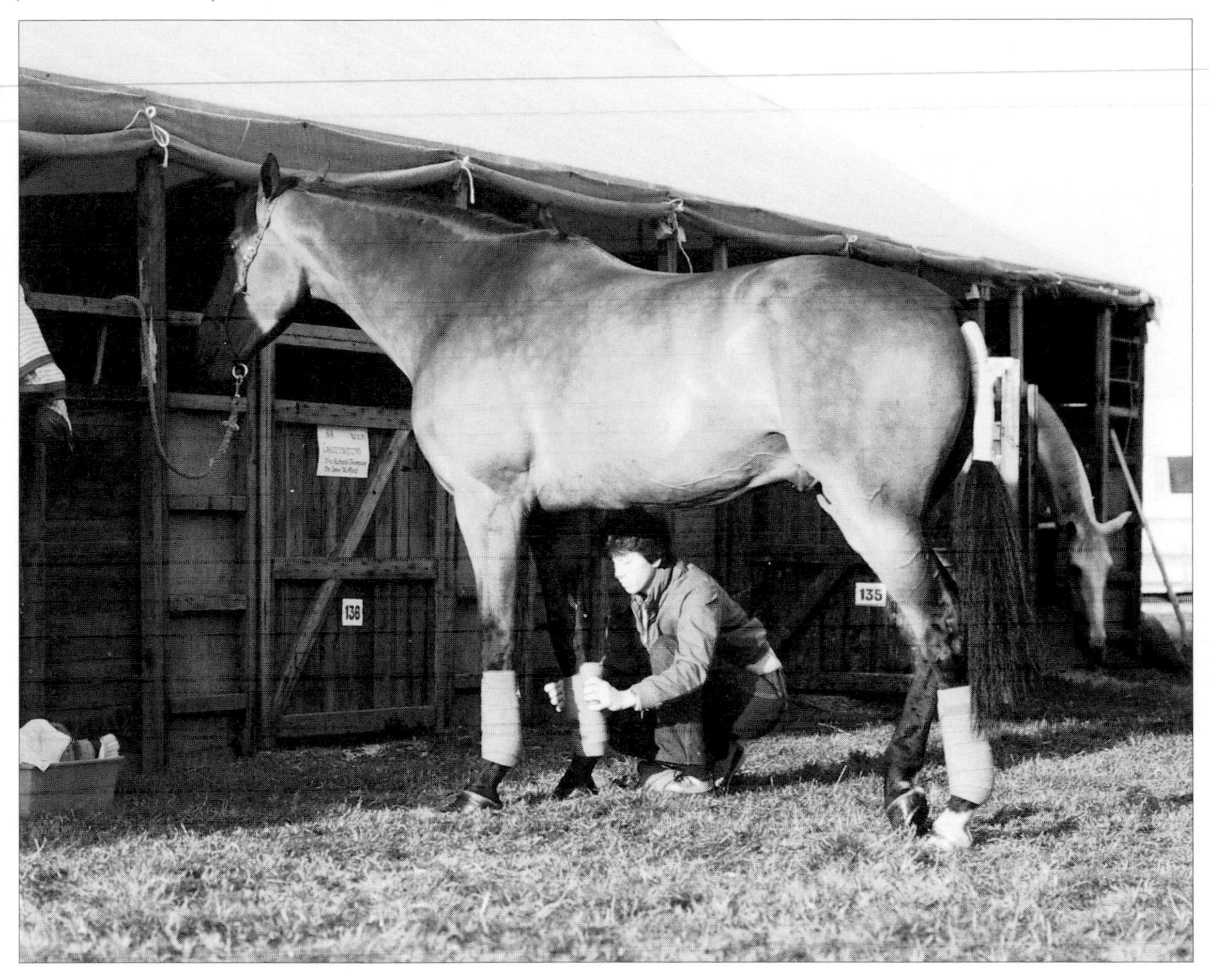

Typical portable stabling used at shows that go on over several days. Here a horse stands calmly as it is prepared to be put away for the night. It is essential to get horses used to staying in locations other than their own home stable so that they do not fret on occasions like this.

PRE-SHOW PREPARATION

Your normal stable and exercise routine should not change in any way in the run-up to a show. The horse is being fed and exercised to keep it in competition fitness so there is no need to vary that, and indeed keeping to your usual routine means that your horse will remain at its most settled. Just before a show I do give my horses a dose of bicarbonate of soda to clean them out and make them more comfortable for travelling.

The day before a show, you should exercise your horse as normal, perhaps going over a few fences if you feel it will make you more confident. But take care not to overface the horse; it would be a shame to upset it before a competition.

Both you and the horse should be immaculately turned out for the show, even if it is only a small local one. Looking and feeling smart will be reflected in your performance. If your classes are late in the morning or in the afternoon, you can do some preparation on the day, but it is more usual that you have to leave home at the crack of dawn, so it is best to get as far advanced as you can the day before.

Make sure your tack is clean and shiny (see page 74). If it is a warm day, you can give your horse a body wash with horse shampoo if you like, or simply wash any white legs or socks. Let them dry naturally and then bandage them to keep them clean. Shampoo the tail, and bandage it (see opposite) while it is still damp to make it as neat as possible. You can keep a tail clean by putting it in an old nylon stocking and then putting a tail bandage on top.

Make sure all your clothes are clean and assembled and make a list of everything you need to take the next day: saddle, bridle, spare stirrup leathers and other items of tack in case of breakages, grooming kit, basic first aid kit. Even Pam still makes a list like this. I've known people forget their tack – girths are a great favourite for getting left behind as they are usually separate from the saddle after cleaning; I've even known someone who turned up to a show without their horse!

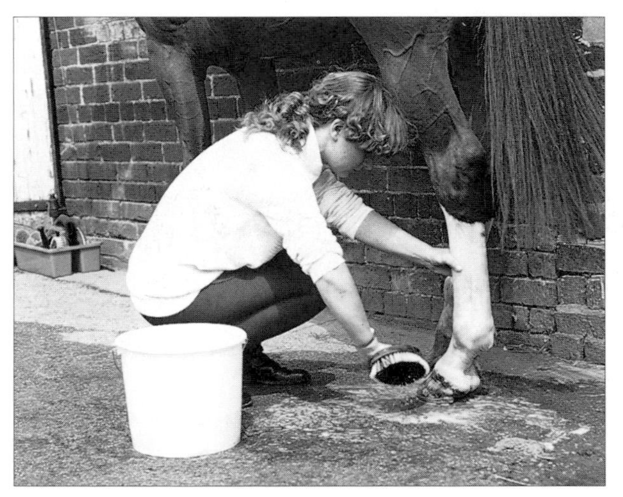

The horse should be immaculate for a show, whatever type of class it is entering. Any white markings should be washed; indeed you can wash the whole of the coat if you like. Use a special horse shampoo and make sure it is all rinsed out of the coat if the instructions state so.

Jennie Lauriston-Clarke, a member of the British dressage team at the 1988 Olympics, and her horse Dutch Courage, provide an excellent example of the perfect turn-out of rider and horse for competition dressage

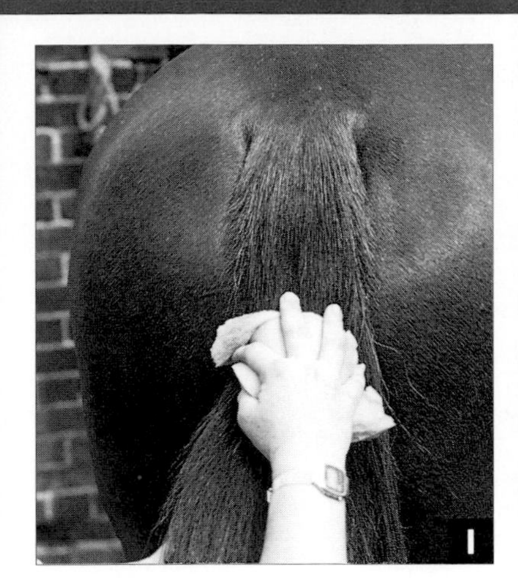

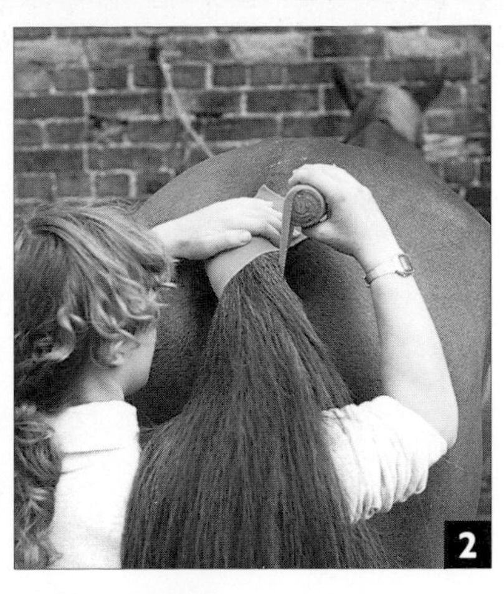

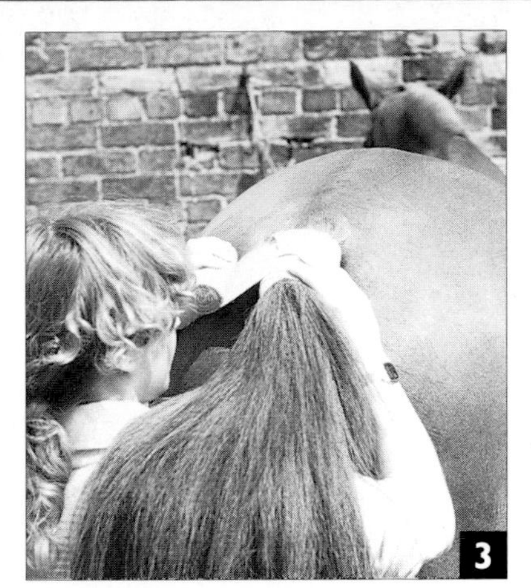

*Bandaging a tail to keep it smart during travelling – the bandage protects the tail if the horse should rub it on the side of the box or the back of the trailer. Begin by laying the hairs with a damp sponge (**1**), then take the elasticated bandage under the top of the tail (**2**). Putting the tail over your shoulder as in the picture (**3**) is a good way of keeping it in position, making the bandaging operation easier. Leave the end of the bandage sticking up at the top of the tail as in the picture then wind the bandage round the tail a couple of times. Fold over the end of the bandage and take another turn over the top. This helps to prevent the bandage slipping. Wind the bandage quite firmly down the tail, slightly diagonally in a herringbone action – this also helps to prevent it slipping – until you reach the end of the dock (**4**). Start winding back*

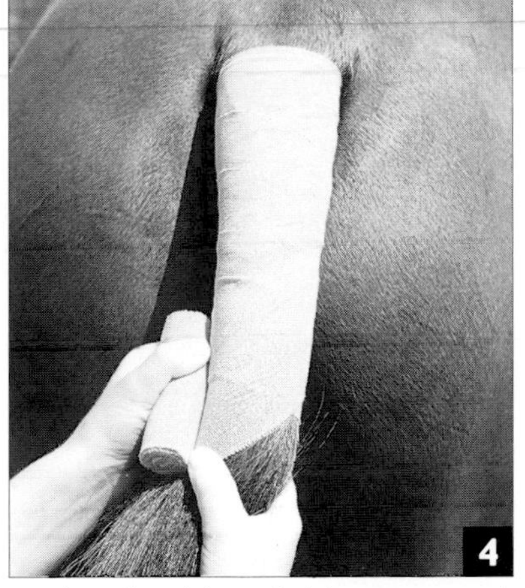

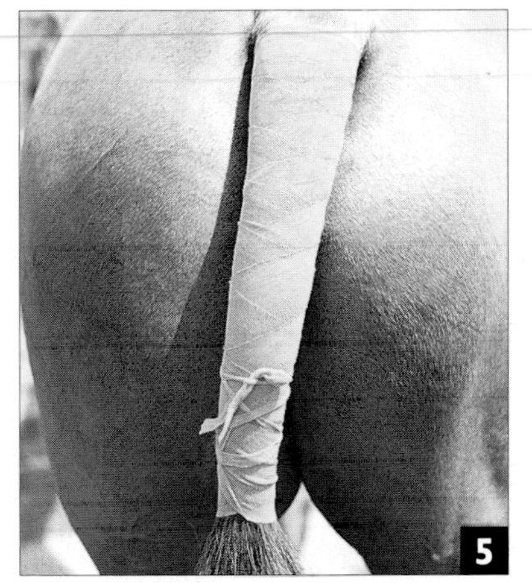

*up the tail and then wind the tapes round the tail in a criss-cross shape before tying with a bow on the outside of the tail (**5**). If you simply wind them tightly round the tail and tie them, you could impede the blood circulation; if this is severe enough the bottom of the dock will quite literally rot off, leaving a shorter dock than there should be. When you have finished bandaging, gently bend the dock back into shape.*

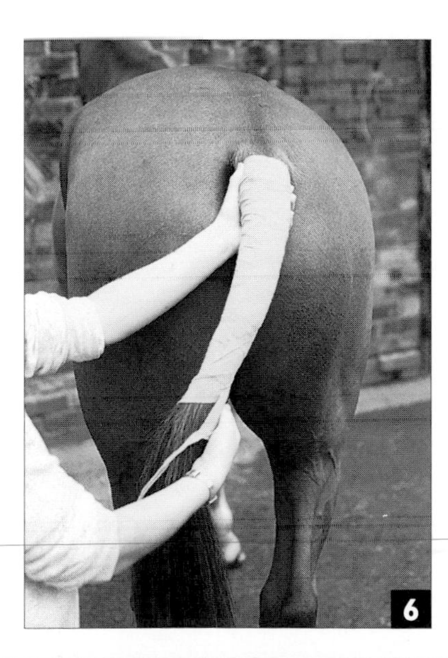

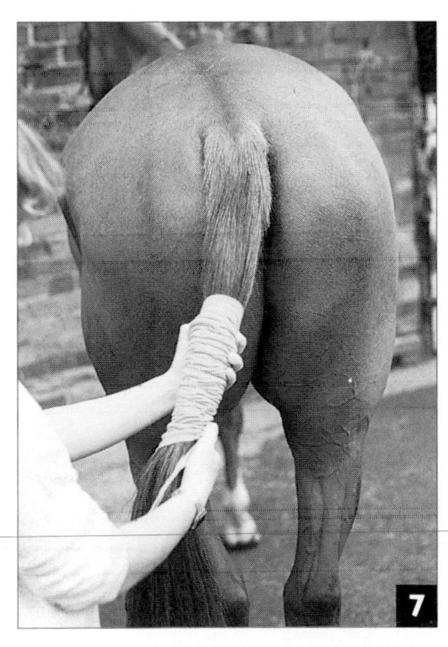

To remove the bandage, untie the tapes and slide the bandage down the tail.

SHOW DAY

Give yourself plenty of time to get ready and leave for the show so that you arrive well before your class is due to begin. If you usually feed your horse at 7.30 am, but need to leave at about 8.00 for the show, get up and feed the horse an hour earlier so it has time to digest the feed before travelling. Never give it anything to eat or drink less than two hours before the competition. Leave it to eat its feed in peace; don't be hovering round it; do everything calmly and slowly so that your horse doesn't feel fussed and bothered.

You will have given your horse a good grooming the day before but give it another one this morning so that it looks fresh and shiny. Remember to take all your grooming kit to the show, including a hoof pick and hoof oil. After grooming put a clean summer sheet on the horse to keep the dust off its coat.Put any travelling rugs on top of this; they are bound to contain some dust from the horse's coat from previous wearings.

If you are going to plait the mane, do so now (see opposite). For show horses this is essential and should be done very carefully and neatly with a needle and thread the same colour as the mane. Show-jumpers do not need to be plaited but it does make them look smart. Most people plait showjumpers using rubber bands which is a quicker method. It is not something you can do the night before because the horse will be bound to rub the plaits out during the night.

Before loading the horse into the box put on whatever you like it to wear in the way of protective leg gear and a tail bandage.

Check everything off on your list as you stow it in the box, trailer or car. Take a bucket so that you can give the horse a drink at the end of the day, and a hay net for the journey home. After giving my horses an early morning feed on a show day, I give them nothing more to eat or drink until after the competition. Certainly they should not be allowed a drink for at least two hours before jumping, however hot the day; that is the quickest way to insure that their jumping won't be at its best.

A plaited mane and forelock are an essential part of the turn-out for a show pony or horse. Show-jumpers do not have to be plaited; it does make for a smarter appearance, however.

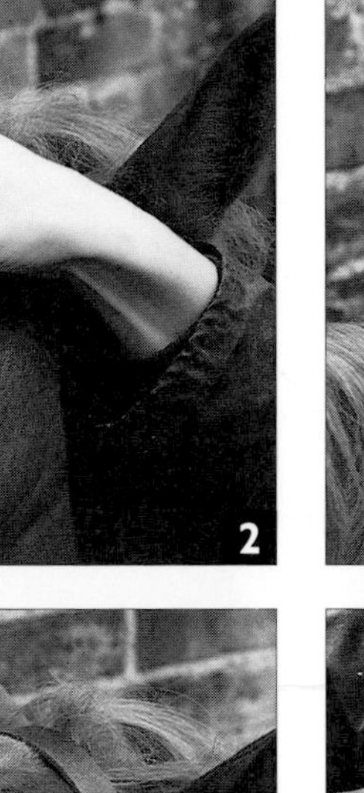

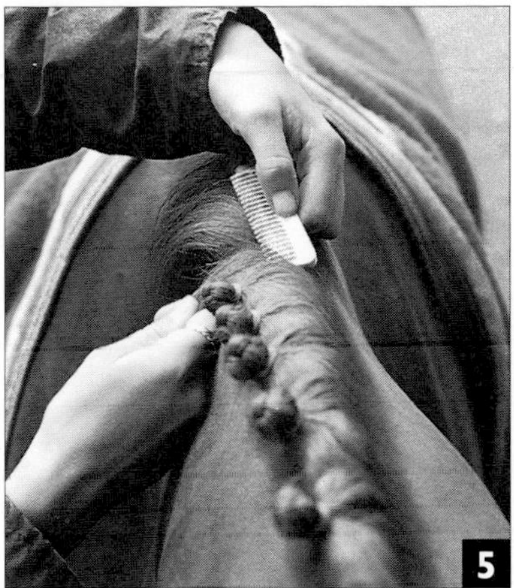

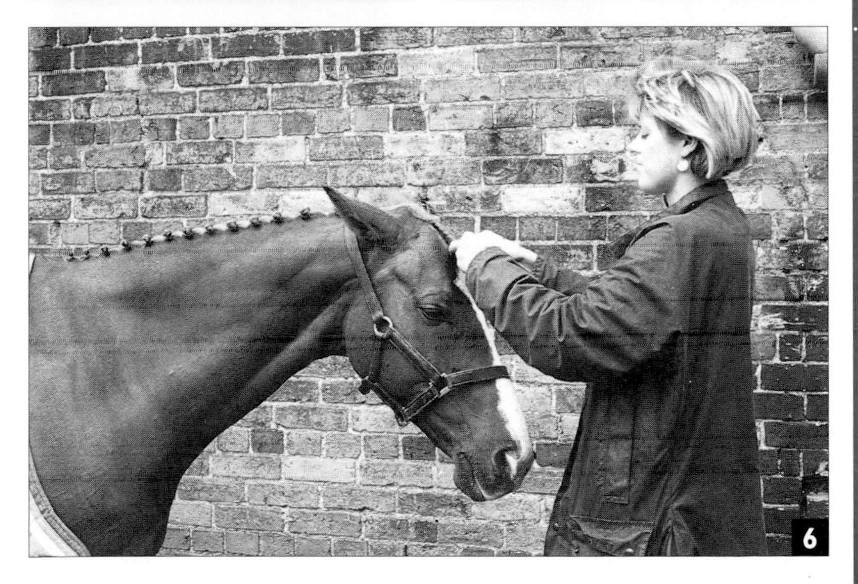

Here Kate, who has worked with us for many years, is demonstrating plaiting a horse's mane. She is standing on a crate as you can see; it is important to be up level with the mane so that you can see what you are doing and so that your arms don't get tired. How many plaits you put in the mane is to some extent a matter of choice; but the more plaits you have, the better the neck will look. I like to have no more than three fingers' width of mane per plait, which can mean thirty or more plaits. You can see Kate measures off the width of mane with a mane comb, and then plaits this section tightly right down to the bottom. She then winds an elastic band round the bottom to secure it, and bends the plait under twice before securing with another rubber band close to the crest of the mane to hold the plait in shape and position. Finally the forelock is plaited in the same way. Plaits can also be held in place using a needle and thread (matching the colour of the mane) and this is the way show horses will generally be plaited. It takes longer to do but gives a neater finish, which is important when the appearance of the horse counts in the competition.

AT THE SHOW

If your horse is a newcomer to shows aim to arrive early, well in advance of your classes, and ride it round quietly at a walk for half an hour or so to settle it and let it have a good look around.

When you arrive at a show you will usually be directed to a parking space by a steward. If not, choose a spot yourself – look for shade if the day is sunny. Check your horse straight away and, providing it won't try to get out, drop the ramp of the lorry or trailer to let the air in.

Next go to the secretary's tent, check your entries and the time of your first class and get your numbers. If the class is quite soon and it is a jumping event of some sort go and walk the course (see page 163). If the course is not yet ready for you to walk it, go back to your trailer or box, get yourself and the horse ready and ride it in for twenty minutes or so; then go and walk the course.

Before a competition, the very worst thing you can do, and yet it is something you often see riders doing, is to go into the collecting ring and sit around on your horse chatting to all your friends. The horse will be making friends, too, and when you take it into the ring and ask it to perform, all it will be thinking about is getting back to its new-found mates! You may see the top riders chatting to one another for a few minutes in the collecting ring, but both they and their horses are used to the competitive environment and atmosphere.

Lungeing is an excellent way to loosen up and settle a horse at a show before its turn to compete. Choose a bit of smooth, flat ground and make sure there is plenty of room. These two people are giving each other a wide berth!

A young event rider waiting to start the course. He is standing a little way from most of the other riders and is keeping his pony quite calm as a result. He should have ridden the pony in for 15 to 20 minutes before this time, so that it is on its toes and ready to go when the moment comes.

I must say that for the uninitiated, going into a collecting ring can be an awful experience, particularly if there are practice jumps in it. There will be people and poles flying in all directions. It is essential if you are entering a jumping competition to have half a dozen warm-up jumps outside the main ring, so you will have to go into the collecting ring for these. Just keep calm and out of people's way. Take a friend with you who can put up the jump if you knock it down. This is essential collecting ring etiquette; if you knock down a fence and leave it down, expect a volley of abuse from all the other riders. Whatever else you do be polite to those around you, however impolite they seem to be to you! It doesn't cost you anything, but it will gain you a good reputation. If you are unsure of what to do – then ask. It is much better than doing the wrong thing.

When your class or classes are over for the day, it is a good idea to be back on the road as soon as possible, taking your horse back to the environment it knows. Make sure your horse is quite cool before decking it out for travel again. Give it a drink before leaving and tie the hay net up for it in the box, well out of reach of its front feet. Once home it can have a good feed and perhaps an easy day the next day, but then it's back to routine as usual.

The procedures we have outlined in this chapter apply to all types of competition. In the next chapter we will look specifically at competitive show-jumping – how to walk the course, ride it and prepare for the jump-off. But whatever kind of equestrian competing you go in for, make sure you are thoroughly acquainted with the rules and the procedures of competition. It is a pity to be eliminated because of a silly infringement of the rules.

7 COMPETITION SHOW-JUMPING

Show-jumping is a sport that can be enjoyed at all levels, from small local shows and clear-round jumping competitions to international events. As in other competitive sports it is sensible to compete at the level where you are likely to have some success – winning a small competition is far more fun than entering, and perhaps making a mess of, a competition where you are really out of your depth. It is also a sport where watching the top riders, by going to shows if possible or watching them on the television if not, can be a very positive help. An inexperienced rider can learn a great deal by watching the techniques of the professionals, both as they get their horses warmed up before entering the ring and as they jump a large and tricky course.

A successful competitive team; Pam is riding Roscoe – possibly the best horse we have ever owned. A small horse, only about 15.1 h.h., he had the most enormous jump, as you can see from the way he is "flying" this huge parallel.

THE RIGHT HORSE

At all levels, from novice to international classes, show-jumping is fiercely competitive. If you want to do anything more than enter small competitions at local shows, you are going to have to invest in a horse with good jumping ability.

A comparatively inexperienced rider should be looking for a horse with jumping experience. Two novices are really not a good mix and, on the whole, it would be a mistake to think that the two of you could learn together, except perhaps when the novice rider is being trained by and is under the guidance of a top professional rider.

Every top show-jumper will have his or her own view on what sort of horse makes a top jumper. I look for a horse with a pleasing appearance, that is brave, level-headed and super-careful. I recognise, though, that my experience is, of course, a great help in coming to a decision.

There is no one breed of horse that always produces good show-jumpers, and riders will have their own preference for English, Irish, American or European bred horses. Remember that a horse with a good temperament will always be easier to *sell on* than one that is mean and spiteful. The same goes for a horse with any of the incurable stable vices – wind-sucking (when a horse grabs the top of the stable door or a rail in the field with its teeth and sucks in air, making gulping noises), crib-biting (biting and chewing up anything wooden) or weaving (swinging the head from side to side, feet apart) – or with any bad scars or blemishes. People often tell me with glee how they have bought such horses "dirt cheap"; that is fine, as long as you want to keep the horse for yourself – for ever. Vices and blemishes do not go away, and not everyone is happy about purchasing a horse possessing them.

A reputable dealer is by far the best person for a novice rider to buy a horse from. There is a kind of distrust of dealers in the UK that is not found in Europe or the USA. It is quite unjustified: a dealer has his reputation to protect and will be anxious to sell you a horse that suits you. And, if he does sell you a horse that you don't get on with, you can generally take it back to him and exchange it. This you can never do after a private sale.

A dealer will get to know you and your capabilities and can then advise you on the sort of horse that will suit you. I once went to buy a horse from Paul Shockemohle; he had 300 horses in work in his yard, all for sale, and yet he would only show me one because he knew this was the one that would suit me.

Kosher, another of our Grade A horses, showing very wide-set eyes. I would describe them as being "right on the corners of his head", which gives him the best possible field of vision. His ears are pricked and alert, showing that he takes an intelligent interest in his surroundings.

The beautiful head of Pam's Grade A show-jumper Durrow. He provides a fine example of a good-looking horse. Although in this picture he is wearing an Abbot Davis for lunging exercise, he has a good natural head carriage, with his head well set on to the end of his neck. Most importantly, he has an intelligent and kind eye. His eyes are set wide apart on the forehead, giving him good all-round vision.

A superb example of the correct conformation for a show-jumper. This is Joe Turi's horse Kruger; he has a beautiful head and well muscled neck set correctly on to the body. The eyes and ears are large and set wide apart, the body is compact and short-coupled, giving a lovely coordinated outline, and the legs are truly set "one at each corner".

FIRST STEPS

You must first get to know your new horse and let it get to know you. So for the first few weeks ride it around at home, practising flat work and grid exercises to gain confidence and trust in one another.

Ask your vet to take a blood sample and assess the worm count so that he can advise you about a worming programme.

The first jumping competition I would advise you to enter is a clear-round event at a local show and you can do this as soon as you feel happy and confident with your new horse. The purpose of the competition at this stage is simply to see what the horse can do and how it goes in the ring. In this type of event, you pay an entrance fee just to jump round the course. If you go clear, you get a rosette. If you don't, you can pay another entrance fee and jump again. We had such a competition at our yard recently, and one girl paid and jumped twelve times before finally going clear and getting her rosette. I wouldn't recommend this, however; the idea is to identify your problems so that you can work on them at home. Don't look on the show-jumping ring as a training ground at this stage, but as a place to establish what your difficulties are.

If you are serious about wanting to take part in competition show-jumping, you should consider going to a good trainer. In America, riders reckon that for every dollar they spend on a horse, they should spend a similar amount on training. This is why they are so successful. Riders in the UK tend not to take this view, which is perhaps why the general standard of riding does not advance and why the UK no longer leads the world in competitive riding in the way that it used to. As soon as we have a win at a show, we think we don't need lessons any more. With that sort of attitude, that win will often be the last as well as the first.

Riders of all ages who want to compete seriously in any equestrian field should seek the help and advice of a trainer. It is impossible for you to see all the mistakes you are making from on the back of a horse, and the experienced eye of someone on the ground can be invaluable in this regard. Pam and I still train each other all the time – criticising all the time, too, although for the sake of domestic harmony we leave it all behind in the manège!

WALKING THE COURSE

Learning how to walk the course, to "read" and recognize the pitfalls the course-builder has set for you, is vitally important in competitive show-jumping. In the first round of a show-jumping competition, it's the rider against the course-builder. Only in the jump-off, when the riders with clear rounds compete against the clock, are you all riding against each other.

The course-builder has to get some sort of result from the first round – after all, he can't have everyone jumping clear rounds. So he's going to build in a few things to try to make you make mistakes. These are not likely to be in the form of very big or wide jumps, or really awkward distances between fences, particularly at novice levels. But he might position a white gate so that, as you approach it, the secretary's tent – also white – is directly behind it, making it a little difficult to see and judge. As you canter towards it, the chances are that the horse will be looking at the tent rather than the gate. Or if the course-builder sees a red car parked by the ring-side, and clearly there for the day, he might build a jump of predominantly red planks in front of it. The fence may be positioned some distance away but if it is almost the same colour as the background it is that much harder for the horse to focus on it. It is possible, too, to build one jump so that, as you approach it, it looks as if you are jumping straight into another one as soon as you land. Another "trick" may be that the final fence is positioned some way from the preceding fence; the horse then knocks it down because it thought it had already finished the round.

So when walking the course be aware of the background and surroundings and the position of the jumps in relation to them. The course-builder's aim is to catch you out, and you must be aware of these catches as it will be up to you to help your horse avoid them or cope with them.

Walk the course in exactly the line that you intend to ride round it, remembering that you want to use as much of the ring as possible, unless you are going to be jumping against the clock. In practice you will probably not end up riding round exactly as you intended, at least to begin with, but try. Learn to walk a step of 90 cm (3 ft) – there are four of these to the average horse's canter stride. (Adjust the length of your step to suit your horse's stride if necessary.) You can then work out exactly how many strides you must take between the different parts of a combination or between two fences placed close together. Begin by standing with your back against the poles of the fence – the back pole if the fence is a spread. Remember that a horse will land a little further over a spread fence than it will over a vertical (see page 167).

The "rules" of walking the course apply even to the greatest! Here David Broome takes time to examine a fence and looks across at the next one, too, to judge how best to take this jump in order to put himself into the best position for the next. The fence you don't like as you walk the course is always going to be the one to catch you out – the one you will have "willed" yourself to fault at – so take extra care when you come to it.

Riders walking the course before an international show-jumping event. Note how each rider is walking on his own, or possibly with a trainer, but not with other riders. It is important to concentrate while you are walking the course, so that you can assess each jump and make decisions about how to approach it. It is not a time to chat with friends, even about the course. And make sure you have really memorized the route; go over it in your mind several times.

RIDING THE COURSE

In Chapter Six we looked at the riding-in of your horse on your arrival at the showground and some general do's and don'ts of collecting ring etiquette and behaviour. Here I want to concentrate on the basic rules for going round a show-jumping course. Each course obviously has to be ridden to suit the particular lay-out, but just as there are general rules for walking a course, so there are for riding one.

Enter the ring quietly so as to keep yourself and your horse as relaxed as possible. Walk or trot around the ring using the time before the bell goes to check the jumps – make sure, for example, that the gate isn't swinging precariously or that a pole isn't resting right on the edge of a cup. You'll soon learn to spot jumps that are not quite correct.

When the bell rings, you must begin your round within thirty seconds. Put the horse into a canter, aiming to keep it in an even, bouncy, lively but controlled stride. Make sure that the horse is alert; I have so often seen novice riders ambling up to the first fence so that the horse is unprepared and just stops. The first fence of the course is one of the most important psychologically. If you jump it well, both of you will feel more confident about the rest of the round. If you refuse it or knock it down, the knowledge that you cannot now get a clear round is likely to make you jump the rest of the course badly.

Aim to go through the start, jump each fence and go through the finish at exactly the same speed. It is a lot to ask, I know. What should in fact happen is that you accelerate very slightly on take-off and decelerate slightly on landing, but no one but the rider should be aware of any change in speed. However, what generally happens, particularly with inexperienced riders, is that they get faster and faster as they go round the course. The inevitable result is that a fence comes down – and the course-builder wins.

Use as much of the ring as possible when you are not jumping against the clock, so as to give your horse the maximum approach room to a jump; as long as you keep in your bouncy canter you will not exceed the time limit.

If you jump clear up until the last fence, there is tremendous pressure on you now: the excitement and tension at this point often prove too much: the rider comes in too fast and the fence goes flying. Perhaps the course-builder has positioned it so that as you approach it you are riding towards the collecting ring, and your horse is distracted and anxious to finish. Always ride especially carefully at the last fence: to have it down when the rest of the course was clear is one of the great disappointments of competitive show-jumping.

A beautiful "roomy" show-jumping course in the large outdoor arena at St Gallen, Switzerland. The rider is obviously enjoying himself, cantering around the course happily.

You should aim to jump each fence of the course as an individual obstacle so as to give it maximum concentration. But at the same time you should be thinking about your approach to the next one. If, after the second jump, say, there is a turn to the right, then between the first and second jump glance over to look at the third, just to remind yourself of it. Apply more pressure with your right leg, so that the horse knows it is to lead away from the jump cantering on the off-fore and is thus ready to turn as soon as it has landed. Here John Carlos Garcia is seen clearly looking over in the direction of the next jump on the course.

A typical competition show-jumping course, with eleven fences – verticals, parallels, a wall, double and treble combinations. When riding the course, use as much of the ring as possible and keep to an even, lively, bouncy canter.

JUMPING PROBLEMS

Small show-jumping competitions are often the best way to find out where you and your horse's jumping problems lie. You can then go home and try to sort them out. In the next few pages we'll look at what some of these problems might be, and at techniques for jumping the various obstacles you are likely to encounter.

Many people when they first come on my show-jumping clinics will tell me proudly how high they have jumped on their horses. But it is being able to jump *round a course of jumps* that counts. Clearing one high jump is not necessarily clever; it may even be very foolish. Going round a whole course of reasonably sized fences of different types, on the other hand, *is* clever.

Always start by jumping low fences, keeping well within your limits and your horse's. If you feel happy jumping fences 90 cm (3 ft) high and no higher, enter classes where this is the maximum height of the jumps – and win. This will give you the confidence to start jumping fences just a little higher. It is much better to win at a lower height than go in for a bigger competition and make a complete mess of it.

There is not a great difference between jumping verticals and jumping spreads. With a vertical fence it is particularly important to keep the horse in that rhythmical, bouncy stride, so that it can, in effect, "bounce" over the fence in the same rhythm. The bouncy stride allows the horse to bascule properly over the fence. As for the rider, if you use your legs too strongly just before a vertical the horse will lengthen its stride and jump in a flatter arc, probably knocking the fence down. Instead, relax your hands a little and slightly decrease the pressure with your legs to allow the horse to bascule.

When approaching a spread fence, hold the horse in a little with your hands and increase the pressure with your legs so that it is tightly wound up, like a spring, ready to uncoil over the jump. By increasing the pressure, you should not increase the speed; the smooth rhythm is still all-important. Instead, the impulsion created by your legs moves the hocks up closer to the shoulders and produces the coiled-up spring effect.

An example of the technique for jumping a high vertical fence. The first picture shows the approach to the jump, and the horse is about to take off. I am in the centre of the point of balance, relaxing my hands to let the horse drop its head to balance itself. In the second picture, I have totally relaxed my hands so that the horse has complete freedom of its head. Although it is not giving the fence a lot of room in front, you will see that it has judged the height correctly so that it just clears the pole. In the final picture I have shifted my weight back over the centre of balance so that the horse can land easily and move forward unimpeded by me.

Compare the horse's position in these pictures, as it jumps a large spread fence, with its position over the vertical. The fence is 4 ft (1.2 m) high by 8 ft (2.4 m) wide and the horse knows it will have to stretch itself to clear the width. You can see that the arc that it naturally makes with its body to cover the width of the jump allows it to clear the fence with considerably more room than it did the vertical. However, the horse is a little more tentative as it takes off, worried about the width of the fence: neither its front legs nor its hind legs are together as a perfect pair as it begins its ascent. Once in the air, confident now that it will make the spread, it has composed itself into a better shape. In these pictures, incidentally, you can see that my stirrup leathers are looped on to the girth to keep them more or less in place. I need a special certificate from the FEI allowing this as the muscles in my legs were severely damaged by an accident I had in the mid-70s.

REFUSING

If you have a horse that refuses to jump any sort of jump – continually – there is only one solution; get rid of it. You must have a horse that wants to please you when it jumps if you are to get anywhere; one that persistently refuses does not want to, and there is simply no point in persevering.

However, it is true to say that horses begin to refuse their fences because they have been badly ridden more than because they are born stoppers. If your horse begins by jumping well, only stopping when it encounters some kind of fence for the first time for example, but then begins to refuse frequently, take a good, hard, honest look at the way you are riding. Are you, for example, not moving up as you get to a fence – particularly a spread – ready to use your legs, so that your horse takes off too early, jumps flat and lands in the middle of it, frightening itself well and truly in the process? I see this happen over and over again. You can sometimes get away with not riding so strongly at a vertical; the horse

If you are having trouble with refusals, putting a small pole 6.4 m (7 yd) in front of a jump helps to position a horse correctly for take-off. However, this sequence illustrates the need for the rider to have impulsion going over the pole, or the horse will still stop. You can see how it has landed much too far away from the fence as it comes over the pole so that, not surprisingly, it stops when it reaches it.

can almost clamber over it. At a spread, however, it will be in trouble if it lacks impetus.

If a horse refuses by running out at a jump, nine times out of ten it's the rider's fault, either for not riding the horse straight, holding it between hand and leg, or because the approach to the fence is unbalanced. Such evasion can quickly become a habit, so you must cure it as quickly as possible. Ride with extra care and concentration at the jump; keep the horse in that even, bouncy canter stride; make sure it arrives at the take-off correctly and in balance. If it still runs out, discourage it by constructing large and elaborate wings to the jump.

This is a tendency that I have seen in many inexperienced riders, and one that they hardly seem aware of. A rider will jump a fence and then turn, always the same way – usually to the left, riding a complete circle before coming in to the next fence. In a show-jumping competition, a circle before a fence counts as a refusal. If it is a habit your horse has adopted, go back to the exercise for pulling up in a straight line after a fence (page 96). When you have practised this, build the fence in the centre of the school, jump it and turn – deliberately – to the right. Come round, jump the fence again, and turn to the left. Do this several times until you feel that the circling habit has been forgotten by both of you.

Refusals happen to everybody at some stage, for a number of reasons: misunderstanding between horse and rider; missing the stride on the approach to the fence so that the horse is unbalanced for take-off; occasionally the fact that the fence is just too large. A horse that refuses consistently should be got rid of – you will never get anywhere together. However, if you have a horse that is normally a willing, careful jumper but suddenly starts refusing or becoming careless over its fences, get your vet to do a blood test; it could be that the horse is anaemic or has a virus or muscle problem. Anaemia is a condition that can come and go in horses and be brought on by such apparently trivial circumstances as changes in the weather, food or environment. Our vet takes a blood sample of all our horses when I know they are fit and well so that if I feel a horse is losing condition or performance the vet can test the blood for anaemia, virus or muscle spasm, comparing the analysis with the healthy sample. Often a horse can have muscle problems in its back or legs which will not make it lame but will be painful enough to put it off jumping.

DITCHES AND WATER

Horses often have a horror of ditches and water jumps, but show-jumping competitions nearly always include one or the other so you must feel confident that your horse will jump them.

If your horse is one that refuses to jump a ditch, the best thing to do is to dig a practice one, if practical. Make it about 4.5 m (5 yd) long, 60 cm (2 ft) wide and 75 cm (2 ft 6 in) deep. You want your horse to get its confidence over this ditch, so let it have a good look at it. Then turn it away and trot up to the ditch; if your horse dithers on the take-off, use your legs and stick and make it jump from a standstill; it can easily do so. Be prepared for a very big leap into the air though – the horse will be wanting to get well away from all the horrors it imagines are lurking in the ditch. Then bring it round again at a trot,then a canter, until it is jumping it easily.

You could try making a water jump at home, too. However, if you are in a hurry to train your horse, you can simulate a water jump by putting blue plastic sheets on the ground, stretched out and held in place by poles. However, it is better to have the real thing, because the best way to teach a horse to jump water is to begin by walking through it so that it stops being frightened.

Once the horse is walking through the water jump happily, bring it round at a trot and ask it to jump it. If it continues to splash through it, put a pole over the top of the water about 45 cm (18 in) high, right in the middle of the jump. Take your horse over it at a trot and a canter. Make sure you include jumping water in its regular jumping practice.

Just occasionally, you get a horse that is truly petrified of water. It is a phobia that needs to be cured. Get the horse used to water by hosing its legs down with running water for ten to fifteen minutes each day, or by tying it up in the yard and leaving the hose pipe running nearby. Then walk the horse through the running water. We once had an event horse sent to us for jumping training that was frightened of water, and we cured it by accident! Somebody left the hose running all night in the sand school and flooded it, so we spent the next day walking, trotting and cantering through the water. Then I built a jump in the flooded sand school and had the horse jumping over that. By the end of the day it was cured.

Peter Robeson – the greatest stylist of all time – demonstrates how to take a water jump in faultless style. Peter has always been an artist and a perfectionist in the sport of show-jumping; a great team man, if he had jumped the course first he would always tell his fellow team members how they could beat him.

My Grade A horse Kosher taking a water jump confidently. Although a proven successful show-jumper, Kosher is still only five years old, so occasionally, as here, I school him in a standing martingale. You will see this item of tack being used less and less in show-jumping events; in fact, England and America are the only countries where its use is still permitted. But although it is generally considered old-fashioned I think the standing martingale still has a use in schooling young horses, helping to position the head and keep the shape right. Of course, it must not be adjusted too tightly; the horse must still have freedom of its head, as Kosher has here.

A novice horse at the same water jump but with the pole removed. If a horse is nervous of the water, let it go right up to it, then keep urging it forward. Be prepared for an enormous leap, and perhaps a splashing, too!

OTHER PROBLEMS

If your horse gets too close to the fence by putting in a short stride before take-off, the problem may be the result of one of three things. Maybe the horse has no "scope," so feels it must get close to the jump to give itself a better chance of getting over it. Or it may have something wrong with its front feet that is causing pain and making it reluctant to jump and hurt itself even more. Or you are riding it badly, allowing it to approach the fence out of balance and in the wrong rhythm.

If you are convinced that it is the first of these that is at the root of the problem, then I'm afraid you have no alternative but to get rid of the horse. Experts have a saying, "No scope, no hope." It is a fundamental problem that will not get better.

If you feel it is your horse's feet that are causing the trouble, stop riding it and consult the vet or the blacksmith.

If you feel that it is your riding that is the problem, go back to the grid exercises (see pages 88-91) until you have really learned how to ride a horse in a rhythmical stride which you can maintain over the grid.

If the horse takes off too early, this is almost always caused by bad riding, usually the result of nervousness in the rider who is anxious to get over the fence as quickly as possible. Again, go back to the grid exercises, practising particularly those ones that help you with seeing a distance (or a stride).

If a horse knocks down a fence that it should have no trouble clearing, it is generally the rider's fault and probably the result of the way the fence has been approached: the horse is likely to knock down the fence with its hind legs if it takes off too early and with its forelegs if it takes off too late. If you think incorrect take-off is the problem, again, go back to the grid exercises.

Another possibility is that you have ridden too fast at the fence, so that the horse has not had a chance to bascule properly over it but has jumped it rather flat. It is again a matter of trying to establish that *rhythm*.

If you feel the horse is simply being careless you can give it a tap with the stick to remind it that you mean business, but in fact it is likely to be you as the rider who is allowing it to be careless.

Perhaps your horse is not on top form (see page 169) and you must be sure that this is not the case before pushing it hard.

There does, of course, come a time when a horse has jumped as high or as wide as it can and, if you ask it to do any more, the result will be a knock-down. My horse Jungle Bunny could clear 2.1 m (7 ft) with apparent ease, but only once in my life did I get him to jump a fence higher than this – and clear it!

Remember, if you do knock a fence down, either at home or in a competition, don't look back. No amount of doing so will put the fence back up, and your concentration is needed for the next obstacle.

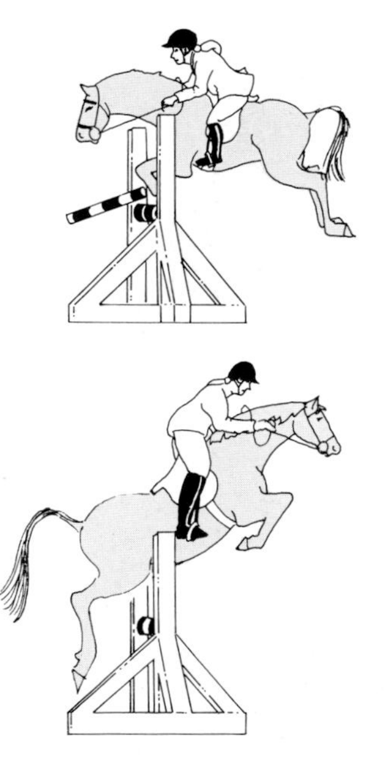

Left *The horse is not trying hard enough, and is knocking down the fence with its forelegs.*

Right *The horse has taken off too early and is getting its front legs tangled in the jump while its back legs are trailing behind it. The rider has been "left behind".*

Left *The horse has put in a short stride and is taking off too close to the fence, launching itself upwards at the last minute.*

Right *The horse is not basculing properly and is knocking down the fence with its stifle.*

…cking down fences happens even to the greats! This will …n be because the horse is a little "over-faced" in a jump-off. …u enter a competition, and your horse knocks down several fences, it is often best to retire from the event and go back to practising at home.

PROBLEMS WITH JUMPING DOUBLES

Typical problems with jumping a double fence are when a horse refuses either part, or rushes through it all, and/or knocks down the second part.

If your horse refuses the jump, look again at the general section on refusing (page 168). Then practise going through the grid (see pages 88-91). Once your horse is happy with this, put another small fence 3.6 m (4 yd) after the small jump at the end of the grid and practise over this. The grid exercise will put your horse in the perfect position for this jump and it will be less likely to refuse it.

Next you can build another fence 7.3 m (8 yd) further on, so that the horse lands after the second small jump, has one non-jumping stride, and then is perfectly positioned for take-off. This exercise should help both of you to judge the distance and take-off as you come into a double and thus cure problems of stopping through being off balance.

If the horse rushes through a combination, your aim is to slow it down. There are two ways in which you can attempt to tackle this. The cure for a horse that continually rushes its fences may, I'm afraid, take some time. Over a period of say six or seven months you should trot up to jumps and not let your horse jump them. You have got to curb its impetuousness, get it to slow down and listen to you. But do make sure it knows you are stopping it; don't let it think it was its own idea! To convey this message you should keep up the grid exercise while never letting your horse jump an individual fence.

When you feel you could try taking your horse to a jump without it rushing it, let it jump, but then ride it to the next fence and make it stop again. Then turn round and jump back over the first fence. Jump it again, and if the horse doesn't go too fast jump the next fence, but then make it stop at the third. Keep on like this, going backwards and forwards, until you really feel you have your horse's attention.

If you feel your horse is not so impetuous as to need this rather drastic treatment, try slowing it down with the "David

An exercise to assist with jumping doubles. A small pole is placed 6.4 m (7 yd) in front of the first fence. Kosher comes in a little fast and you can see he is steadying himself as a result of the pole. This puts him in perfect balance to jump the fence. The "David Broome brake pole" between the fences steadies him again so that he jumps the final fence perfectly too. The brake pole is placed exactly in the middle of the two jumps which are 7.3 m (8 yd) apart.

1

2

3

4

1

Broome brake pole", so called because David Broome was the first to use it.

The brake pole is also the way to deal with a horse that knocks down the second part of a double. The pole makes it look down to where it is going to land and to think about its front feet, and helps to balance it for the second part. If a horse persists in knocking down the second part it is likely to be because it is just looking at the jumps and not judging their height in relation to the ground. Remember, a horse judges the height of a jump from the top to the bottom so it must look down at the ground to get a proper perspective. Try putting up a three-jump combination with a brake pole after each one.

2

3

The same exercise with the first small pole taken away. Here you can see how the brake pole can also become the "accelerator pole". Without the guidance of the pole before the first fence Kosher took this jump far too slowly. As a result he really has to stretch over the pole between the fences, and this puts him in the correct position and balance for the second part.

LENGTHENING AND SHORTENING STRIDES

We have already seen the importance of being able to lengthen and shorten a horse's stride to balance correctly before jumping different types of fences or to ensure you arrive at the right place for take-off in front of a jump (page 110). To jump a complicated course successfully, you need to refine this so that you are completely confident that your horse will lengthen or shorten its stride the instant you ask it to.

The best exercise for this is one that the late George Hobbs, a top international rider for many years, taught me a long time ago when I went to him after not having ridden for eight years. And he made me do it riding thirteen different horses!

You need to set up two vertical fences 18.2 m (20 yd) – four perfect canter strides – apart. Now jump the combination both ways, putting in four strides between landing and take-off. Once you are doing this in perfect rhythm, ask your horse to shorten the stride, so that it puts in five strides between landing and take-off. On a really well schooled horse, you should be able to put in six strides.

Now change one of the fences to a parallel. If jumping from the vertical to the parallel you will find that this distance represents four moving strides or five slightly shorter-than-usual ones. However, from the parallel to the vertical it is four perfect strides and five noticeably shorter ones. The stretch the horse has to make over the parallel fence makes it land a little further away from it than the vertical over which it has – hopefully – basculed.

Whether you are jumping from the vertical to the parallel or vice versa, you should still be able to shorten the stride sufficiently to put in five strides between landing and take-off; you can try six strides again. But you won't be able to do this from the parallel to the vertical.

I have one horse who is so obedient that I can put up my two fences 14.6 m (16 yd) apart, and get him to jump it in two with lengthened strides, in three with normal strides, in four with shortened and steady strides and in five with very short strides. And he's 18 hands high!

Even if you can't quite achieve that, this is an excellent exercise for teaching you about really lengthening and shortening strides as well as seeing a distance. It is a very good exercise for you in controlling a horse, really making it listen and obey you, and it emphasizes the importance of rhythm in jumping.

Above: *By lengthening the number of strides at a trot or canter, you can lessen the number of strides between the fences of a combination.*

Below: *Practise lengthening and shortening strides at trot and canter while out riding, as here, so that you can do so easily when jumping.*

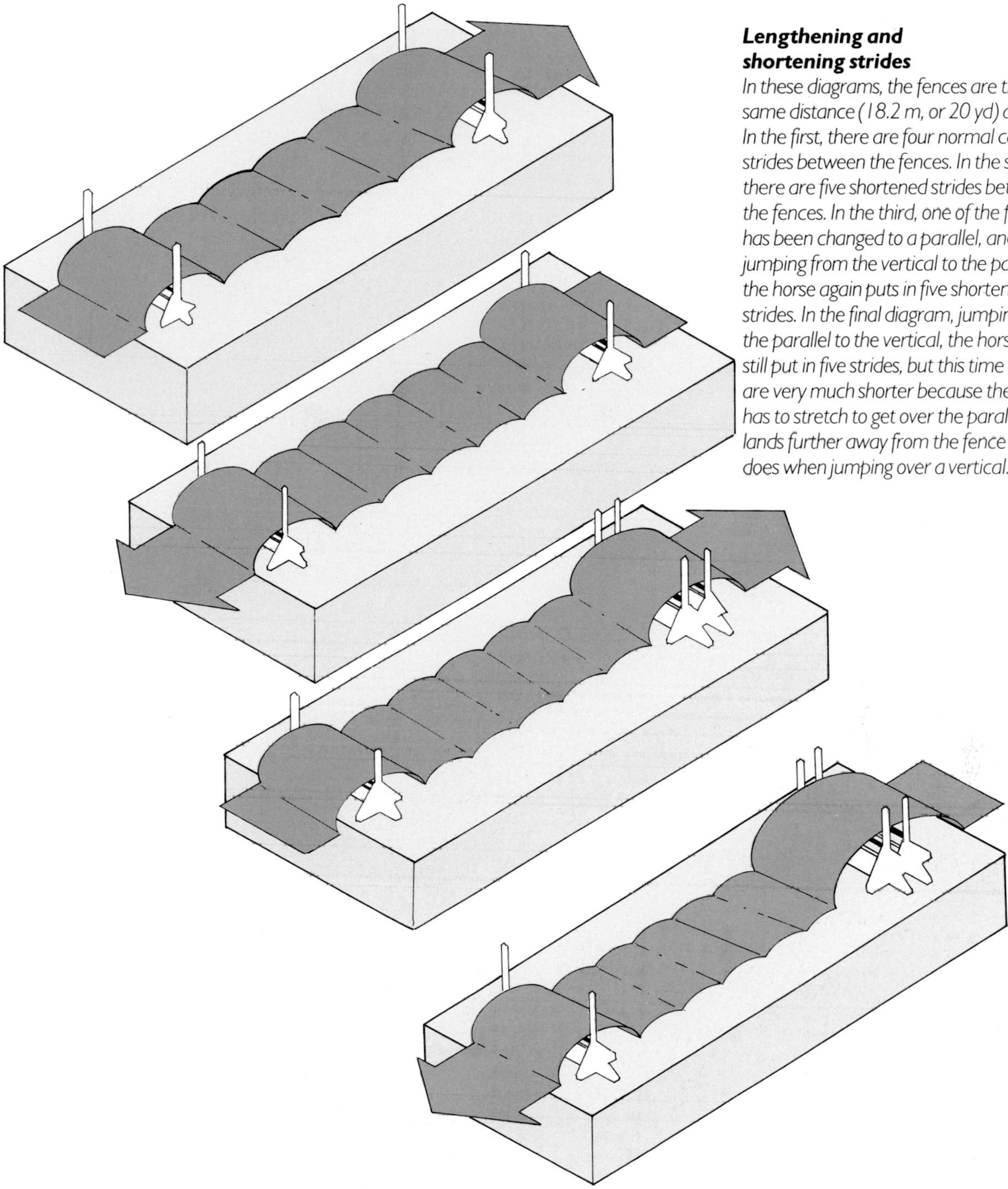

Lengthening and shortening strides

In these diagrams, the fences are the same distance (18.2 m, or 20 yd) apart. In the first, there are four normal canter strides between the fences. In the second, there are five shortened strides between the fences. In the third, one of the fences has been changed to a parallel, and, jumping from the vertical to the parallel, the horse again puts in five shortened strides. In the final diagram, jumping from the parallel to the vertical, the horse can still put in five strides, but this time they are very much shorter because the horse has to stretch to get over the parallel and lands further away from the fence than it does when jumping over a vertical.

FLYING CHANGES IN JUMPING

I talked earlier (page 96) about how to get a horse to land and strike off at the canter on a certain leg over a jump so that it is balanced and ready to begin the approach to the next jump. This is particularly important in speed competitions or a jump-off, where being off balance at any moment can cause seconds' difference in the time taken to go round the course.

The flying changes of a show-jumper are not the beautifully controlled and balanced movements of a dressage horse as discussed in Chapter Five. In dressage, the flying change is actually a very advanced movement and great skill and obedience are required to perform it correctly. A show-jumper's flying change nearly always takes place while it is going over the jump – that is, the horse should land on the new leading leg of the canter – and is used to balance it quickly for the way it's going to go. It will always be accompanied by a move in that direction whereas a dressage horse has to be able to perform flying changes, often one after another in quick succession, while continuing in a straight line down the arena.

I find there are two effective ways of teaching a horse to do a flying change while jumping. The first is to set up a cross-pole, about 45 cm (18 in) high, in the middle of a figure-of-eight, then canter the horse in this movement and as it hops over the pole in the middle to exert pressure with the leg you want it to lead with as it lands. So if you are cantering in a left-handed circle, as the horse goes over the jump use your right leg to ask it to lead with the right or off-fore as it lands. Remember, you are using lateral aids to ask for the change.

Another way is to build a jump about 75 cm (2 ft 6 in) high, preferably a solid one such as a wall or brush fence so that the horse cannot see through it, then construct a vee-shaped fence (see diagram) 4.5 m (5 yd) away, using 3.6 m (4 yd) poles. As you come over the fence, steer the horse towards the left or right part of this construction, and at the same time use the corresponding left or right leg more strongly. If you've jumped to the left side, turn to the left afterwards and you will find the horse has moved away with its left or near-fore leading. It is a near foolproof method.

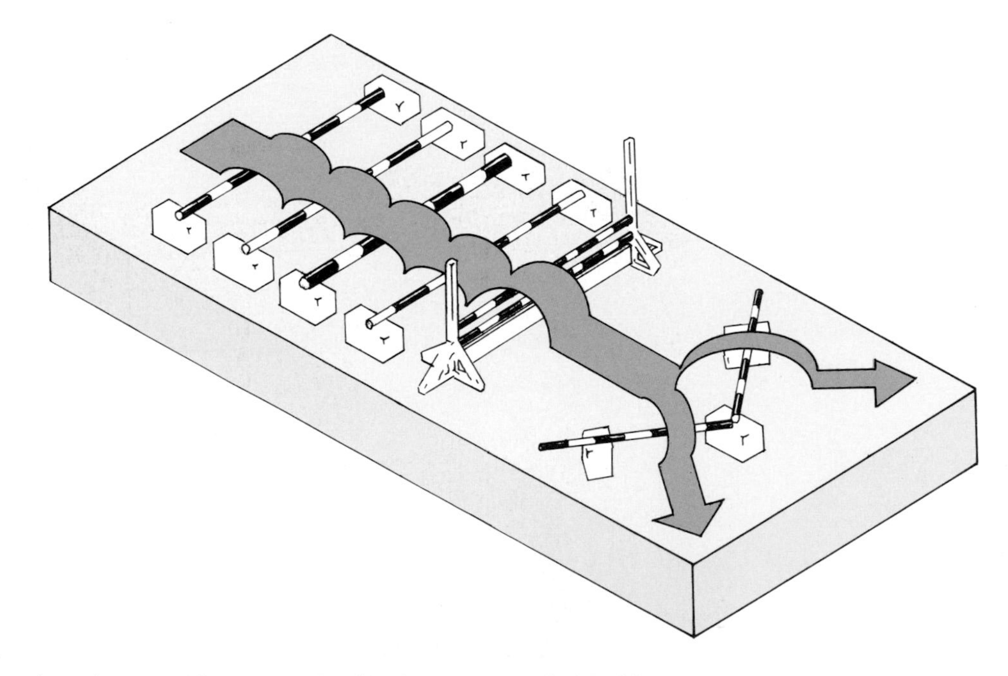

A grid of four poles with a vertical fence and, 4.5 m (5 yd) away, two poles arranged in a V-shape. As the horse goes over the V-pole, it should if necessary perform a flying change and land on the leg of the canter corresponding to the direction in which the rider wants it to go.

*A horse jumping the V-pole. You can see in each picture how the exercise is working; in the first picture **left** the horse will move away from the pole with its near-fore leading and in the second picture **below** it will lead with the off-fore. It is an invaluable – and virtually infallible – exercise for novice horses and riders.*

THE COMPETITION

I now want to take a final look at riding in a competition. Probably one of the principal things you are going to have to combat when you start competing is nervousness. This will be communicated to your horse making it agitated too – the worst possible state for both of you. Difficult though it is to control nerves, it must be done. Just try very hard and consciously to keep calm. It takes time to become used to competing, but keep telling yourself that you are both well prepared for what lies ahead.

When you jump a clear round and there is, say, half an hour before the jump-off, get off your horse, slacken its girth and put a rug over its back if it is a cool day. You may have to hold the horse yourself, but keep out of the collecting ring at this time.

When nearly all the riders have completed their first rounds, you should have an idea of how many clears there will be. If it looks as if there are five or six, then, about ten minutes before you think the jump-off will start, get on your horse and start walking it round. If there is to be a draw for the jump-off, you might find yourself going first and you want to make sure you are prepared for this. As the last horse in the first round goes into the ring, take your horse over a fence or two in the collecting ring so that you are ready to go. If you then find you are last in the draw, that is fine; you can dismount and wait your turn.

If you do get in the prize money, be careful as you go into the ring and during the victory circuit. The horses will know they have done well and will naturally feel pleased with themselves. This, along with the joyous feeling being transmitted from the riders, and the flapping rosettes, may have the horses leaping about in their excitement. You certainly don't want to be on the receiving end of a pair of heels! Be a little restrained and don't get too close to anyone.

We have a rule in our yard; if you have entered a horse for two jumping classes and you win the first, then withdraw it from the second. You can't better a win, and horses aren't stupid; they know if they have jumped well and done their best for you. Why should they be asked to do more on that day? There is a good chance that if you do go in for another class you will not do so well, which would be a real shame after your earlier triumph!

Waiting in the collecting ring for the jump-off is nerve-racking, whether it's at a small local event or an international competition held indoors, under the glare of the lights! Either way, spend the minimum of time there before it is your turn to go.

IN CONCLUSION

As you progress with your show-jumping career and ride different horses, remember that nobody, however brilliant a horseman or woman he or she may be, will get on with and get the best out of every horse. There is no ignominy in admitting this, although many riders seem to think there is. European and American riders seem to be particularly good at recognizing that, just as you don't click with every person you meet, so it is with horses. After all, horses are living things too, and like us have different temperaments and different reactions to different circumstances.

This applies at every level of horse ownership, from the lowliest to the highest. For example, the famous horse Deistar was, as a five-year-old, the leading novice horse in Germany when ridden by Hartwig Steenken. After Hartwig's tragic death, the horse went from yard to yard and nobody really heard anything of him until Gerd Wiltfang got him. But, brilliant though he is as a horseman, Gerd just did not get along with Deistar. Fortunately he recognized the horse's potential and had no hang-ups about not being able to get the best out of him. He passed Deistar on to Paul Shockemohle, and the rest, as they say, is history. Paul has won just about everything there is to win on him.

Another thing to remember is that there are lots of people out there who reckon they know all there is to know about horses and are always ready to give you free advice. Most of this is useless. If you find you are not getting on as well as you think you could and are making mistakes and finding it hard to correct them, put your faith in one person whose riding ability and judgement you trust. Then listen to this person and this person only. If you dither about trying to do what every well meaning, if not well informed, person tells you, you will not know whether you are coming or going, and nor will your horse. Follow one method – the chances are it will work.

If you have decided to make a life with horses, my final advice would be to stick it out. Horses will become a way of life for you, not just a hobby or even a full-time job. There will be hard lessons to learn; one of these is that if you are ambitious and want to progress, but feel your horse is not capable, well, it's time to part company. If horses are your life's work I'm afraid there's not much room for sentimentality – particularly at the top. And all along the road there will be plenty of rough times when you feel like quitting. But there will be many others when the rewards far outweigh the sacrifices.

However many times you win, it still feels good – as Paul Shockemohle's delighted smile confirms, Here he is holding up the Silk Cup Trophy for the winner of the Derby Hickstead.

Paul Shockemohle on Diestar, one of the most difficult of all horses to ride. Paul uses a combination of a snaffle and a bitless bridle to control him. The horse had an interesting and chequered history before he came to Paul; experienced and extremely talented riders had been unable to get anything out of him and it took this great rider to show what the horse was truly capable of.

My great horse, Jungle Bunny, stretching himself to the utmost over this jump in order to win the class – which he did! This fence was placed five strides on from a combination, but in order to beat the time I pushed him to take off after four. He would have been moving at about 48 to 64 km (30 to 40 mi) per hour when he took off for this enormous spread, so if our style leaves a little to be desired that is why!

GLOSSARY

Above the bit When a horse avoids the full action of the bit by raising its head and stretching it forward so that its mouth is above the rider's hands.
Abbott Davis Item of saddlery attached to the reins and girth, used to position a horse's head correctly.
Against the clock A term used in show-jumping competitions in which the final round is timed. The fastest clear round will win, but a clear round will beat a faster round in which fences are knocked down.
Aids Recognized signals given by the rider to convey instructions to the horse. *Natural aids* include the legs, hands, body and voice. *Artificial aids* include whips, sticks, spurs and martingales. *Diagonal aids* are aids in which the rider gives a hand aid in conjunction with the leg on the opposite side, i.e., the right rein is used with the left leg. *Lateral aids* are hand and leg aids given together on the same side.
Anti-cast roller A type of roller (*q.v.*) used to keep stable rugs in place. The roller is connected by an iron hoop or arch either side of the spine; this prevents any pressure on the spine and is also said to prevent a horse from being "cast" (*q.v.*) – that is, unable to get up if it has lain down in the stable.
Bars (of feet) Space between the top of the frog and the outer heel of the foot.
Bars (of mouth) The fleshy areas at the corners of the lower jaw where there are no teeth and where the bit lies.
Bascule The arc action made by a horse's body as it jumps over a fence.
Bedded down Said of a horse that has been fed, watered and had a fresh bed put down for the night.
Behind the bit When a horse evades the full action of the bit by pulling its head in toward its chest.
Bitless bridle A bridle that has no bit. The reins are attached to extensions from the noseband.
Body brush A soft brush used on the horse's coat during grooming to massage the skin and stimulate blood circulation as well as improve the appearance.
Brushing When a horse hits or "brushes" the inside of one leg with the inside of the opposite leg as it moves. May lead to injury and lameness.
Brushing boots Protective boots worn on the lower part of the legs to prevent injury from brushing.
Cast When a horse is lying down in the stable or horse box, and is unable to get up again, due to lack of space or because it has become trapped against a wall.
Cavalletti Adjustable low wooden jump used in the schooling of horse or rider in jumping.
Cavesson Either a simple noseband fitted to a bridle, or a more sophisticated piece of equipment worn by a horse when it is to be lunged (*q.v.*). In the latter, it is sometimes referred to as a *breaking cavesson*.
Clear-round jumping A show-jumping competition in which the aim is simply to achieve a clear round. Can be a useful way to appraise a horse's level of competence.
Collected A horse that is alert and moving in perfect obedience to and in harmony with its rider, with its body very compact so that its paces are shortened, bouncy and elevated.
Counter canter Cantering a circle with the outside fore and hind leg leading the pace, rather than the inside ones, as is usual.
Crib-biting A stable vice in which the horse continually bites at the side of the manger or the top of the stable door. Quite often this is accompanied by windsucking (*q.v.*).
Dandy brush Thick-bristled brush used to remove mud and dried sweat marks from the long coat of a horse or pony.
Disunited (of the canter) When the sequence of leg movement is wrong, so that in the second stride of the pace, the fore and hind leg on the same side, instead of on opposite sides, move at the same time.
Draw reins Reins attached to the girth straps, passing through the bit rings to the rider's hands to give greater control by bringing the horse's head down. Should be used only by experienced riders.
Eventing Riding in a one- or three day event, which combines dressage, cross-country and show-jumping.
Extended A horse that is moving in complete obedience to and in harmony with its rider, with its body "lengthened" so that the strides are as long as possible.
Fence A *combination fence* is a series of fences (usually three) in a show-jumping course, placed to allow only one or two strides between each jump. A *double fence* is two fences in a show-jumping course with the same requirement as the combination. A *drop fence* is an obstacle in which the landing side is considerably lower than the take-off side. A *spread fence* is one in which the main feature is width rather than height, whereas an *upright* is designed to test a horse's ability to jump heights.
Flying change A change of leg at the canter, without coming back to a walk or trot.
Frog V-shaped rubbery part found on the soles of a horse's feet which acts as a shock absorber and as an anti-slip device.
Gamgee Gauze-covered cotton wool used beneath stable or exercise leg bandages for extra warmth or protection.
Grid A series of low poles placed a certain distance apart, for training horse and rider when learning to jump.
Grooming Attention given to a horse – picking out the feet, brushing the coat, legs, tail and mane, sponging the eyes, nostrils and dock, and so on, to improve the horse's appearance, massage the skin and improve the blood circulation.
Hack Term used to describe going out for a ride. Also a showy type of horse, possessing fine conformation.
Half halt Slight check in pace asked for by the rider to alert the horse to be ready to respond to a new instruction.
Headcollar Item of tack, generally with a length of rope attached, placed on the horse's head either to lead it from one place to another or to tie it up for grooming etc.
Hoof oil Oily preparation applied to the horn and underside of the foot to keep it supple and prevent cracking.
Leading rein Long length of leather or rope attached to the bridle or headcollar for the purpose of leading the horse. Usually used in the early stages of being taught to ride.

Loins Part of the horse's spine and surrounding area just behind the area of the saddle, that is particularly sensitive. Weight or pressure should never be placed here.
Long reining Controlling an unridden horse from the ground by using two long reins attached to the bit and taken back through the stirrups or through rings on a roller. The trainer can stand behind the horse and "drive" it forward, or send it in a circle around him.
Lungeing The act of training a horse by directing it around in a circle while on a long lunge rein. The rein may be attached to the bit or to a special lungeing headcollar known as a *cavesson.* (*q.v.*). Schooled horses may be lunged as a form of exercise or during the course of teaching a novice rider.
Manège A marked out area or school used for the teaching, training and schooling of horse and rider.
Martingale Item of saddlery, usually attached at one end to the girth and at the other to the reins or the noseband, to help in positioning a horse's head.
Molars The large grinding teeth that lie near the back of the horse's mouth. These are often worn down unevenly, resulting in sharp points which can cause a horse pain. A check must be kept on them and any sharp points should be filed.
Nations Cup International team show-jumping event held in countries all over the world.
Nearside The left hand side of a horse.
New Zealand rug Waterproof, wool-lined rug for horses to wear when turned out to grass in the winter or in cold, wet weather.
Non-jumping stride Stride or strides taken between the fences of a double or treble combination obstacle.
Numnah A thick pad, generally the shape of the saddle, worn underneath the saddle to protect the horses's back. It may be made of sheepskin, felt or rubber.
Offside The right hand side of a horse.
On the bit When the horse has taken a light hold of the bit in its mouth and is responding completely to the rider's contact through the reins.
One day event An equestrian competition in which all phases of an event – dressage, cross-country jumping and show-jumping – are held on the same day.
Overbent A horse that has arched its neck acutely, thereby bringing its head too far into its chest. Usually caused by a rider exerting too much pressure on the reins while urging the horse forward.
Over-reaching When the horse strikes the heel of the forefeet with the toe of the hind feet. Overreach boots protect the feet from injury when this happens.
Oxer A show-jumping fence consisting of a parallel bar.
Pelham Various types of curb bit with a single mouthpiece to which two reins may be attached. Aims to combine the two bits of a double bridle in a single mouthpiece.
Rein back To instruct the horse to move backward. In order to execute the movement correctly, the horse must move back with the diagonal fore- and hindlegs moving in unison.
Rising trot The action of a rider rising from the saddle in rhythm with a horse's trot.
Roller A strap which passes around the horse's back and belly, used to keep rugs in place.
Running out When a horse evades jumping an obstacle by running out to one or other side.
Saddle, general purpose A comparatively modern design of saddle with a spring tree (*q.v.*), designed for all recreational riding.
Saddle, jumping A saddle designed specifically for jumping. Has a spring tree, a deep seat and padded knee rolls.
Safety stirrups Stirrups designed so that the foot is freed automatically in the event of a fall.
Seeing a distance Term used in jumping, describing the ability to judge the distance at or between fences in relation to the horse's stride.
Snaffle bit A bit that consists of single mouthpiece which may or may not be jointed, used without a curb chain.
Spring tree The inner framework of a saddle, made of highly tempered lengths of steel.
Stable rubber Linen or cotton cloth used at the end of grooming to lay the coat and give it a shine.
Surcingle A webbing strap which passes around a horse's back and belly and is used to keep a rug in place. Show jumpers and jockeys often buckle a surcingle around their saddle as an added precaution against the girth breaking.
Tack Term used to cover all items of saddlery. An abbreviation of *tackle*.
Three day event An equestrian competition in which the three phases of an event – dressage, cross-country riding and jumping and show jumping – are held over three (or sometimes more) days.
Transition The act of changing pace. A walk to a trot and a trot to a canter are known as *upward transitions*. A canter to a trot and a trot to a walk are *downward transitions*.
Windsucking A stable vice in which a horse draws or sucks in air constantly when standing in the stable, generally swallowing it with a gulping sound.
Withers Point at the bottom of the neck of a horse from which a horse's height is measured.

INDEX

Page numbers in *italic* refer to the illustrations

F

I

J

Q

R

S

T

W

ACKNOWLEDGEMENTS

Quarto Publishing would like to thank the following for supplying photographs: **59** (top) Lansdown Rugs, Bath; **117** Landsaver MCP Ltd, Corby.

All other photographs by Kit Houghton
All diagrams by Stephen Frisby

Our thanks also to Judy Bradwell, and to Pam and Lionel Dunning's young pupils, who helped with the riding demonstrations.